BOUNDARIES

OF

FAITH

BOUNDARIES
OF
FAITH

Geographical Perspectives
on Religious Fundamentalism

Roger W. Stump

Human Geography in the New Millennium

ROWMAN & LITTLEFIELD PUBLISHERS, INC.
Lanham • Boulder • New York • Oxford

ROWMAN & LITTLEFIELD PUBLISHERS, INC.

Published in the United States of America
by Rowman and Littlefield Publishers, Inc.
4720 Boston Way, Lanham, Maryland 20706
http://www.rowmanlittlefield.com

12 Hid's Copse Road
Cumnor Hill, Oxford OX2 9JJ, England

British Library Cataloguing in Publication Information Available

Library of Congress Cataloging-in-Publication Data

Stump, Roger, 1951–
    Boundaries of faith : geographical perspectives on religious fundamentalism /
Roger Stump.
        p.   cm.
    Includes bibliographical references and index.
    ISBN 0-8476-9319-8 (alk. paper) — ISBN 0-8476-9320-1 (pbk. : alk. paper)
    1. Religious fundamentalism.   2. Religion and geography.   I. Title.
    BL238.S82   2000
    200'.9'04—dc21   99-057220

Printed in the United States of America

∞ ™ The paper used in this publication meets the minimum requirements of
American National Standard for Information Sciences—Permanence of Paper for
Printed Library Materials, ANSI Z39.48-1992.

CONTENTS

1. Introduction   1

2. Fundamentalist Hearths   23

3. Global Variations in Contemporary Fundamentalism   85

4. Geographical Dimensions of Fundamentalism   157

5. The Impacts of Fundamentalism   213

Glossary of Terms and Groups   231

Selected Bibliography   237

Index   241

About the Author   250

I

INTRODUCTION

Late in 1992, several hundred thousand Hindus gathered in the city of Ayodhya, in India's northern state of Uttar Pradesh, to support construction of a new temple to the Hindu god Ram. India's Supreme Court had ruled that the temple could not be built because its intended site was partially occupied by a sixteenth-century Muslim mosque, but Hindu militants claimed that the mosque sat on the birthplace of Ram and that it should be removed. On the morning of December 6, Hindu demonstrators assembled at the site of the mosque and proceeded to tear it down despite police efforts to stop them. By the end of the day the mosque had been completely destroyed and a small shrine to Ram erected in its place. These events led to widespread violence between Hindus and Muslims throughout India in following weeks.[1]

Christian conservatives gained control of the board of the public school district in Vista, California, following elections in the fall of 1992. Once in office, the board's new Christian majority began to advocate changes in the school district's curriculum, to establish a learning environment more compatible with its Christian beliefs. In August 1993 they approved a controversial set of policies requiring the teaching of biblical creationism in history, social studies, and English classes and encouraging the presentation in science classes of evidence that challenged evolution and other scientific concepts. Public dissatisfaction with these changes led to the removal of the Christian majority the following year and the repeal of its policies.[2]

The Taliban, a militant organization committed to unifying Afghanistan under an Islamic government, took control of the country's capital city of Kabul in September 1996. In the months that followed, the Taliban imposed an exacting version of Islamic law on the city. They required women to be fully veiled when in public and prohibited them from working outside the home. Men were required to grow beards. Various forms of entertainment were banned, including music, television, kite flying, and caged songbirds. The Taliban also enforced traditional punishments associated with Islamic law, such as amputation of a hand for theft, stoning for adultery, and public lashing for premarital sex. Murderers faced public execution by a male relative of their victim.[3]

In the summer of 1997, Israel's Transportation Ministry announced a plan to establish a policy of gender segregation of passengers on several public bus routes running through ultra-Orthodox Jewish neighborhoods in the cities of Jerusalem and Bnei Brak. The plan provided for separate seating areas for male and female passengers and for doorways that would allow men to enter from the front of the bus and women from the back. The Transportation Ministry adopted the plan in response to continuing pressure from the ultra-Orthodox community, whose religious beliefs require the separation of men and women in public. Announcement of the plan drew widespread protests from feminists and secular Jews in Israel.[4]

The above events had no direct connections with one another. They developed in widely separated locations and involved markedly different religious groups. They also had very different consequences for the places where they occurred. Nonetheless, all four incidents can be seen as expressions of a single, far-reaching trend: the spreading influence of religious fundamentalism at the end of the twentieth century. As originally used during the 1920s, the term *fundamentalism* had a much narrower meaning than that implied here, referring only to a particular branch of conservative Protestant Christianity. More recently, however, scholars have applied the term to a diverse array of groups and beliefs, as exemplified in the events described above.[5] Interpreted in this broader sense, religious fundamentalism has become a significant force in the cultural dynamics of contemporary societies around the world.

This book examines the diverse characteristics and impacts of religious fundamentalism through the disciplinary concepts and perspectives of human geography. The extensive scholarly literature dealing with fundamentalism has made relatively little use of explicitly geographical approaches. A large body of research has demonstrated, however, that the disciplinary concerns of geography, such as spatiality, regional variety, diffusion, and the meaning of place, provide important insights into religion as an expression of human culture.[6] In a like manner, the discussion presented here focuses on two geographical themes that are essential to an understanding of the nature of fundamentalism. The first of these themes revolves around the concept of contextuality—the idea that social and cultural phenomena are shaped by the specific geographical settings within which they develop. In a general sense, all expressions of fundamentalism involve interactions between traditional religious beliefs and broad forces of social change, but the causes and consequences of those interactions vary significantly from place to place, as local conditions change. Radical Muslims in Afghanistan and ultra-Orthodox Jews in Israel, for example, have both tried to shape their social surroundings to conform to traditional religious beliefs. But they have done so in very different ways, as distinct groups pursuing their goals in disparate social and cultural settings. In other words, while the spread of fundamentalism can to some extent be considered a global trend, the particular forms that it takes reflect unique circumstances within specific local milieux.[7] The contextual nature of its various manifestations in fact represents a key feature of fundamentalism as a social phenomenon. In essence, fundamentalism only exists within specific contexts as an expression of localized conditions and concerns. Examination of the theme of contextuality thus addresses the significance of the relationships between distinct varieties of religious fundamentalism and the geographical settings where they have developed.

The book's second major theme pertains to the geographical character of the strategies through which fundamentalist movements have responded to the contemporary world. This theme is based on the thesis that the central concerns of religious fundamentalism possess an inherent spatial dimension expressed through assertions of territoriality: that is, through attempts to exert control over the meaning and uses of particular portions of geographical space.[8] Hindu efforts to reclaim possession of a sacred site in Ayodhya and attempts by conservative Christians to revise the curriculum of a local school district in California both illustrate this territorial impulse. The desire to control space is an important characteristic of fundamentalism, reflecting the ways in which fundamentalists define their identity, their distinguishing beliefs, their vision of the ideal society, and their interactions with others outside their own group. The treatment of the theme of territoriality thus examines the varied effects that fundamentalists have had on contemporary societies through the spatial realization of their beliefs and what those effects reveal about the fundamentalists themselves.

These two general themes are not independent of one another, of course. The spatial manifestations of a fundamentalist movement's objectives are intrinsically tied to the nature of the movement's relationship with its specific surroundings. The success of ultra-Orthodox Jews in persuading the government to institute gender segregation on public bus routes, for example, in part reflected the relatively open relationship between the ultra-Orthodox and Israel's ruling political party in the late 1990s. Such a concession would have been less likely to occur under a less sympathetic government. Conversely, the ways in which fundamentalists attempt to express control over geographical space can have significant effects on the broader settings that they inhabit. Thus the Hindu fundamentalist goal of building a temple to Ram in Ayodhya became a recurrent theme in the national elections held in India in 1998, out of which the fundamentalists emerged as the country's dominant political force. Because the diverse geographical settings of fundamentalism are closely intertwined with the strategies that fundamentalists have used to control space, the discussions of these two themes overlap extensively.

In exploring the above themes, the different chapters of this book employ a variety of concepts and perspectives. The great diversity of conceptual approaches encompassed by human geography provides a robust framework for examining a complex phenomenon like religious fundamentalism. Humanist concerns with the meaning of place, for example, are highly relevant in considering fundamentalist attitudes toward sacred space, whereas the feminist concept of gendered space is useful in understanding fundamentalist views concerning the social roles of women. Postmodern concepts of difference and identity help to explain the contrasts that have developed among related fundamentalist groups as well as the attempts of fundamentalists to insulate themselves from other elements of contemporary society. At the same time, the concepts of structuration theory offer insights into the ways in which fundamentalist movements influence the social settings from which they have emerged. Instead of adhering to a single, narrowly defined set of theoretical constructs, then, the following chapters apply diverse approaches in analyzing the nature of religious fundamentalism through the broad themes of contextuality and territoriality.

Before exploring these themes further, however, it is first necessary to lay the groundwork for subsequent chapters by examining in greater detail the distinguishing characteristics of religious fundamentalism. As suggested earlier, the meaning of the term *fundamentalism* has broadened over time and is now used to describe trends within many different religious traditions. The remainder of this chapter examines the features that such trends share in common as expressions of the more general phenomenon of fundamentalism. The discussion focuses in particular on the characteristic attributes of fundamentalist modes of belief, the underlying factors responsible for the rise of fundamentalism, and the various strategies adopted by fundamentalist movements in pursuing their objectives. In addition, the discussion develops a number of concepts related to the geographical themes examined throughout the rest of the book and addresses the importance of these themes in understanding fundamentalism as a global phenomenon.

RELIGIOUS FUNDAMENTALISM: AN INTERPRETATION

The term *fundamentalism* first came into common use in the United States during the 1920s. It was used to describe the beliefs of conservative Protestants who championed certain biblical doctrines, or "fundamentals," in opposing modernist theological trends and the secularization of American society. As the term has been broadened to encompass other groups, however, its meaning has become both more complex and more nebulous. In current usage, the concept of fundamentalism refers not to a specific set of beliefs but to the response of religious traditionalists in general to contemporary social trends. In this context, scholars do not always agree on who should be considered a fundamentalist. In addition, unlike the conservative Protestants who first adopted this label, most people now referred to by others as fundamentalists do not actually identify themselves as such. They may even resent the name, given its connotations of extremism and fanaticism. For these reasons, arriving at a workable definition of religious fundamentalism is not a simple task. According to existing scholarship, such a definition must take a variety of factors into account.

One way to begin defining fundamentalism is to specify what it is not. Again, as the term is currently used, *fundamentalism* does not refer to a particular set of doctrines, such as belief in the literal truth of the Bible. Although biblical inerrancy represents a central tenet of Christian fundamentalism, it clearly has no relevance to Hindu or Buddhist versions of the phenomenon. Fundamentalism also involves more than adherence to traditional beliefs, whatever they might be. For example, the Old Order Amish practice a demanding, traditional form of Christianity that leads them to reject most modern innovations—from automobiles to zippers—and yet they are not generally considered to be fundamentalists. Likewise, fundamentalism does not refer simply to strongly held religious beliefs. Although most fundamentalists are devout practitioners of their faith, so are many nonfundamentalists. Religious belief obviously plays a central role in fundamentalism, but other concerns are also involved.

The most important of these concerns is the impact of social change on religious belief. More specifically, fundamentalists are distinguished in part by their conviction that contemporary social forces threaten the survival of traditional values and beliefs and that only their religion can halt the degeneration of society and restore it to a more principled state. From this perspective, fundamentalism represents a mode of discourse that places religious faith and the contemporary secular world in continual opposition to one another. The fundamentalist viewpoint is further distinguished by its implicit assumption that this conflict can be successfully resolved only through the complete triumph of religion over secular forces, rather than through some form of compromise. Fundamentalist groups differ with respect to the particular religious doctrines that they espouse, of course, but they all believe in the existence of some threat to the social and moral order that must be opposed by true believers.

The sense of threat that motivates fundamentalism arises out of a group's fear that its traditional religious certainties are being weakened or marginalized by forces over which it has no control. The religious certainties perceived to be under attack often involve the traditional sources of authority from which a religious group derives its basic values and beliefs, such as its sacred scriptures. Scientific and theological challenges to the literal interpretation of the Bible, for example, represented a major concern among Christian fundamentalists early in the twentieth century. Similarly, conflicts between social trends originating in Western culture and the spiritual precepts of the Koran have been a recurring theme in Islamic fundamentalism. But the fundamentalist sense of threat can involve other issues as well. Fundamentalist sentiment may arise when a group believes that its traditional religious identity is being eroded or that it is losing its traditional status in society. Hindu fundamentalists assert, for example, that the creation of India as a secular state, in which no religion is favored over any other, has weakened the sense of "Hinduness" that they consider to be the most significant trait of India's people. Fundamentalists may also fear the disintegration of traditional moral values or ethical standards as religion loses its influence in society. For many of Israel's Jewish fundamentalists, for example, the integrity of Judaism is threatened by the widespread disregard for traditional Jewish practices and customs in secular Israeli society. In essence, fundamentalists believe that contemporary trends have endangered the rightful order of things, through their corrosive effects on once unambiguous matters of religious authority, identity, morality, and faith.

The trends identified as threats by fundamentalists generally relate to one of several broad issues. The most basic of these issues is the rise of modernism. This trend involves a change in outlook among individuals and social institutions, in which a growing receptivity to innovation supersedes earlier commitments to tradition and received dogma. The openness to new approaches tends to encourage individuality of thought and belief and to emphasize rationality as the basis for social and cultural progress. This change in outlook has occurred most broadly in societies that have undergone extensive industrialization and urbanization, where processes of innovation have become thoroughly integrated into social structures and institutions. In such societies, the rise of modernism has had widespread impacts on science, the arts, social thought, economic activity, and popular culture. Its main expression in the context of religion has been the attempt by believers to reach an accommodation between religious doctrine and modern rationality. This attempt does not involve a rejection of religion, but rather a reinterpretation of religious beliefs in a manner that is compatible with other contemporary perspectives. A religion's modernist adherents may focus on ethical and moral values rather than specific doctrinal issues and may interpret their religion's sacred writings as allegory or metaphor rather than as literal truth. Fundamentalists, on the other hand, believe that modernist revisionism subverts religious belief by denying the validity of divinely revealed truth. To fundamentalists, the modernist view gives greater credence to rational observation than to the certainty of faith and thus challenges the sources of authority on which such certainty is founded (fig. 1.1). From the fundamentalist perspective, attempts to reconcile traditional beliefs with contemporary perceptions of reality lead to the dilution and marginalization of religion and, inevitably, to social and moral decline.

Figure 1.1   An ultra-Orthodox (left) and a Reform Jew argue over the issue of gender segregation at Jerusalem's Western Wall, one of the most sacred sites in Judaism. Following traditional practice, separate areas have been designated for men and women to pray at the wall. Reform Jews assert that men and women should be allowed to pray together, but the ultra-Orthodox strongly oppose this modernist innovation. Jerusalem, Israel, 1998. *Source:* Debbie Hill/Media Exchange International.

Secularism, a second broad issue of concern to fundamentalists, presents an even more direct challenge to the significance of religion in society. In a setting dominated by modernist attitudes, religion may continue to play an important role, albeit in nontraditional forms. The rise of secularism, on the other hand, eliminates religion as a source of authority in society's various institutions. In a secular setting, the mass media, business, government, science, and education all come to function without reference to religious beliefs or doctrines. The characteristics and objectives of social institutions instead reflect purely humanistic concerns. As secularism spreads within a society, individual religious participation also declines, as does the observance of traditional religious customs. Complete secularization results in the disappearance of religion as a force in the mainstream of society. Scholars disagree about the inevitability of the rise of secularism in the modern world, but most societies that have experienced the transformation from a rural, agricultural organization to an urban, industrial one have seen at least some decline in the influence of religion. Such trends pose a substantial threat to the fundamentalist point of view, again because they challenge traditional sources of authority and create a social context defined by humanistic values rather than divinely revealed principles. Secularism's exclusion of religion from the concerns of everyday life in turn undermines the concept of absolute truth to which fundamentalists are committed. Fundamentalists may also blame the decay of contemporary society on the philosophy of cultural pluralism. Pluralism does not deny the importance of religion, nor does it require that traditional religious beliefs be reinterpreted to conform to contemporary perspectives. Rather, it eliminates any preference in society for one religion over another. No religious group enjoys a position of privilege within a pluralist setting; all religions (or at least all those that are perceived to belong to the social mainstream) are considered to be equally legitimate. In its most extreme version, this view reflects a postmodernist conception of cultural relativism, which denies the possibility of demonstrating that the beliefs of one group are more valid than those of any other. From this perspective, religious truth is essentially relative and has meaning only within the context of a particular religion's worldview. Although fundamentalists oppose the pluralist point of view in part because it rejects the inherent superiority of their particular religious traditions, their objection to pluralism involves more than religious chauvinism. They also oppose the pluralist outlook because it contradicts the very idea of universal truth. Fundamentalists believe that society cannot function without the certainty provided by belief in absolute religious truth, which in their view provides the only valid foundation for ethical and moral standards and indeed for all forms of human activity.

As challenges to a fundamentalist group's religious traditions, modernism, secularism, and pluralism all may originate within the larger society to which the group itself belongs. In such cases, fundamentalists fear that indigenous patterns of social change threaten the continuing status and legitimacy of their religion. A final issue that may provoke a fundamentalist response involves threatening forces of a different sort, imposed from without. These forces include the related processes of colonialism and imperialism. While not of universal concern to fundamentalists, these processes have contributed significantly to the sense of threat felt by fundamentalist groups outside of North America and Europe and must be considered in understanding the motivations of such groups.

Colonialism and imperialism relate to fundamentalist concerns through their extensive impacts on society and culture. Both processes involve the subordination of an indigenous society to a foreign power. In the case of colonialism, the foreign power establishes direct political authority over the colony, while under imperialism the foreign power dominates the indigenous society through economic and political influence rather than direct administrative control. In both cases, the foreign power supports institutions that help to preserve its hegemony over the indigenous society. Such institutions include the government itself in a colonial system; but in both colonial and imperialist contexts many other aspects of the indigenous society may also be involved, including the economic and political systems, education, transportation, and communication. The imposition of foreign institutions in turn places constraints on the underlying structures of the indigenous society and introduces foreign influences into local cultures. As a result, the social norms and cultural customs of the indigenous society may undergo substantial change.

Fundamentalists see such transformations as a threat. In their view, the rise of foreign influences weakens the authentic foundations of their society. The presence of foreign institutions and social structures undermines traditional sources of authority—both secular and spiritual—and the introduction of foreign cultural elements erodes the traditional sources of identity that hold the indigenous society together. Under these circumstances, fundamentalists fear that others will abandon the certainties of their religious faith, which may appear less and less relevant to the organization and operation of contemporary society. Fundamentalists may also see the social transformations associated with colonialism and imperialism as part of a global trend that has relegated their culture to a position of inferiority as the hegemony of a few world powers has spread. A specific concern in this context is that the global dominance of Western ideologies in politics and economics may subvert non-Western ideologies in other realms, such as religion and cultural values. And even if foreign institutions have not had a widespread impact on their particular culture, non-Western fundamentalists are often concerned that their religious traditions may be overwhelmed by the global diffusion of Western popular culture (fig. 1.2).

In denouncing the effects of modernism, secularism, pluralism, colonialism, or imperialism, then, fundamentalists place themselves in direct opposition to processes that, in their view, threaten the integrity of their religious traditions. Indeed, most scholars agree that the oppositional quality of fundamentalism represents one of its most important defining characteristics. Fundamentalism therefore exists only within a context of conflict. In some instances, this context involves conflict between different elements of a single heterogeneous society; in others, it involves conflict between an indigenous society and outside forces. In either case, fundamentalists develop a clearly defined sense of the "other," of an enemy that espouses incompatible values and beliefs, whose influence they must fight in defending religious truth. Whatever form the corrupting influence of the "other" may take, from Western imperialism to modernist theology to secular humanism, fundamentalist movements are defined in part by the specific enemy that they oppose.

A fundamentalist movement thus originates when a self-identified group of true believers draws an ideological boundary between itself and the "other" by which it feels threatened. In defining these "boundaries of faith," fundamentalist groups emphasize the primacy of traditional religious belief and practice. The emphasis on tradition reasserts the group's connections to a distinctive sacred past and the certainties associated with it. Moreover, because it ex-

Figure 1.2   Street Scene in Thailand. The expanding influence of Western secular culture has been a major source of motivation for fundamentalist movements in non-Western countries such as Thailand. *Source:* Weststock.

presses truths revealed by timeless sources of authority, religious tradition provides the group with an incontestable response to threatening forces and trends in contemporary society. The creation of these ideological boundaries thus distinguishes fundamentalist groups from their antagonists, absolutely and unambiguously, in matters of religious belief and practice. Even more importantly, these boundaries set the group apart as the only legitimate moral community, whose beliefs provide the sole means of perfecting contemporary society. The group's sense of its unique moral legitimacy indeed becomes an integral part of its identity and provides the ultimate justification for its subsequent actions.

The emphatic assertion of the primacy of tradition by religious fundamentalists comprises several key elements. Most obviously, it involves an unfaltering commitment to traditional sources of religious authority, particularly in the form of sacred texts such as the Torah in Judaism, the Bible in Christianity, or the Koran in Islam. That commitment often expresses itself as an insistence on literalist interpretations of sacred scripture or on the absolute and unchanging truth of traditional scriptural interpretations. Strict adherence to the teachings of traditional sources of authority thus requires that fundamentalists adopt an epistemology in which human knowledge necessarily derives from divine revelation.

The fundamentalist emphasis on tradition also frequently involves a sense of nostalgia for an idealized past, before the threats inherent within contemporary society had arisen. From the fundamentalist perspective, this idealized past represents a place and time when true beliefs were widely held, when people did not question religious certainties, when modern deviations from traditional teachings had not yet evolved, or when society as a whole functioned in harmony with the requirements of traditional religious belief and practice. The idealized past thus refers to a place and time of religious homogeneity where, at least in theory, the fundamentalist group's beliefs dominated. In addition, it may refer to a time when the group had fewer contacts with—and as a result felt less threatened by—other religious beliefs or secular philosophies. For some groups, the idealized past corresponds to a specific period and location in history; in the case of Islam, for example, the original Islamic society established by Muhammad in the seventh century and maintained by his immediate successors represents such a golden age. More often, however, fundamentalists look back not to a specific time and place, but to a more generalized conception of a past in which religious traditions were not questioned.

A final, crucial feature of the fundamentalist emphasis on tradition is its selectivity. Although fundamentalists typically adhere to a wide range of traditional beliefs and practices, they often focus on a few select issues. Rather than espousing a wholesale return to a traditional past, in other words, fundamentalists concentrate on what they consider to be the most important features of that past in defining the ideological boundary that separates them from others. The particular traditions that they emphasize depend in part on the nature of their beliefs, of course, but they also depend on the specific threats that the fundamentalist group opposes. Certain traditions thus take on profound significance for a fundamentalist group because they unequivocally repudiate the trends by which the group feels threatened. For example, Christian fundamentalists in the 1920s saw the teaching of evolution in American public schools as a key symbol of the rise of modernism. As a result, they declared belief in the literal truth of the biblical account of creation to be one of their distinguishing traits. Islamic fundamentalists, on the other hand, have responded to the spread of Western political and social philosophies by stressing strict adherence to traditional Islamic law in all aspects of daily life. And Hindu fundamentalists have rejected the secularization of Indian society, in which Hinduism is treated as just one religion among many, by emphasizing a more universal conception of Hinduness within their religion's traditional geographical domain.

In contesting change in the contemporary world, then, fundamentalists rely on adherence to those religious traditions that most clearly differentiate their own worldview from that of others. From the fundamentalist perspective, moreover, commitment to these traditions must be unconditional. The adoption of fundamentalist beliefs consequently places strict demands on the believer, in both private and public realms of life. Their absolute commitment to sacred traditions in turn fosters positions of militancy and zealotry among fundamentalists, which are meant to make their beliefs unmistakably apparent to others. Indeed, according to religious scholar Martin Marty, a major goal of fundamentalists in expressing their traditional beliefs is to "cause scandal," to give offense to nonbelievers.[9] In this way, fundamentalists explicitly publicize the ideological boundary that sets them apart from the "other" whose influence they are contesting. At the same time, their zealotry makes it clear that their modes of belief and practice are difficult and uncompromising, accessible only to the truly devoted. For members to adhere to a fundamentalist movement, they must be wholly dedicated to it, and for outsiders to join, they must do so conspicuously and completely.

Ideological boundaries based on fundamentalist traditions are thus sharply drawn and do not allow for compromise. Such boundaries are unambiguously dualistic, with all people on either one side or the other. This dualism echoes the perception of a threatening "other," but it also heightens the sense of community that binds together members of a fundamentalist movement as a self-defined enclave possessing a unique moral legitimacy. As a result, the distinction between those on either side of the ideological boundary is commonly defined by fundamentalists in stark moral terms, as a contrast between absolute good and absolute evil. Convinced of the righteousness of their beliefs, fundamentalists consider all other points of view to be erroneous, depraved, or sinful. Their conflict with the threatening "other" consequently represents more than just a disagreement with those holding different views; it symbolizes the struggle between divinely revealed truth and worldly corruption.

In advancing their side of that struggle, fundamentalists necessarily develop a strong commitment to activism (fig. 1.3). This activist stance in fact represents one of fundamentalism's most important traits, for it defines how fundamentalists interact with and affect the rest of society. Fundamentalist activism takes a variety of forms, but its primary objective is always to counter the forces or trends by which the fundamentalist group feels threatened and thereby to restore society to its rightful order. For some groups, this objective has prophetic overtones; that is, the group conceives of its goals in terms of sacred prophecies or beliefs regarding the end of history, such as the arrival of a millennial golden age or the appearance of a messianic figure. In those cases, fundamentalists believe that their actions possess a special religious urgency because they are part of the process through which the prophecy in question will be realized. In other cases, though, fundamentalist activism is simply directed at preserving the group's view of religious truth, which it believes is threatened by contemporary trends or events.

The specific methods used by fundamentalist groups to pursue the above goals reflect a number of factors, including the group's particular beliefs, the nature of the society that it inhabits, its patterns of interaction with other groups, and the influence of the group's leaders. In their review of fundamentalist movements, Gabriel Almond, Emmanuel Sivan, and R. Scott Appleby

Figure 1.3   Fundamentalist Christians protest at a Gay and Lesbian Pride Celebration. Through public expressions of opposition to the "other" by which they feel threatened, fundamentalists seek both to promote their views and to clarify their distinctiveness from the rest of society. West Hollywood, California, 1999. *Source:* David McNew/ Newsmakers.

have grouped these methods into four broadly defined strategies.[10] The "world conqueror" approach aims at destroying the threat in question by taking total control of the social structures and institutions within which the threat has arisen and imposing the fundamentalists' own beliefs and values on them. This strategy seeks to force all members of society to conform to the fundamentalists' practices. The "world transformer" strategy focuses on a more gradual revision of various elements of a society, such as its laws and institutions, to make it more difficult for others to oppose or ignore the fundamentalists' beliefs. The approach of the "world creator," on the other hand, shuns corrupt social institutions and structures altogether and attempts to create an alternative to them. The goal of this approach is essentially to create a parallel society whose righteousness will attract others to it. Finally, in the "world renouncer" strategy, fundamentalists turn away completely from the society of the "other" and focus on establishing their own independent world. This strategy concentrates on the perfection of the fundamentalist group itself rather than on efforts to compel or persuade others to adopt the group's beliefs.

These four strategies are not mutually exclusive. A single fundamentalist movement may adopt more than one strategy at different stages in its development and may employ two or more at the same time. World conquerors, for example, are also in a sense world creators because like the latter they must thoroughly remake society and its institutions. In addition, the geographical extent of the "world" with which fundamentalists interact varies from group to group. It may encompass the entire globe, or it may comprise only a particular region or country. Either way, this "world" represents the immediate environment of the fundamentalist group, in which it interacts with the threatening "other." The confines of this world are not permanently fixed, but shift in response to changes in the fundamentalist movement's objectives and identity.

Whatever form it takes, fundamentalist activism serves two ultimate purposes. For the fundamentalist group, activism provides a means of confronting the threatening "other" and restoring the proper social and moral order. In this sense, the group's commitment to action reinforces its claim of religious legitimacy, as the agent of the sacred authority on which its beliefs are based. By enforcing a strict interpretation of Islamic law in Afghanistan, for example, the Taliban can assert that they are the genuine followers of Muhammad. At the same time, religious activism allows individuals to demonstrate publicly their dedication to the goals of the fundamentalist movement to which they belong and thus to validate their own religious merit within the context of their larger group. The participation of militant Hindus in the destruction of the mosque in Ayodhya in 1992 not only advanced the objectives of the group as a whole but also verified the religious commitment of the individuals involved. The activist stance of fundamentalism, in other words, both promotes the agenda of a fundamentalist group and enables individuals to declare their religious identity in a conspicuous manner.

To summarize, then, fundamentalist groups possess a number of distinctive features: a conviction that contemporary trends pose a threat to their religious faith and the worldview associated with it; a sense of ideological isolation from the rest of the world; a commitment to the preservation of the certainties embodied in their religious traditions; their resulting self-identification as the only legitimate moral community; and an uncompromising dedication to fighting some "other" that they identify as the enemy of religious truth. All fundamentalist movements are thus characterized by a mixture of oppositionalism, separatism, and activism relative to the rest of the world, a combination of traits that often makes the actions of these movements highly controversial. To fundamentalists, however, the controversy that they generate signifies the righteousness of their cause and as a result represents an important part of their identity.

GEOGRAPHICAL PERSPECTIVES ON RELIGIOUS FUNDAMENTALISM

The preceding discussion describes the general attributes associated with religious fundamentalism in the academic literature. Current scholarship also recognizes, however, that despite their common features fundamentalist movements exhibit great diversity in their specific characteristics. Again, each of the four events described at the beginning of this chapter can be viewed as an expression of fundamentalism, but the details of those events differ substantially, as do the beliefs and objectives of the various groups involved. Thus, while it is clear that fundamentalism represents a useful concept in characterizing certain types of religious belief and behavior, it is equally important to recognize the significant heterogeneity that exists among fundamentalism's actual manifestations.

The primary thesis of this book is that the disciplinary perspectives of human geography provide important insights into the causes and consequences of that heterogeneity. Again, the examination of this thesis in subsequent chapters centers on two main themes: the role of geographical context in the development of diverse forms of religious fundamentalism in different parts of the world, and the relevance of territoriality and related geographical concepts in understanding the varied ways in which fundamentalists define their identities, express their beliefs, and implement strategies for restoring order to the world. Both of these themes address crucial features of religious fundamentalism as a contemporary phenomenon and at the same time relate to significant ideas and issues in human geography. As a prelude to the more detailed discussions that follow, the final section of this chapter introduces some of the key concepts associated with these two themes and considers how they contribute to a fuller understanding of fundamentalism and its effects.

The theme of contextuality provides a useful framework for examining the processes through which individual fundamentalist movements develop. While the rise of fundamentalism can be characterized as a global trend, comprising responses to far-reaching processes of social change, it manifests itself through groups and movements that are embedded in specific places and shaped by local circumstances. Variations in the beliefs and objectives of different fundamentalist movements can thus be interpreted as the product of dialectical interactions between broad global forces and diverse local contexts, a prominent focus of recent geographical research concerning processes of social and cultural change.[11]

Global influences on fundamentalism derive from several sources. Because many of the religious traditions that have produced fundamentalist movements have quite widespread distributions, those traditions are subject to forces and processes that transcend particular local settings. In addition, the inclusive worldview of the major universal religions, including Buddhism, Christianity, and Islam, gives them an explicitly globalizing character. They are not tied to a specific ethnic group or nationality and in fact have established important links among disparate cultural settings. Global concerns may also appear in the strategies adopted by fundamentalist groups, as in the case of missionary activity aimed at acquiring converts in diverse regions of the world. The most prominent global influences on fundamentalism, however, relate to the processes of social change by which fundamentalists feel threatened. The worldwide diffusion of industrialization and modernization, the globalization of the world's economy, and the ubiquity of Western popular culture, to cite only a few examples, have brought the populations of diverse regions of the world into contact with social and economic structures that reflect modernist, secularist, or pluralist perspectives. Although religious traditionalists in different places respond to these trends in different ways, the trends themselves reflect global processes of change. When Christian fundamentalists in California oppose the teaching of evolution, they are reacting against a modernist perspective that has in some way affected most regions of the world. Likewise, conflicts between fundamentalist ideologies and the processes of colonialism and imperialism reflect global patterns in the flow of political and economic influence. The anti-Western stance of most Islamic fundamentalists, for example, represents the rejection not just of foreign influences, but of Western hegemony in global politics, the world economy, and contemporary popular culture. Many of the threats that fundamentalists face, in sum, are not local in origin, but instead derive from broad social transformations operating at a global scale. Indeed, the extensive geographical scope of these threats contributes significantly to the intensity of fundamentalist reactions against them.

In countering those widespread threats, however, fundamentalist movements invariably reflect the influences of the local contexts within which they arise. As a result, fundamentalism is a geographically diverse and inherently contextual phenomenon, varying in the nature of its expression from place to place. Many local variables affect the development of fundamentalism, of course, but several types of factors are especially influential. At the most basic level, variations in the cultural makeup of individual places strongly affect the character of local expressions of fundamentalism. One key variable in this context is religious affiliation itself, which defines the sense of identity out of which fundamentalist movements arise. Because patterns of religious affiliation vary significantly throughout the world, the specific religious certainties defended by fundamentalist groups obviously vary as well. The concerns of fundamentalists in places as disparate as Jerusalem, Kabul, Ayodhya, and Vista, California, thus differ in part because different religious groups populate those locations.

Geographical variations in the role of religion within the local cultural environment also contribute to the inherent contextuality of fundamentalism. In the United States, for example, the principle of religious voluntarism defines religious practice as a personal matter. This principle has created a context for the rise of fundamentalism very different from that which exists in Pakistan, which is officially constituted as an Islamic republic, or in India, where for centuries Hindu beliefs have been incorporated into the dominant structures of social life. Similarly, the status of particular religious groups within their surrounding context affects the character of the fundamentalist movements associated with them. As members of a small religious minority within India, Sikh fundamentalists have thus pursued strategies very different from those adopted by Hindu fundamentalists, who claim to represent the interests of a majority of India's population. Adopting the language of structuration theory, these varying circumstances lead to the development of unique religious "locales" within which interactions between fundamentalists and the rest of the society both shape and are shaped by local social conditions and cultural characteristics.[12] As discussed in chapters 2 and 3, fundamentalism may appear within secular states as well as those with an official or established religion, and it may arise within either majority and minority religious groups. In each of these circumstances, its development is affected differently by local social structures and power relations.

Along with the prevailing cultural environment, processes of social change associated with the rise of fundamentalism have affected different places in different ways. Although they are essentially global forces, modernism and secularism have influenced some regions of the world more profoundly than others. Thus, reactions to these forces are far more prominent among Jewish fundamentalists in Israel than among Buddhist fundamentalists in Sri Lanka. Likewise, reactions to colonialism and imperialism represent an important feature of fundamentalist movements in Asia and Africa, but have little relevance to fundamentalism in North America. Contextual variations in the impacts of these global forces in turn produce different types of interactions between fundamentalists and the "other" by which they are threatened. Islamic fundamentalists in the Middle East and North Africa, for example, view the legacy of European colonialism as a threat in large part because of its connections to continuing Western hegemony in the realms of culture, politics, and economics. Hindu fundamentalist reactions against India's colonial past, on the other hand, focus more on the introduction of secularist and pluralist ideas into Indian society and polity, as evidenced by India's constitution as a secular state when it achieved independence from British rule. The processes of social change that have encouraged the rise of fundamentalism among religious traditionalists thus vary in their impacts from place to place, as discussed in chapter 2.

Finally, the inherent contextuality of fundamentalism in part reflects the influences of local patterns of human agency. Most fundamentalist movements have been shaped by the teachings of charismatic leaders, who differ in their individual approaches to promoting their version of religious truth. The character of group activism also varies in response to local conditions. The strategies employed by fundamentalist groups in a pluralist, democratic society, for example, differ in important ways from those used by groups that are able to wield power autocratically, such as the Taliban in Afghanistan. In addition to affecting the feasibility of particular forms of group activism, local conditions also influence the ways in which the rest of society responds to fundamentalist actions. Jewish fundamentalists in Israel, for example, have faced strong opposition from secular Jews as well as from Palestinian Muslims, and that opposition has to some extent limited the impact of fundamentalism on Israeli society. Islamic fundamentalists in Iran, on the other hand, enjoyed considerable popular support following the Islamic Revolution in the late 1970s and were able to bring about a significant restructuring of their society. In sum, the different ways in which fundamentalists define themselves and pursue their objectives, as groups and as individuals, reflect variations in patterns of human agency and in the interactions between human agency and local social structures. Chapter 3 provides a more thorough treatment of this topic through an examination of contemporary fundamentalist movements in various regions of the world.

The varied religious movements that constitute the phenomenon of fundamentalism thus reflect the diversity of the geographical contexts within which that phenomenon has evolved, and, for this reason, the disciplinary perspectives of human geography provide a useful standpoint from which to interpret how and why different fundamentalist movements have emerged. These perspectives are pertinent as well in understanding the specific beliefs and practices of particular fundamentalist groups. The heterogeneity that is evident among contemporary fundamentalist movements argues against the proposition that they share a common spatiality. Nonetheless, many of the distinguishing attributes of fundamentalist groups have a significant geographical component, which is crucial in understanding the nature of individual fundamentalist groups, and of fundamentalism generally.

Geographical expressions of fundamentalism take many forms, involving varied issues related to religious belief, practice, and identity, but they share a common concern with territoriality in dealing with perceived threats. Three crucial manifestations of this concern are considered in chapter 4. The first category of territorial concern revolves around concepts of sacred space. Sacred space refers to a location to which a group has explicitly ascribed sacred or divine qualities, based on the location's role in the group's beliefs and traditions. This concept is not limited to fundamentalists, of course; virtually all religions assign sacred status to particular sites, such as the birthplaces of key religious figures, important places of worship, or the locations of divine manifestations.[13] Fundamentalists develop a special concern for sacred space, however, when they believe that its sanctity is endangered by the threatening forces that they oppose. The preservation or reclamation of sacred space is thus often a primary goal of fundamentalist groups, especially when that space plays an important role in the group's "fundamental" beliefs. Such efforts may focus on the defense of a site already controlled by the group, to prevent its desecration by others. The protection of Muslim holy places in Jerusalem, for example, has become perhaps the dominant objective of Islamic fundamentalists there. Fundamentalists may also become involved in conflicts with others over the possession or use of a contested site, as seen in the razing of the mosque in Ayodhya by Hindu militants intent on reclaiming the birthplace of Ram. In both types of situation, establishing the boundaries of sacred territory becomes a significant priority for fundamentalists, enabling them to assert control over the site in question and limit its contamination by others.

A second geographical expression of fundamentalism involves efforts to exert territorial control over secular space. Such efforts involve motives different from those underlying fundamentalist concerns with sacred space. In establishing control over secular space, fundamentalists intend to give their moral community a spatial structure. Within this structure they can restore the proper social order, which in their view is threatened by forces outside their control. Their interest here is not in protecting the sanctity of special sites, but rather in ensuring that the everyday use of secular space conforms to their fundamental beliefs. Through such efforts they again create bounded spaces, but in this context the fundamentalists' goal is to regulate the activity space of daily life in accordance with religious doctrine. As with the other geographical expressions of fundamentalism, instances of secular territoriality occur at different scales. Referring back to the sketches that opened this chapter, for example, fundamentalist attempts to control secular space appear both in the Taliban's policing of social activity throughout Afghanistan and in the support among ultra-Orthodox Jews in Israel for gender segregation on public buses. In addition, fundamentalist efforts to control secular space involve highly diverse strategies, from the imposition of religious law on all residents of an area, regardless of their religious affiliation, to the creation of segregated group institutions, such as schools and businesses (fig. 1.4).

The third territorial manifestation of fundamentalism relates to the ideological boundaries that fundamentalist groups establish to define their unique identity. For most groups, this process of boundary making takes on a geographical dimension, either based upon or resulting in the creation of places explicitly identified with their beliefs. In some cases, the integration of territory and fundamentalist identity occurs at a national scale. Christian conservatives, for example, frequently refer to the concept of a "Christian nation" in defining their view of the United States, and the establishment of an "Islamic state" represents a primary objective of Islamic fundamentalists in many Asian and African countries. Fundamentalist concerns with territory and identity are not always tied to political concepts of nationalism, however. The connections between a fundamentalist movement and a particular place may operate at a more local scale, focusing on a particular community or settlement. Finally, a fundamentalist group's identification with a certain place or region may derive from religious belief or from the group's conception of an idealized past. Many Jewish fundamentalists, for example, claim to feel no connection to the state

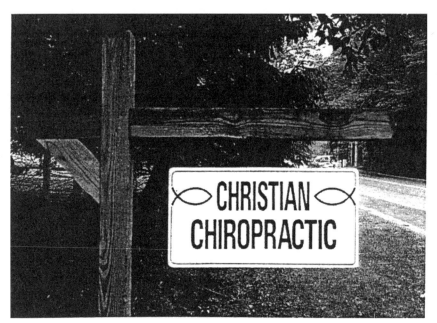

Figure 1.4   Roadside sign identifying a Christian chiropractic practice. Fundamentalists often seek to control their secular surroundings by defining their own group spaces, through the creation of separate places of worship, schools, and businesses. Clifton Park, New York, 1999. *Source:* the author.

of Israel, asserting that they are interested only in the "Land of Israel," the region promised to the Jewish people by divine covenant. In this instance, the territory with which these fundamentalists identify functions essentially as a sacred place. In all of the above cases, however, the attachment of fundamentalists to a certain place and their investment of that place with special meaning represents a central feature of their definition of themselves and shapes their relationship to the rest of the world.

Each of the territorial expressions of fundamentalism previously described has the potential to generate conflict, and all three inevitably produce some sort of reaction from other groups. In general this reaction involves strategies to restrict the power and influence of fundamentalists, but the nature of such strategies varies, again reflecting the diverse impacts of contextual factors. The government of Egypt, for example, has repeatedly imprisoned large numbers of militant Islamic fundamentalists, because it considers their violent activities to be a threat to the stability of Egyptian society. In Malaysia, on the other hand, conflicts between Islamic fundamentalists and their opponents have occurred mainly within the arena of electoral politics and have rarely led to deadly violence. In most settings, however, efforts by others to limit the influence of fundamentalists have had little effect on the persistence of fundamentalism itself. The absolute certainty with which fundamentalists hold their beliefs and their unyielding determination to give their beliefs concrete expression in social space have both contributed to fundamentalism's continuing impacts on societies around the world. Chapter 5 examines in more detail the factors underlying the persistence of conflicts involving fundamentalists, a crucial issue in understanding the future repercussions of the growth of fundamentalism.

In addressing the above-mentioned themes, then, the following chapters explore the nature of fundamentalism by considering the disparate forms that it has taken in different places and its varied spatial impacts on human societies and cultural landscapes. Past scholarship has demonstrated the usefulness of geographical perspectives in interpreting diverse aspects of religious belief and practice. This work contributes to that literature by applying those disciplinary perspectives to what is perhaps the most significant religious trend in contemporary societies around the world. Fundamentalism in its various forms has had profound effects in many different locations and is likely to remain an influential force for the foreseeable future. For this reason, understanding the spatial dimensions of its causes and consequences should be a key concern of human geography.

NOTES

1. Edward A. Gargan, "Hindu Militants Destroy Mosque," *New York Times*, December 7, 1992, 1(A); Scott Steele, "Flames of Intolerance," *Maclean's* (December 21, 1992): 17.

2. David Tuller and Susan Yoachum, "Evolution Debate in San Diego Suburb," *San Francisco Chronicle*, September 14, 1993, 1(A).

3. "The Road to Koranistan," *Economist* (October 5, 1996): 21–4.

4. Haim Shapiro, "Separate Seating Buses to Run in Bnei Brak and Jerusalem," *Jerusalem Post,* July 10, 1997, 1; Judy Dempsey, "Worries Grow over Israel Religious Groups," *Financial Times,* July 26, 1977, 3.

5. See especially the series of volumes edited by Martin E. Marty and R. Scott Appleby, produced as part of the Fundamentalism Project sponsored by the American Academy of Arts and Sciences: *Fundamentalisms Observed* (Chicago: University of Chicago Press, 1991); *Fundamentalisms and Society* (Chicago: University of Chicago Press, 1993); *Fundamentalisms and the State* (Chicago: University of Chicago Press, 1993); *Accounting for Fundamentalisms* (Chicago: University of Chicago Press, 1994); and *Fundamentalisms Comprehended* (Chicago: University of Chicago Press, 1995).

6. For an introduction to this body of research, see David Sopher, *Geography of Religions* (Englewood Cliffs, N.J.: Prentice-Hall, 1967) and Chris C.

Park, *Sacred Worlds: An Introduction to Geography and Religion* (London: Routledge, 1994).

7. On contextuality as a key geographical concept, see Doreen Massey and John Allen, eds., *Geography Matters!: A Reader* (Cambridge: Cambridge University Press, 1984) and R. J. Johnston, J. Hauer, and G. A. Hoekveld, eds., *Regional Geography: Current Developments and Future Prospects* (London: Routledge, 1990).

8. Robert David Sack, *Human Territoriality: Its Theory and History* (Cambridge: Cambridge University Press, 1986).

9. Martin E. Marty, "Fundamentals of Fundamentalism," in *Fundamentalism in Comparative Perspective*, Lawrence Kaplan, ed. (Amherst: University of Massachusetts Press, 1992), 20–1.

10. Gabriel A. Almond, Emmanuel Sivan, and R. Scott Appleby, "Explaining Fundamentalism," in *Fundamentalisms Comprehended,* Martin Marty and R. Scott Appleby, eds., 425–44.

11. For example, see Doreen Massey, "Introduction: Geography Matters," in *Geography Matters!: A Reader*, Doreen Massey and John Allen, eds., 8–10.

12. For useful discussions of the concept of the locale, see Joost Hauer, "What about Regional Geography after Structuration Theory?" in *Regional Geography: Current Developments and Future Prospects*, R. J. Johnston, J. Hauer, and G. A. Hoekveld, eds., 85–102; and Michael Dear and Jennifer Wolch, "How Territory Shapes Social Life," in *The Power of Geography: How Territory Shapes Social Life,* Jennifer Wolch and Michael Dear, eds. (Boston: Unwin Hyman, 1989), 3–18.

13. Richard H. Jackson and Roger Henrie, "Perceptions of Sacred Space," *Journal of Cultural Geography* 3, no. 2 (1983): 94–107.

2

FUNDAMENTALIST HEARTHS

Fundamentalism has attracted widespread attention as a global phenomenon only since the 1970s. Its origins can be traced back much further, however, to a variety of religious movements that developed in different regions of the world during the late nineteenth and early twentieth centuries. The major feature shared by early expressions of fundamentalism was their concern with the effects of unfamiliar patterns of social and cultural change on the traditional certainties of religious belief. Associated primarily with the sweeping transformations brought about by modernization, such patterns of change took various forms, including the growth of scientific inquiry, the restructuring of society through urbanization and industrialization, and the consequences of European colonialism. Early fundamentalist responses to these trends took diverse forms as well, reflecting variations in the religious traditions on which they were based and in the particular issues on which they focused. Fundamentalism thus emerged as a global phenomenon through its development in a variety of independent hearths, each characterized by a distinct set of contextual attributes.

This chapter examines the relationships between fundamentalism and its early hearth areas. The discussion does not investigate all of the historical precursors of contemporary fundamentalism. Rather, it assesses the variety of settings that fostered early expressions of this phenomenon and the ways in which different social and cultural contexts affected its initial development. The analysis of these issues thus examines both the universal factors underlying the rise of early fundamentalist movements and the significant differences among such movements in terms of their motivations, goals, and actions. In the process, this analysis establishes the conceptual groundwork for understanding contextual variations among the present-day fundamentalist movements discussed in subsequent chapters.

The following discussion centers around the thesis that, as a form of cultural innovation, religious fundamentalism arises out of the conjunction of three contextual factors in a specific hearth area. Most obviously, the emergence of fundamentalism requires the presence of a conservative cultural environment in which religious tradition plays a central role. That environment may encompass most or all segments of a society, or it may be associated with a distinctive minority group. In addition, the hearth area's social structures must contain an inherent element of moral or religious conflict, most commonly produced by patterns of social change that have accentuated disparities in the values, goals, or relative power of different groups or that have created friction between local groups and outside influences. For individuals or groups with a strong religious identity, such conflict may result in the perception of a significant threat to the survival of their beliefs, which forms the basis of a fundamentalist response. Human agency represents the final ingredient in this conjunction of contextual factors. Through the efforts of charismatic or visionary leaders and the commitment of self-identified true believers, fundamentalist movements ultimately take shape as the vehicle by which members defend the certainties of their faith.

Of course, each of the above factors—cultural environment, social structure, and human agency—appears in a variety of manifestations. The religious traditions embedded in local cultural environments vary considerably from place to place, reflecting historical patterns of migration and conversion. The role of religion in local social structures also varies, from locales where a dominant official faith influences most aspects of public life, to pluralistic settings where religion remains largely a private matter, to predominantly secular communities where religion holds little significance for most people. Such dissimilarities necessarily lead to different types of conflict between traditional believers and other groups or forces within society. Those varied conflicts in turn lead to different responses among those adopting a fundamentalist stance, ranging from lawful political action to violent terrorism and from aggressive proselytizing to withdrawal from the rest of society. Considered together, the diverse local manifestations of the above-mentioned factors are the main source of variations among the movements that developed in the early hearths of fundamentalism and represent the basic links in the relationships between fundamentalism and place.

To illustrate the impacts of these factors on the rise of fundamentalism, the remainder of this chapter focuses on the hearths of early fundamentalist movements within Christianity, Judaism, Islam, Hinduism, and Sikhism. These hearths differed significantly from one another in terms of their defining social and cultural characteristics and in terms of the sources of conflict that provoked fundamentalist reactions. The Christian fundamentalist movement emerged largely as a reaction among conservative Protestants to the rise of theological modernism and scientific explanation in the United States. Early Jewish fundamentalism rejected both the secularization of Jewish society in Europe and, more specifically, secular interpretations of Jewish history as they related to the formation of a Jewish homeland in Palestine. European colonialism played a central role in the rise of Islamic fundamentalism, which opposed the spread of Western social, political, and economic models to the Islamic world. Similarly, early expressions of Hindu, Islamic, and Sikh fundamentalism in India arose in part as reactions against religious pluralism in Indian society during and after the colonial period. The resulting variations in the goals and strategies of these movements clearly illustrate the contextual nature of fundamentalism, even as similarities in the processes of their formation demonstrate the usefulness of classifying these movements as part of a single, global phenomenon.

PROTESTANT FUNDAMENTALISM IN NORTH AMERICA

In 1909, a Los Angeles oil millionaire named Lyman Stewart recruited the Baptist minister and evangelist A. C. Dixon to begin work on a series of religious booklets entitled *The Fundamentals*. Stewart's goal was to promote the Christian faith by producing a compendium of conservative Protestant doctrines, which would be sent free of charge to ministers, pastors, theological professors, students, and other religious leaders throughout the English-speaking world. To that end, he and his brother Milton committed $300,000 to the publication and distribution of the booklets. The series' editorial committee produced twelve volumes of essays between 1910 and 1915, bringing together contributions from dozens of conservative theologians in North America and Great Britain. The average printing of these volumes ran to around 250,000 copies, and the entire project resulted in the distribution of three million booklets to its intended audience.[1]

The essays included in *The Fundamentals* focused primarily on the defense of the core doctrines of conservative Protestantism. The most prominent of these was belief in the literal truth of the Bible, a concept that had been challenged during the 1800s by a new approach to scriptural interpretation based on the method of "higher criticism," which cast the Bible as a mixture of folklore, history, and poetry rather than as a divinely authored text. To conservatives, the new approach undermined the authority of the Bible and thus threatened the very foundation of Christian belief. Other essays in the series defended the truth of specific doctrines (such as Christ's virgin birth, bodily resurrection, and second coming), presented personal testimonies regarding the power of Christianity, attacked other varieties of Christian belief (including Mormonism, Christian Science, and Roman Catholicism), and discussed the relationship between science and faith. Together these essays outlined the main themes within conservative Protestant belief at the start of the twentieth century. More importantly, though, they represented the first concrete expres-

sion of the emergence of a fundamentalist movement among conservative Protestants in North America as well as the source of the movement's name.[2]
   The perceived need to define and promote the core beliefs of conservative
Protestantism at this time derived from significant changes that had developed
within American Protestantism, and American society generally, since the late
nineteenth century. Throughout most of the 1800s, the religious culture of
the United States had been dominated by the large, evangelical Protestant
denominations, such as the Methodists, Baptists, Presbyterians, Congregationalists, and Disciples of Christ.[3] With their emphasis on revivalism and personal
conversion, these groups had expanded dramatically during the period of rapid
population growth prior to the Civil War, particularly as the settlement frontier
moved westward into the interior of the continent. By the late 1800s, they had
become the nucleus of the country's religious establishment. Their extensive
increases in membership had been accompanied, however, by growth in the
diversity of viewpoints held by their leaders and members. As a result, the
end of the nineteenth century also saw a widening rift within the Protestant
establishment, as liberals and conservatives became increasingly polarized over
the advance of modernist ideas at the expense of traditional beliefs. Reinterpretation of the biblical account of creation to accommodate scientific thought
concerning biological evolution, for example, appealed to some members of
the mainline Protestant churches, but it deeply offended others. The growing
tension within evangelical Protestantism was exacerbated, moreover, by the
development of new threats to Protestant hegemony in the nation's religious
culture, including the expanding impact of secularism on American life and
substantial increases in the number of Catholic and Jewish immigrants from
southern and eastern Europe.
   The conflict between liberals and conservatives within evangelical Protestantism grew out of developments on both sides of the split. Among conservative Protestants, doctrinal orthodoxy became a preeminent concern during the
nineteenth century, leading to a variety of controversies within individual denominations. Perhaps the most significant issue addressed in this context was
the doctrine of biblical inerrancy, the belief that the Bible is the inspired word
of God and is literally and factually true in every detail. The dispute over this
issue arose in a number of denominations, but became particularly intense
among Presbyterians, whose conservative members insisted most strongly on
adherence to this belief. During the 1890s, conservative Presbyterians in fact
brought formal charges of heresy against three prominent seminary professors
who did not strictly follow the doctrine of biblical inerrancy in their scholarship. Two of the professors were subsequently dismissed from the Presbyterian
ministry, and the third later resigned. Conservatives in various denominations
focused on other doctrinal issues as well, including the supernatural elements
of Christian belief, the authenticity of the miracles attributed to Christ in the
Bible, and the significance of particular denominational traditions, such as the

practice of baptism by immersion among Baptists and Disciples.[4] As a result of the controversies generated by these issues, absolute insistence on adherence to orthodoxy became one of the key features of evangelical Protestantism's conservative wing.

A related development within conservative Protestantism in the late nineteenth century was the widespread acceptance of the doctrine of dispensational premillennialism, a supernatural interpretation of history based on a literalist reading of the Book of Daniel and the Book of Revelation in the Old Testament. The first prominent proponent of this doctrine was John Nelson Darby, a British theologian and early leader of the Plymouth Brethren movement who traveled widely in North America. His ideas were further developed and disseminated by a number of influential American ministers and evangelists during the late 1800s and early 1900s. The doctrine that these men articulated asserts that all of history is divided into a series of distinct eras, or dispensations (by most accounts, seven in number). Within each dispensation God poses a test for humanity, which humanity ultimately fails. Each dispensation thus concludes with a catastrophic event, such as the expulsion from Eden, the flood of Genesis, or the crucifixion of Christ.[5] According to this view of history, the present age falls within the sixth or next-to-last dispensation, the "Church Age," in which most people have failed to achieve salvation through the Christian church, which has itself been corrupted by heresy. This dispensation will end, in most versions of this doctrine, with the "rapture" of true Christians, followed by a period of worldly tribulation. The Second Coming will initiate the final dispensation, or "Millennial Age," in which Christ returns to earth and rules for a thousand years. That era will end with the final judgment and the creation of a perfect world, "a new heaven and a new earth," described in the Book of Revelation. Not all conservatives accepted this doctrine, and even those who did often disagreed with respect to its details. Nonetheless, it became one of the most distinctive features of conservative Protestantism at the end of the nineteenth century.

The emergence of new institutional structures fostered the above-mentioned trends among conservative Protestants. Beginning in the 1870s, nondenominational Bible conferences became an important feature of the American religious scene. These meetings brought together conservative theologians, scholars, evangelists, and other believers for several days of Bible study and doctrinal discussion. The most prominent of these, the Niagara Bible Conference (named after its most frequent meeting site, Niagara-on-the-Lake, Ontario), met every year from 1875 to 1900.[6] Large conferences were also organized in many of the major cities of North America, attracting hundreds and even thousands of attendees. The Bible conferences placed a heavy emphasis on the doctrine of biblical inerrancy, the cornerstone of conservative Protestant theology, and they also played a key role in the spread of belief in dispensational premillennialism. In the process, they provided a means for

conservative Protestants from different denominations to develop a sense of
doctrinal unity, at least regarding certain core beliefs.

The doctrinal concerns of conservative Protestantism also found expression
in the formation of nondenominational Bible institutes, schools, and colleges
throughout North America. The most influential of these schools was the
Moody Bible Institute, created in Chicago in 1889 by evangelist Dwight L.
Moody. By the 1920s, several dozen such institutions had been established
throughout the country.[7] At first the Bible institutes focused primarily on the
training of laymen, presenting them with a more Bible-centered education
than students in theological seminaries received, and preparing them for work
as evangelists, preachers, church-school teachers, or missionaries. Eventually,
the Bible institutes and colleges became a primary training ground for conservative Protestant clergy as well. Again, the central concern of the Bible institutes was to oppose modernist culture and promote conservative doctrines,
including biblical inerrancy and authority, Christ's virgin birth and resurrection, and in many cases premillennialism.[8] Like the Bible conferences, the
Bible institutes also provided a source of unity among conservative Protestants
whose own denominations contained many adherents holding theological views
that the conservatives found unacceptable.

Theological divisions within individual denominations in fact became a common feature of evangelical Protestantism in the late nineteenth century, as new
currents of liberal thought developed alongside the conservative trends outlined above.[9] Although liberalism had been an important force in American
Protestantism throughout the 1800s, only after the Civil War did it begin to
influence the evangelical churches significantly, particularly in the northeastern
and Midwestern states. The spread of liberal views within evangelical Protestantism in part reflected a growing receptivity to larger trends in contemporary
thought, particularly in the realm of science. Liberal Protestants accepted the
idea that religious beliefs should be reconciled with modern scientific findings,
even if doing so contradicted traditional doctrines. For example, because the
account of creation in the Book of Genesis, in which God created the world
and humanity in six days, did not conform to the scientific theory of biological
evolution, liberals abandoned the traditional, literalist interpretation of that
account. Liberal thought within the evangelical churches also reflected the influence of new approaches to biblical analysis, such as the historical perspective
of "higher criticism," which approached the Bible as a work of human rather
than divine origin.

In adopting the above perspectives, the liberal wing of the evangelical
churches became less concerned than the conservative wing with the details of
theological doctrine, treating religious dogma as the product of human thought
in a particular time and place, rather than as eternal truth. In place of doctrine,
social and ethical issues became the primary concern of liberals. In this context,
liberal evangelicals strongly emphasized the concept of free will and the human

capacity for altruistic behavior. Unlike their more conservative coreligionists, liberal evangelicals interpreted sin as a form of error or the product of social ills, rather than as an intrinsic component of human nature. The liberal viewpoint also expressed considerable optimism about the future of humanity and the positive impacts of scientific progress and social reform. For most liberals, that optimism fostered belief in humanity's redemption through the spread of Christianity. From their perspective, in other words, the earthly Kingdom of God would be achieved by the historical progress of Christian civilization, not through the catastrophic apocalypse foreseen by many conservatives.

As their understandings of Christianity diverged, liberals and conservatives within the evangelical Protestant denominations became increasingly polarized. Conservative Protestants strongly opposed liberal deviations from traditional orthodoxy, while liberals rejected the conservatives' adherence to what they considered to be outmoded beliefs. Out of this conflict, a distinctly fundamentalist movement gradually emerged among conservative evangelicals, who believed that the certainties of their faith were threatened by liberals within their churches as well as by more widespread forces of modernism and secularism at work in society. The strength of evangelical Protestantism in North America at the end of the nineteenth century provided a large potential constituency for this fundamentalist movement, made up of those who did not question the truth of traditional religious teachings. At the same time, by accommodating significant differences of opinion among their members, the evangelical Protestant denominations provided an institutional context for the conflict between liberals and conservatives, and new institutions such as Bible conferences and institutes provided specific structures for the defense and dissemination of conservative views. The publication of *The Fundamentals*, discussed previously, represented a crucial episode in the emergence of this movement, although its immediate impact was weakened by the onset of World War I, which focused the attentions of most Americans elsewhere. After the war, however, adherents of this new fundamentalist perspective became increasingly active and began to work out specific strategies for combating modernism and promoting the cause of traditional religion.

In their attempts to counter the threat of modernism, American fundamentalists adopted two approaches, one aimed at reforming the evangelical Protestant churches and the other at shaping broader trends in American culture. The initial thrust of fundamentalist action involved attempts to fight the influences of liberal theology within the evangelical Protestant denominations. Growing out of the conservatives' predominant concern with doctrinal orthodoxy, these efforts generated a number of significant intradenominational conflicts. This controversy did not affect all evangelical churches equally, however. The debate over liberalism created little friction within the Congregationalist and Northern Methodist churches, for example, because fundamentalists represented a relatively small minority of their membership. Conversely, the lack of support for liberalism in denominations whose membership was concentrated in the South, such as the Southern Baptists and Southern Presbyterians, prevented the development of significant conflict within those groups. The fundamentalist fight against liberal theology thus became most intense in the Protestant churches where both conservative and liberal viewpoints had large bases of support, including the Northern Presbyterians, the Northern Baptists, and the Disciples of Christ.[10] In each of these groups, however, the diversity of opinions held by group members made it impossible for fundamentalists to achieve unified support for their conservative beliefs.

    Among the Northern Presbyterians, the fundamentalist controversy revolved around the conservative beliefs codified in the 'Five Point Deliverance," a statement of core doctrines adopted by the group's General Assembly in 1910 and reaffirmed in 1916 and 1923. The Five Points included the inerrancy of the Bible, the virgin birth of Christ, Christ's atonement for humanity's sins, the bodily resurrection of Christ, and the authenticity of the miracles described in the Bible. Moderates and liberals within the denomination, along with some conservatives, objected to the acceptance of these points as essential Presbyterian doctrine. In 1924, a group of ministers challenged the necessity of adhering to the Five Points, arguing that they were not a part of the basic teachings of Presbyterianism and that Presbyterian tradition gave ministers some leeway in the area of biblical interpretation. A denominational commission appointed to study the issue subsequently recommended tolerance of diverse viewpoints, and the conservative branch of the denomination gradually lost influence. Many conservatives eventually left the denomination to form their own group, the Orthodox Presbyterian Church, in 1936.

    The debate between conservatives and liberals among the Northern Baptists also focused on the conservative's insistence on a formal statement of doctrine that would unambiguously declare the church's essential beliefs, particularly regarding the issue of biblical inerrancy. The term *fundamentalists* was first used in print in 1920, in an editorial appearing in a conservative Baptist publication, to describe those working toward this goal.[11] Support for an official statement of doctrine faced considerable opposition, however, based in part on the Baptists' tradition of giving individual ministers and congregations considerable freedom of belief. Realizing that their views were not shared by the majority of Northern Baptists, the more militant conservatives began to organize independent institutions. In 1923 they formed the Baptist Bible Union to fight liberal trends within the Northern Baptist Convention; and in 1932, many conservatives left the denomination to form a separate group, the General Association of Regular Baptists.

    Similar debates emerged among the Disciples of Christ during the 1920s, although their impact was mitigated by the earlier departure of many conservative adherents to form the Churches of Christ, in 1906. Those conservatives who did not leave resided for the most part outside the South, where the

Churches of Christ were largely concentrated. They continued to oppose the new trends in liberal theology and biblical criticism, however, and in 1927 formed their own association of congregations within the larger Disciples denomination. In the 1960s, that association formally organized itself as a separate denomination, the Christian Churches and Churches of Christ.[12]

The failure of conservative factions to dominate the mainstream Protestant denominations had several important effects. As previously discussed, it led to the creation of several new religious bodies organized around conservative Christian beliefs. These denominations preserved and promoted conservative doctrine, but they did so for the most part outside the large evangelical churches that had defined the Protestant establishment during the 1800s. At the same time, their inability to prevail within existing denominations added to fundamentalism's growth as a nondenominational movement, drawing followers from various churches as fundamentalists recognized that they had more in common with other fundamentalists in different denominations than they did with modernists and liberals in their own church. The nondenominational character of many of the early Bible institutes and conferences thus became a key feature of new fundamentalist developments, such as the rise in religious broadcasting and televangelism, as the twentieth century progressed.

Finally, the fundamentalists' inability to stop the advance of liberalism within the large Protestant denominations contributed to the emergence of their oppositional stance with respect to contemporary American culture, which they have maintained ever since. Disenchanted with the Protestant establishment, fundamentalists eventually abandoned their goal of reforming the major denominations that had espoused liberal and modernist innovations and instead began to focus on reshaping American culture in general. Their goal in this context was not just to promote private commitment to particular doctrines or beliefs but also to strengthen the influence of conservative Christian principles on the nation's public life. The theological debates of the 1920s were thus accompanied by a second form of fundamentalist activism aimed at combating the impacts of modernism on American life and thought. This form of activism involved a broader coalition of fundamentalists than did the denominational controversies previously described, since it was taken up by many members of the conservative denominations that had not experienced conflicts over liberal theology. In particular, fundamentalists in the southern states played a more active role in this context than they had in the intradenominational disputes, which were concentrated primarily in the northeastern and Midwestern states.

The first major issue that the fundamentalists addressed in their broader attack on modernism in American culture was the teaching in public schools and universities of scientific concepts that contradicted traditional interpretations of the Bible. The most frequently targeted concept in this context was the theory of biological evolution, which many fundamentalists considered to be the most threatening product of modern science. This view was popularized most successfully by William Jennings Bryan, a former presidential candidate and key opponent of modernism in the Presbyterian Church. In a pamphlet entitled "The Menace of Darwinism," Bryan argued that the concept of evolution challenged the biblical account of creation, depicted the universe as a product of random processes rather than a divine plan, and denied the validity of religious revelation as a source of truth. In his view, acceptance of the theory of evolution thus precluded belief in the essential doctrines of Christianity and would inevitably lead to society's moral decay. Bryan's antievolutionism found considerable support among fundamentalists throughout the country and helped to define their goals during the 1920s.[13]

In dealing with the issue of evolution, fundamentalists adopted new strategies to advance their cause, seeking to ban the teaching of evolution through statewide legislation and local school district regulations. Their first success occurred in Oklahoma, which in 1923 passed a law prohibiting the use of textbooks that included discussions of evolution. Florida followed suit later that year with the first state law, which Bryan assisted in drafting, that explicitly prohibited the teaching of evolution in public schools. Tennessee enacted a similar law in 1925, followed by Mississippi in 1926, Arkansas in 1927, and Texas in 1929.[14] Most of these laws banned schools from teaching that humanity was related to other orders of animals, but Tennessee specifically outlawed the teaching of "any theory that denies the story of the divine creation of man as taught in the Bible."[15] Supporters of the antievolution movement also proposed bills in various other states at this time but failed to get them enacted into law. They were considerably more successful at the local level, however. Many local school boards outlawed the teaching of evolution, both in rural areas and in large cities, including Atlanta and Cleveland. By the early 1940s, fewer than half of the high school biology teachers in the United States covered biological evolution in their courses.[16]

The use of state legislatures and local school boards to advance its agenda marked the introduction of fundamentalist activism into the public arena and thus set an important precedent for later developments in fundamentalism in the United States. It also brought greater public attention to the fundamentalists' goals and beliefs and thus initiated a profound conflict between fundamentalism and other strains of thought in American society. During the 1920s, undoubtedly the most important expression of that conflict was the so-called Scopes Monkey Trial, one of the first legal tests of the antievolution laws. John Scopes, a biology teacher in Dayton, Tennessee, had disobeyed that state's law against teaching evolution and was subsequently arrested and tried. The trial itself, which pitted William Jennings Bryan against defense attorney Clarence Darrow, attracted considerable attention throughout the United States and became a major event for the world's news media (fig. 2.1).

Scopes was ultimately convicted, although his conviction was later overturned on technical grounds. But the trial did little to promote the fundamen-

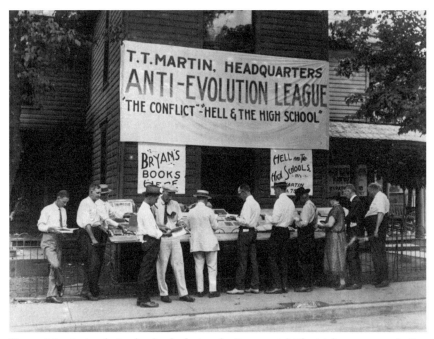

Figure 2.1   Antievolution book sale during the Scopes trial. The trial came to symbolize the conflict between fundamentalist and modernist views in American society but ultimately did little to further the fundamentalists' goal of banning the teaching of evolution in public schools. Dayton, Tennessee, 1925. *Source:* CORBIS/Hulton-Deutsch Co.

talists' cause, as it subjected them to considerable scorn and ridicule from journalists and other outside observers. The most well known of these commentators, H. L. Mencken, was especially caustic in his depiction of the fundamentalists as an ignorant, superstitious lot, a caricature that became widely accepted among nonfundamentalists at the time.[17] Despite the public derision to which they were subjected, fundamentalists continued to pursue their goal of banning the teaching of evolution from public schools during the 1920s. Again, a number of states passed antievolution laws following the Scopes trial; and in Arkansas and Mississippi, such laws remained in effect until 1968, when Arkansas' law was overturned by the U.S. Supreme Court. Many local school boards also continued to enforce antievolution policies. More generally, through the 1950s many states required regular reading from the Bible in public schools, particularly in the South (fig. 2.2).[18] Nonetheless, the fundamentalist movement lost much credibility as a result of the Scopes trial, especially outside the South, and its influence within the broader context of American culture fell sharply. The movement also lost an important spokesman when Bryan died shortly after the conclusion of the trial.

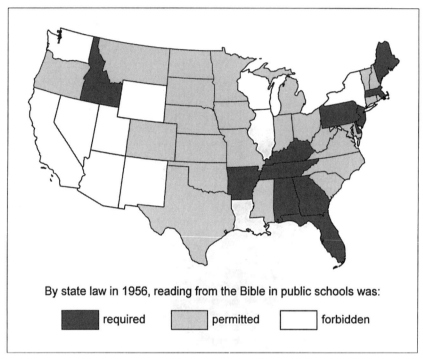

By state law in 1956, reading from the Bible in public schools was:

[dark] required   [gray] permitted   [white] forbidden

Figure 2.2   By the mid-1950s, a number of states still required reading from the Bible in public schools, a practice also permitted in most other states at the time.

As a result, American fundamentalists began to abandon the confrontational approach that had characterized much of their activity up to that point. Instead, they concentrated on strengthening their own institutions, within which they could preserve and promote their traditional religious certainties. In addition to establishing a number of new Protestant denominations during the 1920s and 1930s, they organized many local congregations committed to the tenets of fundamentalism. Some of those local churches developed within the structure of existing denominations, but large numbers operated without an affiliation to any larger organization. The independent Bible institutes and colleges continued to increase in number as well and served as important fundamentalist institutions, providing ministers for independent churches, organizing Bible conferences, and coordinating missionary work. Fundamentalists also played a leading role in the expansion of religious broadcasting that began during the 1930s and 1940s. A number of Bible institutes supported their own radio stations, and many fundamentalist evangelists purchased time on commercial radio stations, paid for by donations from their audiences. The most successful of these radio evangelists broadcast over commercial radio networks to audiences numbering in the millions.[19]

The development of this structure of independent institutions helped to strengthen the fundamentalist movement following the uproar caused by the Scopes trial and consolidated its position as a key element of the American religious landscape. This institutional framework also served two important functions in the continuing development of the fundamentalist movement throughout the rest of the twentieth century. Most importantly, it provided a means of mobilizing new expressions of fundamentalist activism. In essence, fundamentalists had created an institutional infrastructure through which they could continue to promote their cause within the public arena. This factor played an especially important role as the fundamentalists' political influence increased during the 1970s and 1980s. At the same time, the independent nature of this infrastructure clearly placed the fundamentalists in an oppositional position with respect to broader trends within mainstream American culture. As a result, it reinforced the fundamentalists' sense of their own distinctive identity and clarified the ideological boundaries that separated them from their opponents.

Through the above-mentioned processes, then, Protestant fundamentalism in North America arose out of a traditional religious culture rooted in evangelical Christianity. The introduction of modernism into mainstream American institutions, such as evangelical Protestant churches and public schools, created a structural context that threatened the survival of traditional religious beliefs. Unwilling to accept a compromise between tradition and innovation, fundamentalists actively pursued the defeat of modernism by attempting to exclude it from their churches and from the nation's schools and universities. The strategies that they adopted in this struggle proved to be ineffective, however, and so they responded in a new wave of activism aimed at developing an independent network of institutions. Those institutions in turn provided a base for future fundamentalist actions, which are explored in more detail in chapter 3.

SECULARISM, ZIONISM, AND JEWISH FUNDAMENTALISM

The origins of Jewish fundamentalism are difficult to locate precisely, given the extensive geographical transformations that Judaism has experienced since the middle of the nineteenth century. Mass emigration from Europe, the enormous destruction by the Holocaust, and extensive immigration to Israel have significantly reshaped the distribution of the world's Jewish population. Jewish expressions of fundamentalism emerged within the context of this demographic redistribution and so reflected conditions and events in varied locations. Eastern Europe served as the dominant milieu in the early stages of the process, but it was in Palestine, and later Israel, that the two major branches of Jewish fundamentalism reached their fullest development. As an important destination for Jewish migrants since the late 1800s, North America also played a role in the process, but was less important as a hearth of fundamentalist trends. The following discussion thus focuses on the emergence of Jewish fundamentalism in Eastern Europe and its subsequent development in the Middle East.

Changing social and cultural conditions in Europe defined the framework within which Jewish fundamentalism originally emerged. Prior to the late 1700s, European Jews generally lived in isolation within predominantly Christian societies. Laws of exclusion prohibited them from working in many occupations, from owning land, and from voting or holding government office, and residential restrictions produced segregated Jewish ghettos in cities across Europe. Under these conditions, Jews maintained a strong attachment to traditional Judaism, which structured their daily lives and formed the basis for their group identity. By the end of the eighteenth century, however, legal restrictions on Europe's Jews began to be removed. New philosophical trends promoted a more expansive view of civil and political rights and advanced the concept of the separation of church and state, thereby undermining earlier justifications for discrimination against Jews. Subsequent political transformations, from the French Revolution in the late 1700s to the Bolshevik Revolution in 1917, contributed to these changes in perspective. As a result, European states began to revoke the laws that limited Jewish participation in politics, the economy, and society. This process, termed the *Emancipation*, redefined the ways in which Jews interacted with the dominant structures of European society. As the Emancipation spread eastward across Europe during the nineteenth century, it provided Jews with new occupational opportunities, greater residential mobility, and broader involvement in civic life. At the same time, it had important repercussions for the future of the traditional Jewish community, as many Jews sought assimilation in the larger society to which they now had access.[20]

Developments originating within the Jewish community also contributed to a reordering of the character of Judaism in Europe at this time. In response to the changing social and intellectual climate, many Jews became interested in expanding their understanding of contemporary secular knowledge, a task that required a broader knowledge of modern European culture. Some people pursued this goal by thoroughly conforming to their larger cultural surroundings, but others sought to modernize Jewish life without abandoning their religious identity. The latter became the key participants in the Haskalah, or Jewish Enlightenment, a movement to integrate modern European thought and scientific knowledge into Jewish culture.[21] The roots of the Haskalah reach as far back as the seventeenth century, but the movement became most widespread after the onset of the Emancipation, and the two trends reinforced one another as the nineteenth century progressed.

The modernist perspective of the Haskalah also found expression in the

Reform movement, which originated among German Jews in the late 1700s and early 1800s.[22] The adherents of this movement advocated an approach to Judaism that gave human judgment priority over traditional religious laws and customs. More specifically, Reform Jews made a distinction between the eternal aspects of biblical teaching, which they believed were a product of divine inspiration, and the traditional customs associated with Jewish law, which they saw as expressions of human belief grounded in particular times and places. They believed that each generation should adapt Jewish traditions to render them compatible with contemporary conditions. Failure to do so, they argued, would cause many Jews to abandon their religion as modernism spread within the Jewish community. Reform Jews adopted various innovations in religious services during the 1800s, allowing preaching in German and the use of musical instruments in the synagogue, and they rejected traditional customs of daily life that they considered to be outdated, such as dietary restrictions and patterns of dress. They also abandoned the belief that Jewish history would culminate with the appearance of a Messiah who would return the Jews to the promised land. They believed that Jews should see themselves as permanent citizens of their country of residence rather than as exiles from the biblical Land of Israel.

The atmosphere of change associated with these developments was not universally welcomed by European Jews, and a major resurgence in Jewish traditionalism also occurred during the nineteenth century.[23] Traditional believers, who remained in the majority in most parts of Europe throughout the 1800s, asserted that the above-mentioned innovations threatened the survival of authentic Judaism. The traditionalists' primary concern was the threat to traditional Jewish law, but they also viewed many of the freedoms achieved during the Emancipation with suspicion, believing that greater integration into the surrounding society would undermine the integrity of the Jewish community. The traditionalists were not a homogenous group, but they shared a commitment to preserving traditional forms of Jewish life, ritual, and belief, and these objectives laid the foundation for subsequent expressions of fundamentalism.

An early expression of resurgent traditionalism was the Hasidic movement, which originated among Polish Jews during the eighteenth century. Its adherents, the Hasidim, or "pious ones," stressed religious zeal over theoretical knowledge, emphasized salvation through prayer, and incorporated an element of mysticism into Jewish belief and practice. They also relied heavily on the guidance of their religious leaders, the zaddikim, to whom they attributed a spiritually superior character. Although the Hasidim deviated from mainstream Judaism in a number of ways, they adhered to traditional Jewish customs and a strict interpretation of Jewish law and rejected the incorporation of secular elements into Jewish education. As an alternative to the uncertainties of modernization, the movement grew rapidly in Eastern Europe during the nineteenth century, spreading into Russia, Lithuania, and Hungary. The success of

Hasidism among Eastern Europe's large Jewish population contributed to that region's emergence as the leading hearth for resistance to modernist and secularist trends in Judaism.

A more general resurgence of Jewish orthodoxy also developed across Europe during the 1800s, as traditionalists reasserted the importance of strict adherence to the halakhah, Jewish law derived from the Torah and rabbinical teachings. One branch of this movement, known as Neo-Orthodoxy, or "modern" Orthodoxy, insisted on strict observance of Jewish law, but also encouraged secular education, permitted Western dress, and accepted changes in ritual practice, such as preaching in German and other vernacular languages. Neo-Orthodox Jews also departed from tradition by seeking to isolate themselves from the Reform community, a strategy that contradicted the long-standing practice of treating Judaism as a single, unified culture. Because the Neo-Orthodox did not strictly oppose the interaction of Jewish culture with modern secular knowledge, but still maintained a core of traditional beliefs, they found many supporters among Jews who sought a balance between innovation and tradition. Neo-Orthodoxy became especially influential in Western Europe as enthusiasm for the radical innovations of Reform Judaism declined in the second half of the nineteenth century.

A more traditional form of Orthodoxy developed in Eastern Europe, where the Emancipation had proceeded more slowly. The primary hearth of this movement emerged during the early 1800s in Hungary, largely through the leadership of Moses Sofer, the chief rabbi of Pressburg (now Bratislava).[24] Sofer believed that the Torah prohibited any type of innovation and argued that for Jewish tradition to have meaning, it had to be followed in its entirety. He opposed secular education, any modification of worship practices, and the translation of sacred texts from Hebrew into European languages. In his view, segregation from the rest of society offered the only means of preserving the traditional Jewish way of life, which was founded on strict adherence to traditional Jewish law. To promote his views, Sofer founded an influential Orthodox yeshiva (or religious academy) in Pressburg, which excluded any form of study related to the Jewish Enlightenment.

As the leading rabbi in Hungary during the early 1800s, Sofer had considerable influence, and he developed a strong following among traditionalists. After his death in 1839, however, the Reform movement began to attract adherents in Hungary, particularly following the enactment of Emancipation in 1867. In response, some Orthodox leaders adopted a more moderate approach, similar to German Neo-Orthodoxy. But others reasserted the absolute primacy of halakhic tradition and rejected any suggestion of compromise with modern secular culture. The latter group became known as the ultra-Orthodox, the most radical branch of Orthodox Judaism. Their response to the secularization of the Jewish community in Eastern Europe was essentially to isolate themselves from it, preserving traditional Judaism by creating their own institutional structures. They formed and received government recognition for independent Orthodox Jewish communities throughout Hungary and founded a number of yeshivas for training Orthodox rabbis. Along with the Hasidim, they became a major force within the Orthodox Jewish community in Eastern Europe during the second half of the nineteenth century.

As the influence of Hasidism and ultra-Orthodoxy spread, the two groups began to merge into a larger traditionalist community within their Eastern European hearth, and in some areas the groups overlapped considerably. Hasidism contained a stronger folkloric element than did other varieties of Orthodoxy and placed more emphasis on the role of the zaddik, or spiritual leader, while ultra-Orthodoxy stressed law, ritual, Torah study, and the authority of leading yeshiva teachers. The two traditions shared an overriding interest, however, in promoting adherence to Jewish law and opposing the advance of Reform and the Enlightenment. Thus, as the nineteenth century progressed, the differences between these two traditions became less important than their sense of commonality. Along with like-minded Orthodox Jews from other parts of Eastern Europe, these groups gradually came to be recognized as a distinct expression of Jewish culture, now known as the haredim.[25] The term *haredim*, derived from the Torah, can be translated as "the awestruck" or more literally as "those who tremble (at the word of God)." At the time, they included those Orthodox and ultra-Orthodox Jews who followed traditional customs, strictly adhered to the halakhah, and rejected compromise with the modern world. The haredim were not united in any formal association and still today are not a homogeneous group. Nonetheless, they shared an approach to Judaism based on the elevation of tradition and the rejection of innovation.

The early haredim placed great emphasis on the definition of ideological boundaries between themselves and others. These boundaries obviously separated them from those outside their religious tradition, but they also marked increasingly important divisions within the Jewish community. To the haredim, Reform Jews and secular Jews had discarded the central concepts of Judaism: the importance of halakhic traditions, the Jews' unique status as God's chosen people, and the ultimate redemption of the Jews through their return from exile to the promised land. The haredim believed that any compromise with the secular world would eventually destroy their religious identity and their hopes for redemption, and so they isolated themselves from Jews involved in the Reform movement and the Enlightenment. And that isolation was not just ideological. The early haredim also created institutional boundaries between themselves and other Jews, particularly in the Eastern European hearth of Hasidism and Hungarian ultra-Orthodoxy. They established separate communities, which were legally independent from the rest of the Jewish community, and within those communities, they established their own schools, places of worship, and social organizations. While other Jews attempted to distance themselves from the enclave culture of the old Jewish ghettos, the early haredim remained committed to that isolated way of life. As a result, their ideological boundaries took on an explicitly geographical character.

In their efforts to isolate themselves from secular influences, the early haredim marked the beginnings of Jewish fundamentalism. The major threat that they opposed was the dissolution of Jewish identity, and they responded to that threat by reasserting the importance of traditional religious practice and belief. As the nineteenth century progressed, however, a significant new concern developed among these emergent fundamentalists: the rising influence of Zionism. As Jews across Europe acquired basic civil rights and greater access to Western society during the 1800s, most continued to encounter widespread anti-Semitism. As the nineteenth century progressed, some Jewish leaders began to argue that the Jews would always remain outcasts within European society and that the only solution was to establish a Jewish national state in Palestine. Persistent persecution of Jews, especially in the form of Russian pogroms, or massacres, strengthened support for the Zionist cause, as did influential Jewish thinkers such as Leon Pinsker and Theodor Herzl. As the Zionist movement developed, Pinsker became one of the leaders of Hovevei Zion ("Lovers of Zion"), a nationalist movement that supported Jewish settlement in Palestine. More importantly, Herzl organized the First Zionist Congress in Basel, Switzerland, in 1897, which founded the World Zionist Organization to advance the goal of establishing a legally recognized Jewish homeland.

The idea of Zionism, that a political state should be created as a homeland for the Jews, at first glance appears to be consistent with the fundamentalist goal of preserving Jewish identity. But perhaps even more than Reform Judaism and the Enlightenment, secular Zionism represented a grave danger to many traditionalists. In their view, the goal of establishing a Jewish state through political negotiation was heretical, as it directly contradicted a central theme in the sacred history of Judaism: the redemption of the Jews through their divine restoration to the promised land. These traditionalists saw Zionism as an attempt to bring about by human means a result that could be achieved only by God and thus as a direct challenge to divine authority. They also opposed the Zionist movement because it had extensive support among secular Jews, who seemed intent on substituting nationalism for religious belief as the core of Jewish life. An emerging fundamentalist view thus asserted that Jews should seek their redemption through strict adherence to religious law, not by forming a political state in which Jews would be defined as a secular nationality, like the Dutch or the French.

Their shared opposition to Zionism produced a growing sense of unity among adherents of different Orthodox and traditionalist groups. Eventually the common concerns of these groups led to the formation of an Orthodox political association known as Agudat Israel ("Union of Israel"), or simply the Agudah, established in 1912 at a conference of Orthodox leaders. Its members were drawn from diverse backgrounds, including German Neo-Orthodoxy,

Hasidism, and traditionalist forms of Orthodoxy that had developed among Hungarian, Polish, and Lithuanian Jews. Although these groups differed in many ways, they all stressed strict adherence to Jewish law and rabbinical authority, and they strongly objected to the goals of Reform, the Enlightenment, and secular Zionism.[26] They further believed that authentic Judaism could be preserved most effectively by following the traditional patterns of Jewish life that had developed in Central and Eastern Europe. As a result, they disapproved of many features of the secular culture developing in the Zionist settlements of Palestine. Zionists had, for example, revived Hebrew as the language of daily life in Palestine, a practice that the Agudah opposed because it diminished Hebrew's status as the sacred language of Judaism.

Agudat Israel became the primary institutional focus of Orthodox Judaism during the early 1900s and a leading fundamentalist organization. It also established itself as an influential political party in Poland and Latvia and later on in Israel. The Agudah did not represent the entire spectrum of Jewish fundamentalism, however. Some of the more extreme Orthodox Jews in Eastern Europe viewed the political character of Agudat Israel as an unacceptable compromise with modern secular culture and rejected any form of association with it. In addition, a separate expression of Jewish fundamentalism that had appeared in the early 1900s did not support the Agudah's anti-Zionist position. This movement instead promoted the philosophy of religious Zionism. Its followers believed that the religious objectives of Orthodox Judaism could be advanced through the creation of a Jewish state in Palestine. In their view, this act would not preempt God's work, but would prepare for it by establishing an independent society where Jews could gather to live under traditional law.

The first formal organization of religious Zionists appeared in 1902. Named Mizrachi, an abbreviation of the Hebrew term *merkaz ruhani* ("spiritual center"), it sought both to perpetuate Jewish traditions and to promote religious Zionism within the Orthodox community. Mizrachi originated essentially as the religious branch of the World Zionist Organization, but conflicts soon arose between the two groups over the association between Zionism and secularism. Mizrachi's members accepted the Zionist movement as the practical instrument by which a Jewish state could be created, but they wanted the society that developed there to function according to Orthodox Jewish principles, which many secular Zionists had rejected. Some religious Zionists thus left the World Zionist Organization and in fact played a role in the formation of Agudat Israel. Others maintained ties with the Zionist movement but remained at odds with the secular majority in that group over religious issues.

The fundamentalist response to Zionism thus developed in the European context along two distinct paths—one defined by anti-Zionist haredim, the other by religious Zionists. This duality subsequently shaped the evolution of Jewish fundamentalism in its second major hearth in Palestine, and later Israel, as both approaches became established there. The migration of traditionalist

Jews from Europe to Palestine had in fact begun during the late 1700s. These early migrants were motivated by the belief that *Eretz Israel*, the sacred "Land of Israel," provided the best setting for leading an authentic Jewish life and for awaiting the redemption of the Jewish people. This migration remained fairly small, numbering only in the thousands for most of the nineteenth century, but it succeeded in establishing an Orthodox presence in the region before the rise of Zionist immigration in the 1880s.[27] The influence of this community eventually declined as the Zionist population in Palestine grew. During the early twentieth century, however, adherents of both branches of Jewish fundamentalism also began to migrate to Palestine, where they advanced the cause of traditional Judaism in different ways.[28]

The religious Zionists of the Mizrachi movement began to arrive in Palestine during the early 1900s alongside the much larger immigration of secular Zionists. Although religious Zionists disagreed with secularists over the role of religion in the Jewish community, they supported the creation of a Zionist state. As a result, they came to Palestine intent on furthering that process and cooperated in a number of ways with the secular Zionists in building a Jewish society there. By 1918 the Mizrachi movement had become officially organized in Palestine, and in 1920 it relocated its world center to Jerusalem. Mizrachi migration to Palestine gained momentum after World War I with the establishment of the British Mandate, which gave the proposed Zionist state a territorial identity and legitimized the political structure being erected by the Zionist-led National Council. From the religious Zionists' perspective, this process of creating a national homeland for the Jews marked a divinely inspired step forward in the progress of Jewish sacred history (fig. 2.3).

Mizrachi never achieved a dominant position within Israeli politics, but it did play a major role in the formation of the official structures of Judaism in Palestine.[29] As it prepared to take control of the region, the National Council sought to develop an administrative arrangement for handling Jewish religious affairs, and it delegated this responsibility to Mizrachi, the Zionists' main source of support within the religious community. Mizrachi favored a centralized institutional organization, an approach that would reinforce the bonds between nationalism and religious observance. The national religious structure that the Zionists established thus concentrated authority in the institution of the Chief Rabbinate. The latter consisted of two chief rabbis, one representing Jews with ties to Northern and Eastern Europe (the Ashkenazim) and the other representing Jews from the Mediterranean world (the Sephardim). In addition, the nation's religious structure included a court of appeals that had the authority to rule on the judgments of local rabbinical courts.

Through these institutions, religious Zionists outside of Mizrachi also influenced the development of fundamentalist thought in Palestine. The first European chief rabbi, Abraham Kook, contributed significantly to the spread of religious Zionism, advocating an explicitly religious interpretation of the mean-

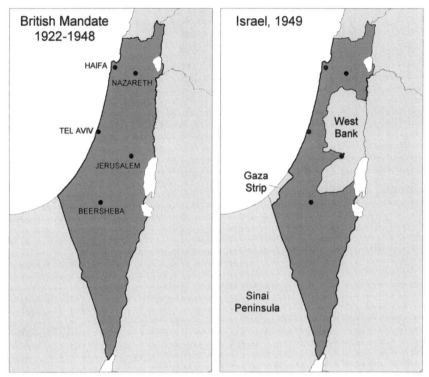

Figure 2.3   The establishment of the British Mandate in 1922 marked the beginning of the development of a Jewish state in Palestine. Religious Zionists viewed this process as part of the divine redemption of the Jewish people and played an important role in the religious institutions of the emerging state. The boundaries established in 1949 by an armistice between Israel and its Arab neighbors excluded Gaza and the West Bank, areas that Israel reoccupied following the Six-Day War in 1967. Religious Zionists assigned great significance to the retaking of the West Bank, since that region contains the biblical lands of Judaea and Samaria, key elements of the sacred Land of Israel.

ing of the emerging Jewish state. In his view, the creation of the state of Israel was an expression of the divine will, not of human arrogance; and he believed that even the secular Jews who did not acknowledge God's plan were unwitting participants in it. He further asserted that the return of Jews to *Eretz Israel* indicated that the process of redemption had in fact already begun. Kook faulted the secular Zionists for disregarding the spiritual aspects of Jewish nationalism, however, and his followers opposed many trends in secular society. Kook also had some differences with Mizrachi, which in his view limited its concerns to pragmatic, political matters rather than deeper religious issues. Members of the Mizrachi movement, on the other hand, did not fully accept Kook's complex interpretation of Judaism, including his messianic belief that the process of redemption had already started. And Kook's views were even more objectionable to the anti-Zionist haredim, who rejected his religious interpretation of Zionism and his collaboration with Zionist leaders.

Despite these controversies, Kook introduced new theological currents into the religious Zionist wing of Jewish fundamentalism during his tenure as chief rabbi. In emphasizing the role of the state of Israel in the imminent redemption of the Jewish people, Kook offered a more radical interpretation of Jewish history than that supported by Mizrachi.[30] To promote his views, Kook established an influential yeshiva in Jerusalem, which trained many subsequent leaders of the religious Zionist movement. His ideas continued to be promulgated after this death by his son, Zvi Yehudah Kook, whose followers later established Gush Emunim, the foremost expression of religious Zionist fundamentalism at the end of the twentieth century. Through these means, Kook's version of religious Zionism added to the varied character of Jewish fundamentalism as Israel emerged as an independent state, and for the rest of the twentieth century it continued to evolve alongside and often in conjunction with the beliefs of Mizrachi and its successor, the National Religious Party.

Important developments also occurred in the anti-Zionist branch of Jewish fundamentalism in Palestine. Despite their opposition to Zionism, a growing number of haredim migrated to Palestine in the years before World War I, but for reasons quite different from those of the religious Zionists. Much like the traditional Jews who had moved there from Europe during the previous century, the haredim sought religious fulfillment in *Eretz Israel*. They believed that by settling in this sacred region, they could achieve a way of life that conformed more closely to the traditional tenets of Judaism (fig. 2.4). They had no interest in the political struggle to establish a Jewish state, and even after migration they remained strongly anti-Zionist. They also attempted to remain apart from the surrounding Zionist society. Most haredi migrants were affiliated with Agudat Israel, particularly with its more traditionalist, Eastern European component. They thus formally established the Agudah in Palestine in 1912, after which it became an important institutional focus of haredi society and helped the haredim to maintain their sense of community.

The political dominance of Palestine's secular Zionist majority created a challenging social environment for the haredi minority. Again, the secular Zionists' primary concern was to establish a Jewish homeland, not to promote religious tradition. They did not support the haredi goal of creating a society based on Jewish law, and many of the social structures that they created reflected their more secular orientation. The most traditional of the haredim responded by adopting a policy of strict separation not only from the Zionists themselves but from any of the institutions that they had founded. One crucial issue in this context was the relationship of the haredim to the religious structures established by the National Council in consultation with Mizrachi. The haredim

Figure 2.4 Jews praying at the Western Wall during the 1920s. Even though they opposed the creation of a secular Jewish state, many traditionalist Jews migrated to Palestine during the early 1900s to be close to the hearth of Jewish sacred history, as embodied in the Western Wall, the only surviving portion of Jerusalem's Second Temple. Jerusalem, Israel, 1920s. *Source:* Weststock.

rejected the authority of these religious institutions, because to do otherwise would put them in contact with nonbelievers and heretics. They also resisted any attempt to be grouped with nonharedi Jews following the capture of Jerusalem by the British in 1917, and to ensure their isolation from Zionist society, they formed a separate religious organization, Edah Haredit ("Haredi Community").[31] The primary goal of Edah Haredit was to defend the ideological boundaries that separated it from the much larger Zionist community in Palestine. Although it did not receive official recognition as a distinct religious group, it functioned independently from the Zionists' religious structures and established a communal bureaucracy to provide its members with religious services involving matters such as marriage and dietary practices.[32] Following the creation of the Chief Rabbinate in the early 1920s, to which the haredim objected, Edah Haredit became more or less identical to Agudat Israel in Palestine, and together they defined the core of the anti-Zionist branch of Jewish fundamentalism.

Over time, however, the relationship between Agudat Israel and Edah Haredit became strained by the difficulties faced by the haredim as a religious minority within Palestine's Jewish community. During the late 1920s and 1930s, some members of the Agudah began to favor a degree of reconciliation with the Zionists, whose success in building a Jewish society in Palestine made the separatist stance of the haredim increasingly problematic. Arab attacks on the Jewish community in 1929 also convinced many Agudists that cooperation with the Zionists was necessary to provide for their own self-defense. In addition, the worsening situation for Jews in Germany and Poland during the 1930s provoked an increase in migration from those countries to Palestine, including many European members of Agudat Israel; and these newer immigrants accepted the necessity of cooperating with the Zionists to ensure their escape from the menace of Nazism. The newly arrived Agudists had also led a less segregated life in Europe than had earlier immigrants from the Eastern European hearth of haredi fundamentalism, and as a result, they were less committed to remaining apart from the Zionists in Palestine. Finally, the growing danger to Jews living in Europe during the late 1930s caused many members of Agudat Israel to abandon their opposition to the creation of a Jewish state. As a result, Agudat Israel adopted a new position of cooperation with national institutions during World War II, and, in preparation for Israeli independence, became part of the new nation's Provisional Council of State. After independence, Agudat Israel became active as a religious political party and focused on shaping the nation's religious character and on ensuring that the government did not interfere with its members' traditional way of life.[33]

The expanding interactions between Agudat Israel and secular Zionist society proved unacceptable to many members of Edah Haredit. Separatists within Edah Haredit continued to avoid contact with the nonharedi majority and condemned the Agudah for not doing the same. They also opposed certain innovations that the Agudah had adopted, such as the use of Hebrew as the language of instruction in girls' schools. The haredim thus began to split into two camps: those who remained strictly anti-Zionist and separatist, who came to identify more closely with Edah Haredit, and those willing to participate in the reality of a Jewish state, who came to identify more closely with Agudat Israel. In 1935, this division resulted in the withdrawal of a number of militant haredim from Agudat Israel. These militants established a radical movement within Edah Haredit unequivocally committed to remaining separate from mainstream Zionist society. Several years later, this group took as its name the Aramaic term *Neturei Karta* ("Guardians of the City"), drawn from a passage in the Talmud that identifies religious scholars rather than armed guards as the true defenders of the city.[34] Neturei Karta asserted that the effort to create a

Jewish state was a sacrilege and that strict religious observance offered the only means of safeguarding authentic Judaism.

The adherents of Neturei Karta accounted for only a small minority of Edah Haredit's membership, but they wielded considerable influence within the haredi community. During the 1940s they became increasingly critical of Agudat Israel's position regarding separation from the Zionists, and in 1945 they succeeded in expelling members of the Agudah from Edah Haredit by initiating a rule barring membership to those whose daughters received instruction in Hebrew. After Israel became an independent state in 1948, Neturei Karta retained its militant stance toward Zionism. It refused to recognize Israel's existence and prohibited its members from voting in national elections or accepting financial support from the government. The group's most radical members have refused to accept national identity cards or to acknowledge the authority of Israel's court system, and they have isolated themselves geographically in a few segregated neighborhoods of Jerusalem and Bnei Brak. In the realm of public life, they have opposed the use of religious legislation to integrate Judaism into Israel's civil institutions, a strategy favored by Agudat Israel and other religious political parties. To Neturei Karta, commitment to a political state and its laws cannot coexist with adherence to Judaism, and thus efforts to promote Judaism legislatively desecrate the faith by placing it under secular control.[35] Again, while many adherents of Edah Haredit did not fully accept the more radical positions of Neturei Karta, the latter did establish a model of pious activism for other haredim (including some members of the Agudah), who have often sided with Neturei Karta in specific religious controversies.

Despite the strong similarities in their views, however, the different organizational structures of Neturei Karta and Edah Haredit eventually led to tension between the two groups. As a communal organization, Edah Haredit maintained a bureaucracy to serve its members' needs, and this structure could not operate in complete isolation from the state. Functions such as the legalization of marriages and divorces, or the acquisition of food from nonharedi sources, required minimal interactions with outside society. Neturei Karta, on the other hand, did not function as a formal organization. Because its more loosely structured activities did not intersect with government functions, it could maintain a stricter separation from the rest of Israeli society. The different approaches of the two groups gradually led to increasing alienation between them, and eventually the most militant of members of Neturei Karta rejected the authority of Edah Haredit.

Conditions in Zionist Palestine, and later in Israel, thus had a major effect on the haredi branch of Jewish fundamentalism and over time contributed to development of groups with different conceptions of how to promote authentic Judaism. All of the haredi groups remained committed to the preservation of traditional Judaism and strict adherence to Jewish law, and all of them opposed any attempt to cast the history of the state of Israel in religious terms. They differed primarily in their willingness to recognize the authority of the state in secular matters and in their acceptance of contact with the government and secular society. Agudat Israel comprised the most accommodating of the haredi fundamentalists. In a sense, its members changed from anti-Zionists to non-Zionists after the 1930s, neither supporting nor fighting the reality of a Jewish state. This shift effectively illustrates the selectivity typical of fundamentalist movements, in terms of the specific issues on which they choose to focus. At the other extreme, Neturei Karta promoted an unyielding commitment to complete separation from the mainstream of Israeli society and refused to acknowledge the legitimacy of the state of Israel. Between these two groups, and not entirely distinct from either one, Edah Haredit occupied a middle position, perhaps closer ideologically to Neturei Karta but forced by the needs of its members to accept minimal contacts with the outside world.

By the middle of the twentieth century, then, Israel had become the center of both branches of Jewish fundamentalism—the haredim and the religious Zionists. They shared a common concern with maintaining religious tradition, and each rejected the secularization of Jewish culture. The two branches differed in their views of Jewish sacred history and its relationship to Jewish settlement in Israel. To the haredim, the unfolding of sacred events could not be advanced through human agency. Their presence in *Eretz Israel* allowed them to adhere more scrupulously to Jewish law, but it had no theological significance. The religious Zionists, on the other hand, saw their settlement in Israel as an active contribution to the fulfillment of Jewish sacred history. These divergent perspectives caused the two branches of Jewish fundamentalism to focus on different types of issues and to define the boundaries that separated them from the rest of society in different ways. In addition, these divergent perspectives produced very different types of activism within the two branches, which is discussed in more detail in chapters 3 and 4.

ISLAMIC FUNDAMENTALISM AND THE IMPACTS OF IMPERIALISM

The conditions under which Islamic fundamentalism emerged differed in important ways from those associated with early Christian and Jewish fundamentalist movements. The latter groups originally defined themselves largely in terms of their opposition to innovations within their own religious cultures, such as modernist Protestant theology or Reform Judaism. The ideological boundaries that they established separated them from other adherents of the same faith who had rejected traditional beliefs. The first expressions of Islamic fundamentalism, on the other hand, focused on subversive influences originating in other regions of the world, particularly those spread through Western imperialism. Like their Christian and Jewish counterparts, early Islamic fundamentalists sought to prevent the erosion of traditional beliefs, but the forces that they opposed derived more from external sources than from innovations evolving within the Islamic community.

Early fundamentalist Muslims especially feared the pollution of Islam by foreign ideas, and not only in the context of religion. One of their central beliefs was that Islam represented a comprehensive way of life, encompassing all facets of human existence, and as a result, they saw any attempt to impose alien ideologies on Islamic society as an attack on their faith.[36] During the early 1900s, they considered economic and political interventions by Europeans to be particularly threatening, because these processes undermined traditional sources of authority and identity in the Islamic world. Islamic fundamentalists thus tended to create ideological boundaries in broad geographical terms, as a barrier separating the Islamic world from the West. As a result, even in countries where they are in control, Islamic fundamentalists have defined themselves in terms of their struggle against external forces, in particular against Western hegemony. Their concern with threats originating outside of their own culture has also accounted in part for the use of extreme forms of political action, including terrorism, by some Islamic fundamentalists.

The early Islamic fundamentalists did not focus solely on external threats, of course. They were concerned as well with deviations from tradition within the Islamic community, and in this sense they represented a modern manifestation of the revivalist movements that have arisen within Islam throughout its history.[37] These movements have typically revolved around charismatic leaders seeking to purify Islamic practice by returning to the sharia, Islamic law based on the Koran and traditions associated with Islam's prophet, Muhammad. Some revivalists also focused on missionary efforts, while others adopted military or political means of promoting Islamic identity. This extensive history of revivalism thus helped to establish a cultural context that later legitimized the fundamentalists' stance of militant Islamic traditionalism.

Another antecedent of Islamic fundamentalism was Islamic reformism, a movement that developed during the late 1800s in response to the impacts of European culture and politics on the Islamic world.[38] Jamal al-Din al-Afghani, a widely traveled Muslim writer, began to advocate social reform after his observations of the Islamic world convinced him that it had entered a period of decline as European imperialism had expanded. Afghani's ideas influenced intellectuals throughout the Islamic world, but particularly in Egypt, the principal center of the reformist movement by the end of the nineteenth century. The reformists asserted that an uncritical devotion to tradition had caused Islamic societies to fall behind Europe in terms of economic development, political power, science, and technology. They further believed that the growing weakness of the Islamic world would cause it to become increasingly subordinate to the West. In their efforts to modernize Islamic society, however, the reformists rejected the usefulness of economic and political models based on European experience. They saw Islam as the only acceptable foundation for social renewal. Afghani argued that Islamic culture had once been a powerful force and that it could be again if Muslims renewed their commitment to authentic Islam. He recognized that the Islamic world would not achieve parity with Europe without scientific and technical expertise, but he asserted that Muslims did not have to abandon their religious identity to excel in these areas. Afghani in fact argued for the integration of Islam and scientific inquiry; in his view, Islam was a rational religion, based on reason and natural law, and so was entirely compatible with modern science.

Despite their emphasis on the role of Islam in social renewal, however, Afghani and his followers were not strict traditionalists and cannot be considered true fundamentalists. They opposed the unquestioning acceptance of traditional customs and beliefs, asserting that this practice had led to stagnation within the Islamic community. They also advocated an open attitude toward innovation, particularly within the elite classes of society. Similarly, they stressed the need for continual reinterpretation of Islamic texts and the traditions derived from them. According to Afghani, this approach provided the only means of sustaining the vitality of Islam in a modern setting. Muhammad Abduh, Afghani's most influential disciple, further developed the modernist component of reformism, asserting that Islamic law should be rationally evaluated with regard to the public interest and adapted to meet the needs of contemporary society. Unlike Afghani, Abduh also thought that Muslims should model their efforts to modernize on Europe's example. He believed that some elements of European thought were in fact compatible with Islam and should be adopted as Islamic society advanced.

Some reformists opposed the modernist trend within their movement, however, claiming that emulation of the material success of Europe would detract from the renewal of Islamic belief. Muhammad Rashid Rida, one of Abduh's students, played a key role in promoting this more conservative point of view, arguing that the modernists had overstated the compatibility between Islam and Western ideas. He also advocated stricter adherence to the principles of Islamic law, although he still favored the use of independent reason in applying those principles to contemporary society. Rida did not attract a large or influential following at first, but his more conservative approach helped lay the groundwork for the emergence of Islamic fundamentalism during the 1920s and 1930s.

The fundamentalist turn in Islamic thought first began to gain momentum during and after World War I in reaction to a series of critical events within the Islamic world. In 1914, at the start of the war, Great Britain declared Egypt to be a British protectorate. The British had in fact occupied Egypt militarily since 1882, even though it officially remained part of the Ottoman Empire. When the Ottomans entered World War I on the side of Germany and Austria, however, the British officially claimed possession of Egypt. This move provoked a significant rise in Egyptian nationalism and intensified Muslim concern over the threat of European imperialism. That concern was reinforced by the defeat of the Ottomans at the end of World War I, which eliminated the world's last major Islamic empire. Among Muslims, this defeat was seen as a critical blow to Islam in its ongoing struggle against expanding Western hegemony.

The challenges to Islam continued when Turkey, the former core of the Ottoman Empire, declared its independence in 1922 and embarked on a program of radical modernization under the leadership of Mustafa Kemal Atatürk.[39] Atatürk followed an explicitly Western model in planning Turkey's development and enforced the adoption of Western customs and institutions. He also sought to establish Turkey as a secular state. Within a few years of taking power, his government had closed Islamic schools, dissolved Islamic religious orders, and replaced the sharia with a new civil code. Atatürk's most serious attack on traditional Islam came in 1924, however, when he abolished the Caliphate.[40] The Caliphate, or office of the caliph, had been created in 632 following the death of Muhammad and represented one of the central institutions of Islam. The caliph originally served as both the political and spiritual leader of the Muslim community, but the specific duties of the office varied throughout history in response to changing circumstances, and the title of caliph was used by various rulers at different times. The Ottoman sultans had claimed the title since the late 1700s, and many Muslims considered them to be the true leaders of Islam. When the new Turkish republic abolished the sultanate in 1922, it at first preserved the Caliphate as a purely religious office; but by 1924, Atatürk decided that the Caliphate too should be eliminated, to sever completely the ties between Islam and politics. To traditionalist Muslims, this decision threatened the integrity of the Islamic world.

As the above-mentioned events unfolded, traditional Islam also faced a more diffuse threat from the continuing impacts of Westernization. Political circumstances during the early twentieth century had led to a rise in secular nationalism, particularly in Egypt, and to growing acceptance of European social and political models even among those fighting the effects of European imperialism. Atatürk's success in establishing Turkey as an independent state provided additional support for the adoption of Western modernization as a strategy in addressing the backwardness of the Islamic world.[41] As a result, a growing number of secularists rejected the ideas of the Islamic reformists and began to look beyond Islam for the means to improve society.

These developments produced a strong counterreaction among Muslims still committed to the idea of a society rooted in Islam, and their attempts to realize such a society represented the first integral expressions of Islamic fundamentalism. The strict supporters of Islam condemned European imperialism, but they also fought the spread of Western culture within the Islamic world and refused to accept European models of social and political organization. They argued that Islamic reformism had failed not because it placed too much emphasis on Islam, but because it had absorbed too much influence from the West. The emergent fundamentalists contended that a rigid ideological boundary separated Islam from the West and that Muslim society could return to a position of strength only through strict observance of Islamic law in all aspects of life. They further asserted that a return to authentic Islam would require militant activism on the part of true believers, both to counter external influences and to challenge voices of compromise within the Muslim community. The early fundamentalists thus organized their movements around the concept of social action and by the 1930s and 1940s had begun to attract significant followings in various parts of the Islamic world.

The first major expression of this militant activism developed in Egypt. The presence of the British there since the 1880s had strengthened Western influences on the region, particularly in the Suez Canal Zone and Cairo. These influences resulted in the adoption by the urban classes of Western ways that conflicted with Islam, such as the consumption of alcohol. The secular and modernist character of many of the cultural institutions founded by the British also challenged Islamic tradition. At the same time, Egypt had long been a major center of the Islamic world and had seen a major rise in nationalist sentiment early in the twentieth century. As the primary hearth of the reformist movement, Egypt also provided a fertile intellectual environment for Muslim thinkers. The conflict between Islam and the West thus became a central theme in Egyptian culture, resulting in a vigorous fundamentalist response during the 1920s and 1930s.

The leading figure in this response was Hasan al-Banna. Banna was raised in a religious family and as a youth had become involved with various groups that promoted strict adherence to Islam and sought to counter the effects of Christian missionary activity. While still in school, he also joined a religious order of Sufism, the mystical branch of Islam. His education at first focused on classical Islamic learning, but later included broad exposure to the modern sciences. After completing his studies in Cairo, he became a teacher in the state school system and took his first position in 1927 in the city of Ismailia, the British headquarters in the Suez Canal Zone. There as in Cairo he concluded that Egyptian society had been corrupted through its encounters with the West. Although this conclusion reinforced his support for Egyptian independence, he believed that the most important force in the revival of Egyptian society would be a return to authentic Islam. He further believed that Muslim society had become too passive and that a return to Islam would necessarily depend on positive social action. Thus, in addition to his regular teaching duties, he began spending evenings in schools, mosques, and coffeehouses instructing adults in the details of Islamic belief. Eventually he decided to establish a formal organization to continue this work and in 1928 founded the Muslim Brotherhood (al-Ikhwan al-Muslimun), a fundamentalist group that developed widespread influence in Egypt and throughout the Arab world.[42]

The Muslim Brotherhood at first drew its support mainly from its hearth in the Suez Canal Zone, where it focused primarily on social reform and Islamic education. To advance this work, the brotherhood created a dispersed network of social and cultural institutions, including schools, mosques, and clubs. It also supported the establishment of home industries, such as small textile workshops, to foster economic autonomy and improve living conditions. Banna believed that the brotherhood had to establish its own organizational structure to protect itself from the corruption that he saw in other Islamic institutions. Moreover, the brotherhood found that this strategy provided an effective means of spreading its message, particularly among the urban lower middle class, and within a few years the group had established major centers in Port Said and Suez City and smaller branches throughout the region.

The brotherhood's message of Islamic renewal attracted interest in other parts of Egypt, and in 1933 Banna moved the group's center of operations to Cairo. As support for the organization grew, so did its infrastructure. The brotherhood founded schools and mosques throughout the country, created new businesses, and organized a wide range of social services to provide food and medical care to the needy. This pragmatic activism gave the group considerable popular credibility, and its membership increased rapidly. By the late 1930s, roughly 500 local branches of the brotherhood had been established. As it grew, the Muslim Brotherhood also developed a new political focus, which extended its interests into the larger Arab world. This process of politicization began in 1936, when Palestinian Arabs rebelled against British occupation and Zionist expansion. Over the next several years, the brotherhood provided both moral and financial support to the Palestinians. Such efforts established contacts between the brotherhood and Muslim traditionalists outside of Egypt and eventually led to the formation of related organizations in other countries.[43]

The rise in political activism within the Muslim Brotherhood reflected Banna's belief in the ideological totality of Islam. He made no distinction between political or social issues and the concerns of religion, since he believed that Islam contained within it all of the principles by which governments and societies should be organized.[44] He thus argued that the goals of the Muslim Brotherhood should include the creation of a true Islamic state. Banna did not define in detail the political structure of such a state, but he did insist that it must be based on the sharia. Banna's concept of the ideal state was based, in other words, on the original Islamic society established by Muhammad and expanded by his immediate successors (fig. 2.5). Banna believed that such a state would not only recognize the authority of Islam but would actively promote adherence to Islamic belief and practice and ultimately produce a truly virtuous society. Many Egyptians found this new political message to be highly appealing, and again the brotherhood's influence grew. By the late 1940s, it claimed 500 thousand active members and an equal number of sympathizers, and, according to some sources, its total membership actually numbered over two million. The group had also established nearly two thousand local branches

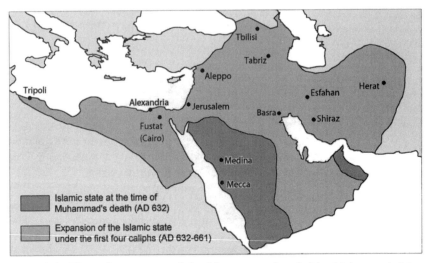

Figure 2.5   The early expansion of the Islamic state founded by Muhammad. Most Islamic fundamentalists base their concept of an ideal social order on this empire, as ruled by Muhammad and the first four caliphs.

by this time, and its social, medical, and economic efforts had continued to expand.[45]

The brotherhood's political turn also led to growing conflict with Egypt's existing government. During the mid-1940s, this conflict contributed to the rise of a radical element within the brotherhood, exemplified by the "secret apparatus," a clandestine group within the organization that employed violent forms of activism. The use of violence by the brotherhood expanded after the Arab-Israeli War in 1948, during which the group formed a paramilitary unit to fight on the Arab side. Returning to Egypt with arms and military experience, as well as an intensified bitterness against British imperialism, members of the brotherhood became increasingly involved in terrorist activity in the late 1940s. In December 1948 the Egyptian government responded to the growing violence by dissolving the Muslim Brotherhood. The brotherhood's secret apparatus subsequently assassinated Egypt's prime minister, and two months later Hasan al-Banna was shot and killed by Egyptian police.

After a period of disarray, the brotherhood regained its legal status as a religious organization in the early 1950s and resumed its political activities. It reorganized a paramilitary unit to join in the guerrilla war against British control of the Suez Canal, and its members participated in rioting against Western interests in Cairo. Although not involved in its planning or execution, the brotherhood also supported the military revolution in 1952 that deposed Egypt's ruling monarch, King Farouk, and led to the creation of an Egyptian republic. The brotherhood approved of the revolutionaries' efforts to free Egypt from British control, but grew disillusioned when it appeared that the new regime intended to establish a state based on secular principles. The Muslim Brotherhood thus returned to its oppositional stance, openly agitating against the new government and its secular policies. Early in 1954, the new regime again dissolved the brotherhood, stating that the latter had become a political organization and had to disband under a law prohibiting political parties. The government also arrested several hundred Muslim brothers, including most of their leaders. Later that year, a Muslim brother retaliated by attempting to assassinate Egypt's prime minister, Gamal Abdel Nasser. Nasser's government moved quickly to crush the brotherhood, jailing thousands of its members and executing six Muslim brothers involved in the assassination attempt.[46] Several thousand other Muslim brothers went into exile in other Arab states.

Their experiences in prison and in exile changed the fundamentalist character of the Muslim Brotherhood, as members adopted a more militant position against the Egyptian government and against secular nationalism in general. The intellectual framework for the new militancy derived from the writings of Sayyid Qutb, an early supporter of nationalism who had joined the Muslim Brotherhood in 1951. After being imprisoned in the mid-1950s, Qutb developed a new interpretation of the relationship between Islam and contemporary society. In his view, the political states that governed the Islamic world were all in a condition of "unbelief," such as existed before the rise of Islam. By creating their own laws and standards of behavior, these unbelieving states and the secular societies associated with them disregarded divine authority and thus had no moral legitimacy. Qutb further believed that to counter the effects of unbelief, a vanguard of true believers must initiate a jihad ("holy war") against society. In his view, jihad offered the only means of reestablishing an authentic Islamic order. Qutb argued that this approach would not require the forced conversion of unbelievers to Islam, because given the opportunity unbelievers would convert to Islam as a matter of course. He further believed that once the jihad had begun, it would continue until Islam governed the entire world.

Qutb based these views on Islamic sacred history, in particular on the experiences of the first generation of Muslims under Muhammad's leadership: their persecution by unbelievers in Mecca, their flight to Medina, where they gathered strength, and their armed jihad against their enemies, which led to the creation of an authentic Islamic society.[47] Qutb contended that true believers must model their activities on these events, preparing for jihad by isolating themselves mentally and spiritually from the mainstream of society. He rejected the populist approach adopted by the Muslim Brotherhood in its early years and instead advocated the development of a tightly knit core of activists dedicated to the destruction of the existing government. Qutb's ideas thus refined the ideological boundaries of Islamic fundamentalism, distinguishing among an inner core of activists, the main body of practicing Muslims, the corrupt societies and governments of the Islamic world, and the corrupting influences of the West. Qutb was released from prison along with many other Muslim brothers in 1964, as part of a government effort to foster popular opposition to communism in Egypt. The brotherhood resumed its antigovernment activities, however, and Qutb was subsequently convicted of plotting against the government and was executed in 1966 along with a number of other fundamentalist leaders. Nonetheless, Qutb's writings remained widely influential among Islamic militants and provided an ideological foundation for the radical fundamentalist movements that developed in Egypt in subsequent decades. Qutb has had considerable influence among Islamic fundamentalists in other parts of the Arab world as well and represents a major forerunner of contemporary Islamic radicalism.

Egypt thus became a key hearth area in the development of Islamic fundamentalism. The interactions in Egypt among traditional Islam, Western imperialism, the rise of nationalism, and the general processes of modernization produced a social environment particularly conducive to fundamentalist thought and action. Egypt's influence within the Islamic world also contributed to the broader dissemination of fundamentalism to other countries. As a center of education within the Arab world, Egypt attracted many foreign students, who helped spread the ideas of Banna and Qutb. Through its contacts with Muslim traditionalists outside of Egypt, the Muslim Brotherhood also inspired the formation of analogous organizations in other countries, including Syria, Jordan, Sudan, Morocco, and Saudi Arabia. These organizations generally adopted similar goals, but their specific actions have varied in response to local circumstances. In Syria, for example, the Muslim Brotherhood has engaged in violent conflicts with the national government, while in Jordan it has adopted a less extreme approach and has at times maintained a cooperative relationship with the nation's rulers. In all of its manifestations, however, the Muslim Brotherhood has sought to encourage adherence to authentic Islamic values and rejection of Western influences.

Fundamentalist movements not directly tied to the Muslim Brotherhood also developed elsewhere in the Islamic world, again largely in response to conflicts between Islam and external influences. The Islamic Revolution in Iran in 1979 and the rise of the Taliban movement in Afghanistan during the 1990s represent two recent examples, and they are examined in the discussion of contemporary fundamentalist movements in chapter 3. Earlier in the twentieth century, however, the leading hearth of Islamic fundamentalism outside of Egypt developed in South Asia, where distinctive conditions produced a fundamentalist response among Muslims different from that which had emerged in Egypt.[48]

During the late 1800s and early 1900s, conditions in South Asia in some ways resembled those that threatened traditional Islam in other parts of the world. British imperialism had established a colonial structure that limited the political power of indigenous peoples and weakened the authority of their traditional cultures. In addition, the British had introduced Western attitudes and technological advances, which encouraged strong support for modernization among some indigenous elites. In dealing with these developments, however, Muslims in South Asia faced an additional complication: their minority status within the region's indigenous population. In trying to protect their interests, they faced potential conflicts not only with the British but with the much larger Hindu majority as well. The boundaries between the Hindu and Muslim communities were not in fact impermeable, but the two groups had developed distinct concerns and experiences under British colonialism. Hindus had been more active than Muslims in acquiring Western learning, for example, and adapted more readily to the social structures established by the British. At the same time, the colonial period produced a resurgence of nationalism and religious revivalism among Hindus reacting against recent British domination as well as earlier centuries of Muslim rule. Given the potential for conflict with the Hindu majority, Muslims in British India inhabited a more complex social and political context than did Muslims in Egypt or other Arab states.

Some Muslim leaders responded to these circumstances by advocating modernization. These progressives argued that Islam was compatible with Western concepts of scientific progress and political liberalism and that the Muslim community should embrace these concepts to promote its social and political interests. They further believed that these goals took on a special urgency given the social transformations that were likely to occur after the region achieved independence from British rule. The progressives thus advocated the adoption of a distinctly modernist perspective, with strong secular overtones. Some traditionalist Muslims, on the other hand, rejected any sort of reconciliation with the forces of modernization and paid little attention to the potential for change suggested by the prospect of British decolonization. Their primary concern was simply to maintain the status quo by preserving existing Islamic traditions and institutions in the region. As a result, followers of this passive form of traditionalism did not adopt the activist stance typical of fundamentalism.

Islamic fundamentalism developed in South Asia as an alternative to both modernism and passive traditionalism. Specifically, it involved absolute commitment to the original teachings of Islam but was expressed in relation to the complex political situation in which South Asian Muslims were situated. These fundamentalists did not reject technological or scientific advances from the West, but they opposed the secular outlook that modernism tended to encourage. They believed that Islam should serve as the guiding principle for the contemporary Muslim community. They had little interest in the institutions supported by passive traditionalists, however, which they saw as historical remnants from an earlier period of Muslim dominance that had been undermined by British colonialism. Instead, the fundamentalists focused on restoring a purified form of Islamic belief among the Muslim masses in the region. This strategy, they believed, offered the only means of preserving the cultural identity of the Muslim community within South Asia's changing political context.

The leading thinker of this fundamentalist movement was Mawlana Abul Ala Mawdudi. Although a devout Muslim from a religious family, Mawdudi was not trained in traditional Islamic schools. His father at first directed his education, and later Mawdudi studied widely on his own. In the process, he developed an extensive familiarity with Islamic scholarship, but was not tied to the traditional perspectives of established Islamic institutions in India. Throughout his life he continued to develop his ideas regarding the role of Islam in the modern world, particularly with respect to its political dimensions and its self-sufficiency as a social and religious system. He insisted that Islam was superior to Western ideologies and that it did not have to be justified by demonstrating its compatibility with Western thought, which he considered to be morally corrupt. He did not reject the utility of scientific knowledge, but he believed that technological advances should be adopted to promote the interests of Islam. He also believed that Muslims should interpret and develop Islam through an understanding of its original fundamentals and should not be bound by traditions and institutions based merely on historical practice.

For Mawdudi, the defense of Muslim identity in South Asia required the restoration of authentic Islam, a process that depended on two related factors: belief in the authority of Islamic law in all domains of life and the application of that belief in acquiring political power. Mawdudi asserted that Islam represented a comprehensive ideology that would be weakened if it were compartmentalized to cover only certain aspects of life. He thus believed that Muslims had to recognize the political dimensions of Islam, particularly within the complex conditions that arose in South Asia as the British colonial period ended. Mawdudi further concluded that Muslims could achieve political influence only through disciplined organization, specifically through the creation of a small cadre of leaders committed both to political action and to uncompromising religious standards. By functioning as a pure Islamic community, this group would provide a model for the larger Muslim community and ultimately win its support in reshaping Islamic society.

To achieve these goals, Mawdudi formed the Jamaat-e-Islami ("Islamic Society") in 1941.[49] Originally comprising seventy-five founding members, the Jamaat was organized as a "holy community" committed to the preservation of Islam. Its members believed that a number of factors threatened Islam in India: the Muslims' minority status within the existing British colony, the rise of Hindu nationalism, the attempt to impose Western political structures on South Asia after decolonization, and the corruption of Islam by historical practices not derived from its fundamental tenets. They further believed that the crucial first step in responding to these threats was to lead individual Muslims back to the practice of authentic Islam. In their view, this process would ulti-mately lead to the creation of a true Islamic state, but that goal did not repre-sent their first priority, which was the purification of Islamic practice and belief.

Changing conditions in India during the 1940s forced the Jamaat to become more actively concerned with politics, however. Debate over the prospect of decolonization raised important questions for the Muslim community. The Muslim League, which since the early 1900s had been the dominant Muslim political party, had generally supported the idea of continued British rule. It was concerned that complete independence for India would lead to oppression of the Muslim minority by the region's Hindu majority. Supporters of indepen-dence proposed various safeguards to protect Muslim interests in a Hindu-dominated state, but most Muslims remained unconvinced that these safe-guards would prove effective. As Hindu nationalists continued to push for inde-pendence, therefore, the Muslim League changed its position and in 1940 announced its support for the creation of an independent Muslim state con-taining those areas of British India in which Muslims represented a majority. The Hindu majority in India opposed the partition plan, but in the end, the divergent concerns of the region's two main religious communities led to the creation in 1947 of two independent states, predominantly Muslim Pakistan and predominantly Hindu India.

This outcome proved to be problematic for Mawdudi and the Jamaat-e-Islami. Mawdudi objected to the concept of Muslim nationalism because he considered Islam to be a universal religion, open to all. As a result, he did not actively support the creation of a separate Muslim state in South Asia. He also felt that many supporters of the creation of Pakistan, such as the leaders of the Muslim League, had adopted Westernized, secular perspectives incompatible with Islam. Pakistan, he feared, would become a Muslim state in name only and would not incorporate Islamic principles into its political, social, and eco-nomic systems. To Mawdudi and his followers in the Jamaat, the creation of Pakistan in 1947 thus did not represent an unequivocal victory. Rather, it cre-ated a new set of challenges for the Jamaat as it continued to work toward its goal of Islamic purification.

One challenge for the Jamaat was that the partition of British India isolated members in India from those in Pakistan. Antagonisms between the govern-ments of the two countries made it impossible for the Jamaat to remain united and thus a separate Jamaat organization developed in each state. Moreover, the disparate social contexts in which the two organizations were located contrib-uted to different patterns of development. India's Jamaat-e-Islami was smaller than its Pakistani counterpart and in the long run proved to be less fundamen-talist in character. It continued to promote adherence to authentic Islam within the Muslim community, but it also worked to protect the religious rights of Muslims within the surrounding society. Although India was constituted as a secular state, giving preference to no particular religion, Muslims often felt threatened by the overwhelming size of the Hindu majority. As a result, the Indian Jamaat became a strong supporter of India's secularist policies, since they offered legal protections to the Muslim minority, which accounted for only about 11 percent of India's population.[50]

The Jamaat-e-Islami in Pakistan, on the other hand, developed a more fundamentalist character in responding to the challenges that it faced. Although many of its members were native to the regions united as Pakistan, an even greater number (including Mawdudi himself) were part of the vast stream of refugees from India who fled to Pakistan following partition (fig. 2.6). The members of the Jamaat who regrouped in Pakistan found themselves in circumstances very different from those of their counterparts in India. Pakistan's Jamaat operated within a state that had been nominally established as a Muslim polity. The creation of Pakistan thus presented an obvious opportunity for the Jamaat to promote its goal of forming a state that conformed to the dictates of Islamic law. The political leaders of Pakistan did not share that goal, however. Although they acknowledged the importance of Islam in Pakistani society, these leaders were mostly Western-educated modernists and were not primarily concerned with religious objectives. Their priorities instead reflected the political realities of decolonization and focused on promoting the social and economic development of Pakistan, generally in accordance with Western principles. The lingering impact of Western colonialism thus posed significant challenges to the Jamaat-e-Islami as it pursued its goal of creating a purified Islamic state.

In response to these challenges, the Jamaat-e-Islami adopted the development of an Islamic constitution for Pakistan as one of its major objectives. Such a document would establish the sharia as the nation's legal code and forbid the government from adopting un-Islamic policies. The fundamentalists' insistence on an Islamic constitution defined a clear ideological boundary that separated them from the modernists. The latter were willing to incorporate the spirit of Islam into Pakistan's political structures, but they opposed placing religious constraints on civil law. During the late 1940s, however, the Jamaat received considerable support for its position, particularly from Muslim refugees from India and from a growing population of educated urban dwellers. As a result, the Jamaat became the leading voice of Islamic fundamentalism in Pakistan. The government of Pakistan viewed the growing popularity of the Jamaat's demand for an Islamic constitution as a threat and imprisoned Mawdudi during the late 1940s. Nonetheless, Mawdudi and the Jamaat continued to argue that the logical outcome of Pakistan's liberation from colonialism should be the creation of a true Islamic state, and they continued to push for the adoption of an Islamic constitution throughout the early 1950s.

The constitutional issue was not the only matter than concerned fundamentalists at this time. The Jamaat also continued to promote authentic Islam among the people of Pakistan through public meetings, popular publications,

Figure 2.6   Muslim Indians seeking transportation from India to Pakistan following independence. The partition of the Indian subcontinent into two independent states transformed the region's social character and led to massive migrations of Muslims from India to Pakistan and of Hindus from Pakistan to India. This political restructuring also had important consequences for fundamentalist movements in both countries. New Delhi, India, 1947. *Source:* CORBIS/Bettmann.

and social welfare activities. As a result of their concern for the purity of Islam in Pakistan, the Jamaat became involved in a broader conflict involving the Ahmadiya movement, an Islamic sect whose leader claimed to be a holy prophet who had received divine revelation. This claim contradicted the Islamic belief that Muhammad was the final prophet and thus engendered strong opposition to the sect among many traditional Muslims and provoked deadly anti-Ahmadiya riots in 1953. Mawdudi and the Jamaat did not support this violent response, but their public opposition to the Ahmadiya movement again led to Mawdudi's imprisonment on a charge of inciting the riots. Originally sentenced to death, Mawdudi was released several years later when the courts ruled that he had been detained unlawfully.

At the same time that the conflict over the Ahmadiya movement developed, progress had been made toward the creation of Pakistan's constitution, which was finally adopted in 1956. The constitution represented at least a partial victory for the Jamaat, as it established Islam as the nation's guiding ideology. The constitution prohibited the enactment of laws that violated the basic tenets of Islam and required that existing laws be amended to satisfy this policy. At the same time, the constitution included provisions organizing the government as a Western-style parliamentary democracy, and it left the matter of deciding what did or did not contradict Islam to the parliament rather than to the clergy or to religious societies like the Jamaat. Nonetheless, the Jamaat generally approved of the constitution's pro-Islamic spirit and saw it as a first step in establishing Pakistan as a genuinely Islamic state.[51]

That process encountered a major setback in 1958, when a military coup replaced Pakistan's constitutional government with martial law, under the leadership of General Muhammad Ayub Khan. Mawdudi saw the coup as an attempt by secularists to prevent the Jamaat-e-Islami from gaining political power, and indeed for a number of years the military government banned all political parties in Pakistan. The Jamaat survived as a social and religious organization, but could not further its goal of creating an Islamic state under the regime of Ayub Khan. His major concerns were to promote nationalism and economic prosperity and, in the process, to modernize the practice of Islam in Pakistan. As a religious modernist, Ayub Khan thus became a new opponent for the Jamaat, and throughout his rule during the 1960s the group represented a major source of opposition to the government.

Since the 1960s, the relationship between the Jamaat-e-Islami and the Pakistani government has varied, depending on the attitudes of military and civilian leaders toward the Islamization of Pakistan. For the most part, though, the Jamaat has operated as a voice of opposition and has repeatedly criticized the governments in power as being insufficiently Islamic. As a political party, the Jamaat never amassed a large popular following and has not developed strong ties with the traditional Muslim clergy in Pakistan. It continues to have considerable influence among educated Muslims, however. Branches of the Jamaat-e-Islami have also wielded influence in other places, including India, Bangladesh, the disputed territory of Kashmir, and Afghanistan, although not to the same extent as in Pakistan. More generally, Mawdudi's ideas have been an important source of inspiration for fundamentalists in various parts of the Islamic world.

In its origins, then, the Jamaat-e-Islami differed in important ways from Egypt's Muslim Brotherhood. Both faced challenges created by European colonialism, but the nature of those challenges differed, as did the groups' responses to them. Because of Egypt's greater proximity to Europe, Muslims there experienced more extensive interactions with European culture and faced stronger pressures to adopt Western ways of life and incorporate Western ideologies into their worldview. The British presence in Egypt had also encouraged the rise of Egyptian nationalism early in the century, which eventually produced a radical anti-British movement. The fundamentalist task adopted by the Muslim Brotherhood thus contained two key components: to remove the British from Egypt as a political force and to remove corrupting Western influences from Islamic society and culture in Egypt. To achieve this task, they organized as a popular movement and acquired a substantial membership.

The Jamaat-e-Islami, on the other hand, did not at first oppose the British presence in South Asia; indeed, its members believed that in some ways the colonial status quo provided safeguards for the Muslim minority in the region. Their concerns turned political mainly in response to the process of decolonization, when the establishment of Pakistan as a Muslim state made their goal of establishing an authentic Islamic society more feasible. Like the Muslim Brotherhood, the Jamaat-e-Islami was committed to the purification of Islamic belief, but the Jamaat was more interested in removing incidental historical traditions and restoring the concept of Islam as a complete way of life than in fighting the corrupting effects of foreign ideas. The Jamaat believed that its goals could best be achieved through the example of an elite group of dedicated members and so did not adopt the populist approach used by the Muslim Brotherhood.

The two movements, both influential as models for other Islamic fundamentalists, thus emerged in different ways out of the interactions between Islamic traditionalism and European colonialism. The differences between the two groups, and between more recent developments that are discussed in the following chapter, clearly illustrate the diversity that exists within Islamic fundamentalism and demonstrate the importance of context in understanding fundamentalism's development and impacts.

PLURALISM AND FUNDAMENTALISM IN INDIA

India's distinctive religious character has played a key role in the development of fundamentalist movements within several different religious traditions. As discussed previously, the Jamaat-e-Islami first appeared in British India, in part as a response to the process of decolonization. Religious circumstances not directly related to colonialism also contributed to the emergence of important expressions of fundamentalism in India, however. In particular, the religious pluralism that characterizes Indian culture has been a major factor in the development of several fundamentalist movements.[52] That pluralism is rooted in the inherent diversity within Hinduism, the region's dominant religion. Over the course of several millennia, religious and philosophical concepts expressed in Hinduism's sacred writings have mixed with the traditional beliefs and rituals of local cultures across India. In the process, no central authority or institutional structure developed to standardize Hindu theology, and its beliefs and practices continue to display considerable heterogeneity among geographical regions and social classes. Hinduism's implicit flexibility also contributed to the emergence of several distinct religions, including Jainism in the sixth century B.C., Buddhism in the fifth century B.C., and Sikhism in the fifteenth century A.D., all of which incorporated elements of Hindu philosophy and belief.

The spread of Islam into the Indian subcontinent during the twelfth century A.D., primarily through Muslim invasions from central Asia and the missionary activities of Sufi mystics, expanded the complexity of the region's religious character. The syncretistic nature of India's indigenous religious culture, in which local traditions freely absorbed external religious influences, in theory clashed with Islam's insistence on orthodoxy. Indeed, this conflict inspired an unsuccessful attempt by the Muslim Mogul Empire to impose orthodox Islam across India in the late 1600s, an effort that antagonized both Hindus and Sikhs and contributed to the empire's demise. Moreover, many of those who converted from Hinduism to Islam during the period of Muslim rule remained unconcerned with matters of orthodoxy and retained elements of Hindu ritual and folk belief in their religious life. Similarly, many Hindus incorporated aspects of Islamic belief into their practice of Hinduism during the period of Muslim rule.[53] Thus, while the boundary between Hindus and Muslims became increasingly important in a political sense after the fall of the Mogul dynasty and the rise of British colonialism, the religious divisions between the two groups were not absolute.

India's pluralistic religious environment was further complicated by the British during their colonial occupation.[54] The British adopted a policy of religious neutrality, but as part of that policy they attempted to formalize the region's diversity by defining distinct communities on the basis of religion. The development of different legal systems for Hindu and Muslim communities under British rule, for example, represented an attempt to institutionalize the colony's religious diversity. Such efforts politicized the meaning of religious identity, but they failed to resolve the conflicts and contradictions inherent in India's complex religious culture. As a result, the region's pluralistic character ultimately produced fundamentalist impulses among various religious groups during and after the colonial period. For these incipient fundamentalist movements, the major threat to their faith was not the spread of modernism or secularism within their own community, or the imposition of Western values. Rather, their concerns focused on questions of religious identity, rooted in the mutability of India's diverse religious traditions.

The fundamentalist impulses that developed within this pluralistic context took two distinct forms, distinguished by their approaches to defining the boundaries of their religious groups. One type of fundamentalist response appeared among the minority religious communities of the Muslims and Sikhs. These incipient fundamentalist movements concluded that their beliefs had been corrupted through the processes of syncretism, or cultural borrowing, that characterized India's religious culture. Their primary goals were thus to define the boundaries of their faith more exclusively and to purify its beliefs and practices, particularly by removing Hindu influences. Most Islamic fundamentalists in colonial India eventually became concerned with political issues as well, as discussed earlier in relation to the rise of the Jamaat-e-Islami, but the goal of religious purification did remain preeminent among some of India's Muslims. This goal played an even larger role in the emergence of Sikh fundamentalism. Because Sikhism had historical connections to Hinduism, and because non-Sikhs (both European and Hindu) often considered Sikhism to be a form of Hinduism, many Sikhs became concerned with clarifying their distinct identity as a religious group and eliminating any residual connections to Hinduism.

A second type of fundamentalist response to India's religious pluralism developed within the Hindu majority. This response also focused on the question of religious identity, but in trying to define the boundaries of Hindu identity it adopted a more inclusive approach. That approach was made necessary by the significant diversity that existed within Hinduism, which throughout much of its history lacked a clearly articulated identity as a single religious system.[55] The incorporation of some elements of Hinduism into more recently developed religions further complicated the concept of Hindu identity, as did the European practice of designating all indigenous residents of British India as Hindus. The challenge to early Hindu fundamentalists, then, was to define those features of their religion that united its diverse adherents under the rubric of Hinduism. The lack of a single scriptural authority made this task especially difficult, leading some Hindu reformers in the nineteenth century to insist on a purer adherence to the ancient Vedic texts. During the twentieth century, however, the dominant expressions of Hindu fundamentalism focused more on the question of establishing an inclusive Hindu identity than on issues of scriptural authority or theological orthodoxy.

As in the other hearths of fundamentalism discussed in this chapter, the fundamentalist impulses provoked by the above concerns eventually led to the formation of specific religious movements. Again, each of these movements was distinguished by motives generally related to issues of identity, but they also reflected the circumstances of the particular religious tradition that they represented and the beliefs of their individual leaders. As a result, the early fundamentalist movements that emerged in response to India's religious pluralism differed significantly in terms of their strategies and their effects on Indian society.

Among Indian Muslims, the Jamaat-e-Islami provided an important outlet for fundamentalist sentiments, as discussed above; but that group focused more on the political complexities facing the Muslim community than on the threat to Islam in India posed by its syncretistic relationship to Hinduism. The latter issue became the primary focus of a separate group, the Tablighi Jamaat ("Missionary Society"), or simply the Tabligh, established in 1927. Its founder, Muhammad Ilyas, was an Islamic teacher concerned by the deviations from orthodox Islam that he observed among Indian Muslims living in the northern district of Mewat.[56] Descended largely from Hindu ancestors who had converted to Islam during the Mogul dynasty, these Muslims followed a folk form of Islam with strong Hindu overtones. Ilyas and his followers believed that this practice would eventually eliminate the distinctions between Islam and Hinduism in India, presumably through the absorption of the former by the latter. The Tablighi Jamaat thus devoted itself primarily to missionary work, aimed at persuading "strayed" Muslims to abandon beliefs and rituals derived from Hinduism, to follow the sharia rather than local custom in matters relating to marriage, divorce, and inheritance, and to adhere more strictly to the religious duties specified in the Koran, such as regular prayer in a mosque. Personal piety rather than political objectives were their main concern.

The Tabligh spread their message of Islamic purification using a grassroots approach based on personal interactions between small itinerant groups of members and local villagers or townspeople. Ilyas developed this approach after concluding that formal institutions had failed to promote Islamic education. He also believed that the involvement of Tabligh members in missionary activity would purify their own faith in Islam as well as that of the other Muslims they reached. Missionary journeys lasting several days, or even weeks, during which participants concentrated solely on religious matters, thus became an accepted duty of the group's members. These activities proved to be effective in reinforcing members' commitment to Islam, in attracting new members to the society, and in increasing Muslim adherence to orthodox Islamic practices, first in the district of Mewat and then throughout other parts of India and beyond. Again, the Tablighi Jamaat did not try to convert non-Muslims; its sole concern was to spread authentic Islamic practices among existing Muslims.

By undertaking this effort, the Tabligh grew into one of the largest international Muslim organizations, with millions of followers worldwide. It has expressed a continuing disinterest in political matters, however, which it considers to be of little importance relative to the religious life of the individual. This apolitical stance has allowed the Tabligh to operate in contexts where more militantly political Islamic groups have been suppressed, but it has also limited the group's impact beyond its own closed community. For this reason, scholars have disagreed over the validity of identifying the Tablighi Jamaat as a fundamentalist movement. Some claim that the Tabligh's literal interpretation of the Koran and hostility toward liberal theological innovations mark it as a fundamentalist group. Others argue that it is too informally organized and too little involved with political activism to be considered a true expression of fundamentalism.[57] In either case, the Tablighi Jamaat clearly illustrates the relationship between India's syncretistic religious environment and the development of fundamentalist impulses within a religious minority concerned with maintaining its distinct identity.

A second illustration of that relationship, and one that conforms more clearly to a strict definition of fundamentalism, involves the Sikh minority concentrated in the Punjab region of northern India (fig. 2.7). The difficulties faced by the Sikhs in India's plural religious culture differed in important ways

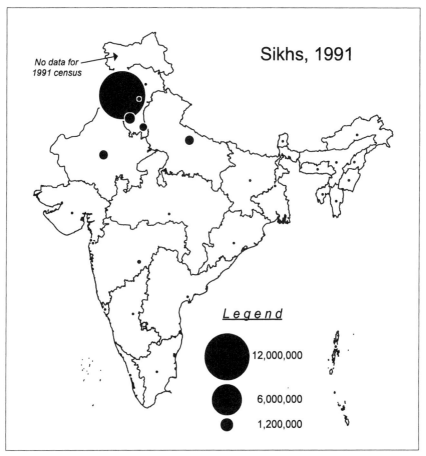

Figure 2.7   The distribution of Sikhs in India in 1991. The heaviest concentration of Sikhs is located in the state of Punjab and surrounding provinces. *Data source:* Census of India, 1991.

from those addressed by the Tablighi Jamaat. Founded in the late 1400s by the Hindu guru Nanak, the Sikh religion (*sikh* being the Hindi word meaning "disciple") brought together elements of Hinduism and Islam, along with the original insights of its founder. As Sikhism evolved, it retained much of its syncretistic character even as its leaders sought to clarify its unique identity. The most important development in that process occurred late in the 1600s, under the guru Gobind Singh, with the emergence of the concept of the Khalsa, or "community of the pure." Gobind Singh identified himself as the final Sikh guru and stated that after his death the primary sources of authority for the Sikhs would be their sacred scriptures (the Granth) and the entire Sikh brotherhood as represented in the Khalsa.[58] Not all Sikhs followed the ways of the Khalsa, which took on an openly militaristic aspect, but those who did identified themselves as the true core of Sikhism and used various means to identify themselves as a distinct community. Members of the Khalsa brotherhood all took the name Singh ("lion"), for example, and underwent a baptism ceremony. They also observed strict rules of conduct that prohibited men from cutting their hair or beard and required them to wear a wooden comb, iron bracelet, and breeches and to carry a sword. In asserting their separate religious identity, the Khalsa Sikhs introduced a sense of nationalism distinct from that of Hindus.

Their separate identity was not entirely secure, however, in part because some practicing Sikhs were not baptized and did not participate in the Khalsa, and in part because Hindu elements remained an important part of Sikhism. Sikh identity also faced a serious challenge when the Sikh Empire, which had been formally established by the early 1800s through an agreement with the British, was subsequently absorbed by British India in 1849. This event led to a temporary decline in the influence of the Khalsa and an associated growth in the influence of Hinduism within the Sikh community, even among those who remained practicing Sikhs.[59] An increase in Christian missionary activity at this time also made inroads on Sikhism. The period of British colonialism had complex implications for Sikh identity, however. While annexation of the Sikh Empire at first reduced the influence of the Khalsa, the British eventually reinforced the notion of a distinctive Sikh identity by their efforts to recruit Khalsa Sikhs for the Indian colonial army and police. The Khalsa's militaristic character had given its members a reputation as effective soldiers, which the British attempted to exploit by treating the Sikhs as a distinct group. The resurgence of the Khalsa brought about by British colonial policies was accompanied by a growing concern among some Sikhs with reforming their religious practices and countering Christian missionary activity. A reassertion of Sikh identity thus developed during the late 1800s and early 1900s, leading to new confrontations with India's pluralistic religious culture.

During the late 1800s, religious reform within the Sikh community was associated most strongly with the Singh Sabha ("Singh Assembly") movement. The first Singh Sabha was established in Amritsar in 1873, and a second appeared in Lahore in 1879. By the end of the century, well over a hundred such organizations existed throughout Punjab and adjacent regions of northern India. The first Sabhas did not heavily stress the distinctions between Sikhs and Hindus, and some members actually considered the Sikhs to be part of the Hindu community. As the century ended, however, the rise of Hindu nationalism and attempts by Hindu traditionalists to promote Hindu practices among unbaptized Sikhs provoked a counterreaction among the Khalsa Sikhs, who insisted on their distinctiveness as a religious community. An important expression of Sikh separatism appeared in 1898, with the publication of an influential pamphlet titled (in translation) *We Are Not Hindus*, written by Sikh scholar Kahan Singh. This pamphlet argued that Sikhism was a distinct religion, not simply a version of Hinduism, and it provided a rationale for establishing an ideological boundary separating Khalsa Sikhs from those with residual ties to Hinduism.[60] In 1902, the various Singh Sabhas reinforced that boundary by uniting as a single association, the Chief Khalsa Diwan. The Chief Khalsa Diwan essentially defined Sikhism in terms of the traditions of the Khalsa brotherhood and sought to purify Sikhism by eliminating Hindu elements. Its first significant victory came in 1905, when it succeeded in having Hindu idols removed from the most sacred Sikh place of worship, the Golden Temple in Amritsar (fig. 2.8). It also supported the legal establishment in 1909 of a separate marriage ritual for Sikhs, who had previously observed Hindu marriage ceremonies.

Following these successes, the Chief Khalsa Diwan increasingly focused on the goal of controlling Sikh temples, or gurdwaras ("gateways to the guru"), as a means of purifying Sikhism. From the period of Mogul rule, the gurdwaras had been managed by hereditary temple custodians who generally professed Sikhism but did not belong to the Khalsa. Under British colonial law, the gurdwaras remained under the control of these custodians, who in turn were expected to express loyalty to the British. As in earlier times, the vast majority of the temple custodians under British rule were either unbaptized Sikhs or even practicing Hindus (which accounted for the presence of Hindu idols in Sikh temples).[61] The British colonial government also established special controls over the Golden Temple, placing its secular administration under local British authorities and assigning its spiritual direction to a British-appointed Sikh. These arrangements for the management of the gurdwaras derived from the pluralistic context within which Sikhism arose, in which the Sikh masses accepted the custodial role of non-Khalsa Sikhs and Hindus in the temples. As a more fundamentalist approach to Sikh identity developed in the twentieth century, however, these arrangements became unacceptable to the Khalsa Sikhs. Bringing the gurdwaras under the control of Khalsa Sikhs thus became a primary objective of many members of the Chief Khalsa Diwan and led to a continuing dispute with the colonial regime during the early 1920s.

That dispute resulted in the formation of two new organizations by the

Figure 2.8 The Golden Temple, located in the middle of a large reflecting pool, represents the Sikhs' most important place of worship. During the 1920s, control of the Golden Temple and other Sikh shrines became a major objective of Sikh fundamentalists. Amritsar, India, early 1900s. *Source:* CORBIS/Hulton-Deutsch Co.

Khalsa Sikhs: the Shiromani Gurdwara Prabandhak Committee (or SGPC), established in 1920 as an elected body that would become responsible for managing all Sikh temples and shrines, and the Akali Dal ("Band of Immortals"), a political group formed in 1921 with the goal of removing the hereditary custodians from the gurdwaras by direct action. These groups eventually became more influential than the Chief Khalsa Diwan, and the formation of the activist Akali Dal in particular represented the emergence of the first explicitly fundamentalist movement within Sikhism. The Akali Dal subsequently mounted a nonviolent protest campaign aimed at bringing the gurdwaras under the control of the SGPC, and a number of temple custodians agreed to the Akalis' demands. Other custodians refused to yield control of the shrines, however, and on a number of occasions the authorities used violence to suppress Akali demonstrations. The nonviolent stance of the Akali Dal in the face of such opposition increased support for their cause, however, among both Sikhs and non-Sikhs. As a result, in 1925 the Punjab Legislative Council passed the Gurdwara Reform Act, which ceded control of all Sikh temples and shrines to the SGPC.

This victory validated the efforts of the Akali Dal and other Khalsa Sikhs to redefine their identity within the larger context of India's pluralistic religious culture. It also reinforced the inherently fundamentalist perspective of the Akali Dal and its interest in maintaining a strict ideological boundary between Sikhs and Hindus. As the postcolonial era approached, moreover, the Akali Dal became the Sikhs' leading political voice. Within this context, the formation of a separate Sikh state became a prominent theme within the identity politics of Sikh fundamentalists. They did not succeed in achieving this goal, but many members of the Akali Dal remained committed to political independence after British India had been divided into the independent states of Pakistan and India. Eventually the goal of establishing a separate Sikh state was taken up by a more radical group of Sikh fundamentalists, as discussed in the following chapter, but the foundation of that group's ideology was established by the Akali Dal.

As an expression of fundamentalism, the Akali Dal differed from the Tablighi Jamaat through its commitment to political action, first in reforming the system of gurdwara supervision and later by representing Sikh political interests regionally and nationally. As a result, it better fits the accepted definition of fundamentalism than does the Tablighi Jamaat. Nonetheless, the two groups resemble one another in their insistence on the purity of their religious tradition within the larger context of Indian pluralism and in their concern with the elimination of elements of religious practice that blur their exclusive identities.

The pluralism inherent within India's religious culture contributed as well to the emergence of fundamentalist sentiments among the Hindu majority. Hindu fundamentalism has also focused on the issue of identity, but from a perspective different from those of the Tablighi Jamaat and Akali Dal. Because Hinduism comprises a great variety of traditions and practices associated with particular places and social castes, and because it contains diverse scriptural expressions, its "fundamentals" are considerably more difficult to specify than are those of the other religions discussed in this chapter. In trying to prevent the erosion of Hinduism's central position within Indian society, Hindu fundamentalists thus adopted a distinctive approach in which they defined their religion's key "fundamental" as Hindu identity itself. The concept of a unified Hindu sense of identity in fact represented something of an innovation, as India's long tradition of religious pluralism had established neither the need nor the ideological basis for a precise definition of what it meant to be a Hindu. The British division of Indian society into separate Hindu and Muslim communities during the colonial period created a context in which the issue of Hindu identity took on greater meaning, however.[62] The postcolonial establishment of

India as a constitutionally secular state reinforced the need to articulate and protect Hindu interests. Hindu fundamentalist responses to India's pluralistic religious context thus represent a distinctly modern phenomenon and required new conceptions of the nature of Hinduism.

As in many of the other religious traditions discussed thus far, the roots of Hindu fundamentalism can be traced back to expressions of reformism that emerged in the nineteenth century in response to increasing Western influences. The most important such development in Hinduism was the founding of the Arya Samaj ("Society of Nobles") in 1875. As a reform movement, the Arya Samaj promoted the compatibility of Hinduism with concepts of modernity imported from the West, while at the same time trying to preserve the core of Hindu tradition. The Aryas undertook these efforts in response to two primary concerns: a perceived decline in Hindu society that had begun under Muslim rule and continued under British colonialism, and the threat to Hinduism posed by Christian missionary activity and the expansion of the Muslim and Sikh communities. The Arya Samaj thus exhibited a fundamentalist concern with perceived dangers that challenged its religious community.

Specific beliefs of the Arya Samaj also displayed a distinctly fundamentalist character. The group placed special emphasis on the authority of the Vedas, the original sacred texts of Hinduism. Its members rejected elements of Hinduism that were based on sources other than the Vedas or that were inconsistent with Vedic teachings, such as the caste system, image worship, and polytheism.[63] They believed that such deviations from Vedic tradition had led to Hinduism's decline following its contacts with Islam and Christianity and that Hinduism would thrive only after those elements had been removed. The Aryas thus attempted to purify Hinduism by emphasizing strict adherence to a specific scriptural tradition, mirroring the efforts of Christian and Islamic fundamentalists to purify their own faiths. In the process, however, the Arya Samaj rejected many practices associated with orthodox Hinduism, significantly weakening their movement's appeal among the majority of Hindus whose beliefs and practices contained post-Vedic elements. In this sense, the Arya Samaj represented a movement away from many Hindu traditions, suggesting that it does not exactly fit the definition of a fundamentalist movement.

The Arya Samaj does not conform to the fundamentalism model in other ways as well. The group supported radical social reforms that countered traditional Hindu customs; for example, it favored education for both sexes and marriage by choice rather than by familial arrangement. Support for such reforms reflected the Aryas' desire to modernize Hindu social practices and demonstrates the complex relationship in their beliefs between cultural preservation and accommodation to the modern world. The Arya Samaj also instituted some religious innovations, such as their redefinition of the *shuddhi*, a purification ritual for high caste Hindus, which the Aryas transformed into a conversion procedure for people of Hindu ancestry who had converted to another religion. Traditional Hinduism did not possess procedures for acquiring converts, and so the creation of this ceremony represented a major departure from past practices. This innovation grew out of the Aryas' desire to combat Christian missionary activity in India, but it also represented part of a more general emulation of Western practices, as seen in the Aryas' concern with establishing the Vedas as scriptural canon.[64] The Arya Samaj thus contained some fundamentalist elements, but on the whole it is more accurately described as an expression of reformism. Indeed, some members of the Arya Samaj considered it to be a distinct religious group, identified with Vedic tradition rather than with the whole of Hinduism.

As the political situation in British India became more volatile during the 1920s and 1930s, however, the Arya Samaj came to identify more closely with the broader Hindu community and participated in the growth of Hindu nationalism. In the process, some of its members became involved in organizations that took on more decisively fundamentalist characteristics. Most importantly, members of Arya Samaj were involved in the formation of the Hindu Mahasabha ("Hindu Great Council"), a national political party promoting Hindu interests. Founded in the 1910s in response to the growing political organization of the Muslim community, particularly in the form of the Muslim League, the Hindu Mahasabha became a leading political voice of the conservative Hindu community and played a major role in representing Hindu concerns during the process of decolonization. During the 1920s and 1930s it drew many of its leaders from the Arya Samaj, but it also came to support a distinctive view of Hinduism that provided the foundation for further expressions of Hindu fundamentalism.

The Mahasabha's view of Hindu culture derived primarily from the writings of V. D. Savarkar. Savarkar's militant activism in support of Indian independence led to his imprisonment by the British from 1910 to 1923. While in prison, he developed a distinctive conception of Hindu identity, which he outlined in a work titled *Hindutva*, published in 1923 shortly before his release. The concept of *Hindutva*, commonly translated as "Hinduness," quickly gained acceptance as an ideological basis for Hindu nationalism and became widely influential among members of the Mahasabha and later fundamentalist groups. In essence, Savarkar tied Hindu identity to three fundamental elements: geography, ancestry, and culture. In geographical terms, Savarkar associated *Hindutva* with those people living in the traditional domain of the Aryans who settled India, bounded by the Indus River, the Himalayan Mountains, and the oceans to the south. Within this region, *Hindutva* was associated specifically with those whose ancestry could be traced, at least in part, to the ancient Aryan society from which Hinduism arose, and who also participated in a common Hindu culture. The definition of the latter centered on certain rituals, social rules, and languages (in particular, Sanskrit and Hindi) associated with Hindu tradition but did not require adherence to any particular version of Hindu orthodoxy. Indeed, *Hindutva* could be attributed to indigenous adherents of any of the Indic family of religions, including Jainism, Sikhism, and Buddhism. In Savarkar's conception, the term *Hindutva* thus applied not just to practitioners of Hinduism but to all those who considered the traditional geographical domain of Hindu culture to be both their "fatherland" and their "holy land."[65]

An important feature of Savarkar's definition of Hindu identity was its inclusiveness. Unlike the Sikh and Muslim concepts of religious identity discussed earlier, the notion of *Hindutva* focused on the clarification of group affiliation in a broader historical and geographical context rather than on the purification of religious beliefs. The assertion that *Hindutva* defined the character of the Hindu community still involved the establishment of ideological boundaries, but with an emphasis on inclusion rather than exclusion. This approach defined Hindu identity in a way that both recognized and sanctioned Hindu diversity and thus represented a radical departure from the ideas of the Arya Samaj. Those who adopted the idea of *Hindutva* in fact came to see inclusiveness as the essential core of Hindu doctrine and *Hindutva*'s accommodation of various specific religions as a definitive aspect of Hindu culture.[66] They also saw *Hindutva*'s tolerance of religious diversity as evidence of the inherent spiritual superiority of the Hindu tradition over the exclusiveness of Islam and Christianity, an assertion emphasized by later Hindu fundamentalists.

In formulating an inclusive definition of Hindu identity, Savarkar also provided support for the development of Hindu nationalism, particularly as expressed in the concept of the *Hindu Rashtra*, or "Hindu Nation." Savarkar believed that the people who possess *Hindutva* represent a distinct ethnoreligious nation bound to its homeland in the Indian subcontinent. He opposed the creation of a free India as a pluralistic, secular state defined only by its territorial extent. Instead, he argued that India, as a political state, should be explicitly organized around the *Hindu Rashtra*, the national community sharing the culture of *Hindutva*. In this regard, the acceptance of Savarkar's ideas among Hindu fundamentalists represented a response not just to India's religious pluralism but to the politicization of that pluralism as the process of decolonization unfolded. To the fundamentalists, that process contained two related threats to the integrity of Hindu culture: political competition among different religious communities, in particular between Hindus and Muslims, and the institutionalization of secularism as a national policy, which would deny Hinduism its central place in Indian life. The concepts of *Hindutva* and *Hindu Rashtra* provided an ideological standpoint from which Hindu fundamentalists could oppose those threats and reassert their religious identity.

Savarkar's ideas thus produced a dramatic reorientation within the emerging fundamentalist community regarding both the nature of Hindu identity and the importance of the issue of identity in promoting Hindu interests. Again, unlike their Sikh and Muslim counterparts, later Hindu fundamentalists were not primarily concerned with the impacts of syncretism on their religious culture or with the purification of Hindu doctrine and ritual.[67] They focused instead on the creation of a unified Hindu nation that would preserve the religious diversity inherent within *Hindutva* itself. As a result, while they shared the concern with religious identity found in other forms of fundamentalism in the region, Hindu fundamentalists addressed that concern by adopting distinctive strategies and goals that reflected both the numerical superiority of their religious community and its internal variety.

A highly influential fundamentalist organization based on the concepts of *Hindutva* and *Hindu Rashtra* appeared in 1925 as the Rashtriya Swayamsevak Sangh ("National Union of Volunteers"), or RSS. Its founder, K. B. Hedgewar, also belonged to the Hindu Mahasabha, but he believed that the revitalization of the Hindu community required more than traditional political action. He thus established the RSS as a cultural organization focusing on the spiritual and physical training of young men, which would prepare them for a lifelong commitment to *Hindutva*. Hedgewar looked to the martial tradition of the northern Indian region of Maharashtra as the historical model for his organization and in particular to the example of Shivaji, a seventeenth-century hero who led a revolt against Mogul rule.[68] In Hedgewar's view, the vitality of the Hindu community in the twentieth century depended both on the adoption of military values of discipline and physical strength and on a continuing commitment to the spiritual values encompassed by *Hindutva*. By incorporating both elements into the activities of the RSS, he intended for it to serve as a model for the rest of the Hindu community and eventually to become the vanguard of a revitalized and unified Hindu nation.

A key feature of the RSS, and in the long run one of the reasons for its widespread influence, was its focus on developing strong local branches, or *sakhas*.[69] The *sakhas* gave the RSS an institutional presence in thousands of communities across India, providing a local context for the processes of training, indoctrination, and male bonding among RSS recruits. These processes involved various forms of physical activity as well as character-building exercises designed to instill Hindu values. Members of the local *sakha* met daily to reinforce group discipline and solidarity, and, starting in the 1930s, larger groups of members began to organize RSS religious festivals, based on Hindu tradition but incorporating a strong element of nationalism.[70] Through such activities, the RSS created a durable sense of group identity among its recruits. After completing their period of training, usually by their mid-twenties, some recruits remained in the RSS as leaders, but most went on to other activities in the secular world. Those who gave up active participation in the RSS typically remained in contact with the men with whom they had trained, however, and together they provided a vast reservoir of support for the group's activities. This strategy of building closely knit local communities of current and former members proved to be highly successful, and by the late 1940s the RSS had a core of roughly 200 thousand fully active members and a broader following of around 5 million, including all adult Swayemsevaks and young boys who had not yet achieved full membership.[71]

As the RSS grew in membership, so did its importance as an expression of Hindu fundamentalism. Its influence within Indian society derived largely from its militant support for Hindu nationalism, a position that became increasingly popular among Hindus during the early and mid-1940s as Muslim support expanded for the partition of British India into two independent states—India and Pakistan. The situation changed in 1948, however, after a former member of the RSS assassinated the Indian leader Mohandas Gandhi, ostensibly because the latter demanded that India compensate Pakistan for losses suffered in the conflicts that arose at the time of partition. Although the RSS was not implicated in Gandhi's murder, this event produced strong public and government reactions against the more extreme expressions of Hindu nationalism and resulted in the arrests of thousands of RSS members and the banning of the RSS itself for a brief period.[72]

After the ban was lifted, the RSS readjusted to the new political reality of Indian independence and began to reestablish its base of support. It remained committed to the concept of *Hindutva* and to the creation of a vital Hindu nation, but now operated within the context of a secular but predominantly Hindu state rather than a diverse European colony. Within this new context, it developed two strategies to rebuild its popular appeal. On one hand, it adopted a position of patriotic support for India in conflicts with Pakistan in 1950 and China and 1962 and declared that as a Hindu cultural organization it had no interest in the country's internal politics.[73] At the same time, it used its extensive local network and well-developed organizational skills to support the formation of a variety of new Hindu groups, including the political party Jana Sangh in 1951 and the Vishwa Hindu Parishad ("World Hindu Society," or VHP) in 1964. These organizations, along with a student association, labor union, societies to support peasants' rights and rural education, and a number of other groups, constituted an informal system of institutions associated with the RSS. Known as the Sangh Parivar ("Union Family"), this cluster of organizations significantly extended the influence of the RSS and its fundamentalist ideology within Indian society. Membership in the RSS also continued to grow, to roughly a million fully active members by the late 1970s and nearly twice that number a decade later.[74]

Through its success in rebuilding popular support during the 1950s and 1960s and the declining influence of earlier groups such as the Arya Samaj and Hindu Mahasabha, the RSS became the central organization within Hindu fundamentalism in the second half of the twentieth century. As such, it continued to define the goals of the Hindu fundamentalist movement in terms of the inclusivist perspective of Savarkar's concept of *Hindutva*. Those goals remained focused specifically on the development of a unified Hindu community,

but now within the context of India as a secular state. From the Hindu fundamentalists' point of view, India's constitutional secularism represented a threat
not to religious belief in general but to Hindu identity in particular, since government policies appeared to place greater emphasis on protecting the rights
of religious minorities than on preserving the central place of Hinduism in
Indian society. The primary danger perceived by Hindu fundamentalists, in
other words, was not the secularization of Indian society after independence,
but rather the weakening of the Hindu majority by pluralist policies that denied
Hinduism's cultural primacy. As a result, their core objectives involved the
promotion of *Hindutva* and the creation of a strong Hindu nation.

  Again, this response to India's pluralistic religious culture differed significantly from the focus on religious purification that developed among Sikh and
Muslim fundamentalists in the same hearth area, but it reflected an equally
powerful concern with the interactions between group identity and the region's
complex religious context. The striking conjunction of diverse religious traditions within India thus presented a challenge to majority and minority groups
alike. As a result, questions of religious identity became an especially important
issue for fundamentalist groups in the region as they sought to preserve their
particular traditions.

CONCLUSIONS

  The cases discussed above reveal important similarities among the hearths
of fundamentalism and the processes through which fundamentalist movements have arisen during the past century. Within the hearth areas discussed,
fundamentalist movements emerged out of conflicts between established religious traditions and newly developing processes of social change. Many adherents of the religions examined here tried to reconcile their beliefs to changing
secular conditions. Others believed, however, that the subordination of religious tradition to the demands of the modern world would undermine the
certainties of their faith, and must be resisted; and the latter conviction provided the basis for fundamentalist responses to change. Such responses involved two key elements: the development of a strong sense of shared identity
among those who perceived threats against their religious traditions and the
group's belief in the importance of those traditions as a guiding moral force or
organizing principle within society. Individual leaders played important roles
in shaping and articulating fundamentalist thought, but in each hearth fundamentalism itself emerged as a group phenomenon, uniting a community of
believers who shared a certain conception of religious tradition and its role in
society. The rise of fundamentalism thus centered on the definition of distinct
ideological boundaries around those who adhered to a religion's "authentic"
form. The creation of such boundaries represented the first step in protecting

threatened religious traditions and provided a foundation for subsequent actions by the group in defense of its faith.

The cases examined in this chapter further reveal that the ways in which early fundamentalist groups defined their ideological boundaries varied from hearth to hearth, as did the threats that made the creation of such boundaries necessary. These variations resulted in part from the distinctive beliefs considered to be "fundamental" by each group. The concepts of Jewish sacred history, Islamic law, and Hindu identity raised very different kinds of issues for fundamentalists in these three traditions and led to the development of distinctive ideological strategies. Variations among the early expressions of fundamentalism also reflected social and political differences among the local settings within which they developed. The impact of modernization on North America and Europe during the 1800s, for example, created a context in which fundamentalist groups arose in opposition to trends within their own societies, such as modernist theological innovations and the decline of religion's influence on secular life. As a result, these groups often focused on strategies to redirect the course of society from within, through legislation or the reformation of religious institutions. In the hearths scattered from northern Africa to southern Asia, on the other hand, the concerns of early fundamentalists more often related to the corruption of their indigenous societies by foreign influences imposed through the processes of colonialism. In these cases, nationalism often became a crucial theme within the larger fundamentalist discourse and at least implicitly engaged fundamentalists in a struggle against outside influences. The rise of fundamentalism has thus been a widespread phenomenon during the past century, but one that has been intrinsically contextual, tied to particular religious traditions and their distinctive interactions with local processes of social change.

Out of these diverse beginnings, religious fundamentalism has emerged as a potent force in the contemporary world. Through their underlying concern with the influence of religion in society, fundamentalists in various settings have played major roles in defining the terms of important social conflicts. Often these conflicts have focused on specific issues, such as the teaching of evolution in American public schools or the adoption of the Koran as the basis for civil law in Muslim countries; but in a broader sense, they reflect a more basic and far-reaching debate in modern societies concerning the legitimacy of religious authority. Fundamentalists have also defined the interactions between different societies in religious terms and thus have had significant effects on both internal and international political conflicts, such as the establishment of Jewish settlements on the West Bank of the Jordan River or the efforts of militant Sikhs to create an independent Sikh state. Again, such conflicts appear to focus on narrowly defined issues, but they raise much larger questions about the impact of religious belief on political policies. Fundamentalists' involvement in such conflicts has extended the impact of their concerns far beyond their own religious communities. As a result, fundamentalism in its various expressions has become an important source of friction in societies around the globe.

The two following chapters examine in greater detail the contemporary impacts of fundamentalism and its relationship to the contextual frameworks in which it has evolved. Chapter 3 focuses on global diversity in contemporary expressions of fundamentalism, in particular on the various objectives and strategies that fundamentalists have adopted in their interactions with their surrounding contexts. Chapter 4 elaborates on this theme through a more detailed examination of the geographical dimensions of fundamentalism and an assessment of what those dimensions reveal about the nature of fundamentalism itself.

NOTES

1. Ernest R. Sandeen, *The Roots of Fundamentalism: British and American Millenarianism, 1800–1930* (Chicago: University of Chicago Press, 1970), 188–206.

2. George M. Marsden, *Fundamentalism and American Culture* (New York: Oxford University Press, 1980), 118–23; Sidney E. Ahlstrom, *A Religious History of the American People* (New Haven, Conn.: Yale University Press, 1972), 815–16.

3. Ahlstrom, *A Religious History*, 843–8; Robert T. Handy, *A Christian America: Protestant Hopes and Historical Realities* (London: Oxford University Press, 1971), 27–64.

4. Marsden, *Fundamentalism and American Culture*, 102–18; Ahlstrom, *A Religious History*, 812–15; Robert T. Handy, *A History of the Churches in the United States and Canada* (New York: Oxford University Press, 1976), 286–94.

5. Marsden, *Fundamentalism and American Culture*, 62–8.

6. Sandeen, *Roots of Fundamentalism*, 132–7.

7. Stewart G. Cole, *The History of Fundamentalism* (New York: Harper and Row, 1931), 246; Marsden, *Fundamentalism and American Culture*, 128–9.

8. Sandeen, *Roots of Fundamentalism*, 181–3, 241–3.

9. Ahlstrom, *A Religious History*, 763–84.

10. Ibid., 910–15; Marsden, *Fundamentalism and American Culture*, 164–70.

11. Cole, *History of Fundamentalism*, 66–8.

12. D. Newell Williams, "How and Why the Disciples Have Changed in Relation to American Culture," in *A Case Study of Mainstream Protestantism: The Disciples' Relation to American Culture, 1880–1989*, D. Newell Williams, ed. (Grand Rapids, Mich.: William B. Eerdmans, 1991), 3–25; Roger W.

Stump, "Spatial Patterns of Growth and Decline among the Disciples of Christ, 1890–1980," in *Case Study of Mainstream Protestantism*, D. Newell Williams, ed., 445–68.

13. Willard B. Gatewood Jr., ed., *Controversy in the Twenties: Fundamentalism, Modernism and Evolution* (Nashville, Tenn.: Vanderbilt University Press, 1969), 113–16; Bruce B. Lawrence, *Defenders of God: The Fundamentalist Revolt against the Modern Age* (San Francisco: Harper and Row, 1989), 170–88; Lawrence W. Levine, *Defender of the Faith: William Jennings Bryan: The Last Decades, 1915–1925* (New York: Oxford University Press, 1965), 260–6.

14. Alvin W. Johnson and Frank H. Yost, *Separation of Church and State in the United States* (Minneapolis: University of Minnesota Press, 1934), 165–174; Cole, *History of Fundamentalism*, 313; Ahlstrom, *A Religious History*, 909–10.

15. Cited in Johnson and Frank, *Separation of Church and State*, 166.

16. Eugene F. Provenzo Jr., *Religious Fundamentalism and American Education: The Battle for the Public Schools* (Albany: State University of New York Press, 1990), 52.

17. Marsden, *Fundamentalism and American Culture*, 185–9.

18. Don Conway, "Religion and Public Education in the States," *International Journal of Religious Education* 32 (March 1956): 34–40.

19. Ben Armstrong, *The Electric Church* (Nashville, Tenn.: Thomas Nelson Publishers, 1979), 31–52.

20. Samuel C. Heilman and Menachem Friedman, "Religious Fundamentalism and Religious Jews: The Case of the Haredim," in *Fundamentalisms Observed*, Martin E. Marty and R. Scott Appleby, eds. (Chicago: University of Chicago Press, 1991), 200.

21. Dan Cohn-Sherbok, *Modern Judaism* (New York: St. Martin's Press, 1996), 73–7; Dan Cohn-Sherbok, *Atlas of Jewish History* (Routledge: London, 1994), 144–51.

22. Joseph L. Blau, *Modern Varieties of Judaism* (New York: Columbia University Press, 1966), 28–39.

23. Phillip Sigal, *Judaism: The Evolution of a Faith* (William B. Eerdmans: Grand Rapids, Mich., 1988), 204–14.

24. Michael K. Silber, "The Emergence of Ultra-Orthodoxy: The Invention of a Tradition," in *The Uses of Tradition: Jewish Continuity in the Modern Era*, Jack Wertheimer, ed. (New York: Jewish Theological Seminary of America, 1992), 23–84.

25. Samuel Heilman, *Defenders of the Faith: Inside Ultra-Orthodox Jewry* (New York: Schocken Books, 1992), 11–39.

26. Alan L. Mittleman, "Fundamentalism and Political Development: The Case of Agudat Israel," in *Jewish Fundamentalism in Comparative Perspective: Religion, Ideology and the Crisis of Modernity*, Laurence J. Silberstein, ed.

(New York: New York University Press, 1993), 216–37; Gilles Kepel, *The Revenge of God: The Resurgence of Islam, Christianity and Judaism in the Modern World* (University Park: Pennsylvania State University Press, 1994), 175.

27. Jeff Halper, *Between Redemption and Revival: The Jewish Yishuv of Jerusalem in the Nineteenth Century* (Boulder, Colo.: Westview Press, 1991), 7.

28. Heilman and Friedman, "Religious Fundamentalism and Religious Jews," 222–34.

29. Emile Marmorstein, *Heaven at Bay: The Jewish Kulturkampf in the Holy Land* (London: Oxford University Press, 1969), 80–3; Charles S. Liebman and Eliezer Don-Yehiya, *Religion and Politics in Israel* (Bloomington: Indiana University Press, 1984), 32–7.

30. Aviezer Ravitzky, *Messianism, Zionism and Jewish Religious Radicalism* (Chicago: University of Chicago Press, 1996), 86–96.

31. Gary S. Schiff, *Tradition and Politics: The Religious Parties of Israel* (Detroit, Mich.: Wayne State University Press, 1977), 71.

32. S. Clement Leslie, *The Rift in Israel: Religious Authority and Secular Democracy* (London: Routledge and Kegan Paul, 1971); Menachem Friedman, "Jewish Zealots: Conservative Versus Innovative," in *Fundamentalism in Comparative Perspective*, Lawrence Kaplan, ed. (Amherst: University of Massachusetts Press, 1992), 160–3.

33. Schiff, *Tradition and Politics*, 81.

34. The choice of this name reflected the group's opposition to a tax imposed in 1938 on all Jewish residents to support their defense against Arab attacks. Neturei Karta opposed the tax based on their principle of separation. See S. Zalman Abramov, *Perpetual Dilemma: Jewish Religion in the Jewish State* (London: Associated University Presses, 1976), 154–7.

35. Ravitzky, *Messianism, Zionism and Jewish Religious Radicalism*, 60–73.

36. G. H. Jansen, *Militant Islam* (New York: Harper and Row, 1979), 17–30.

37. R. Hrair Dekmejian, *Islam in Revolution: Fundamentalism in the Arab World* (Syracuse, N.Y.: Syracuse University Press, 1985), 2–23; Dilip Hiro, *Holy Wars: The Rise of Islamic Fundamentalism* (New York: Routledge, 1989), 26–43.

38. Youssef M. Choueiri, *Islamic Fundamentalism* (London: Pinter Publishers, 1990), 31–52; Jansen, *Militant Islam*, 91–4.

39. Jansen, *Militant Islam*, 114–20; Choueiri, *Islamic Fundamentalism*, 64.

40. Sami Zubaida, "Islamic Fundamentalism in Egypt and Iran," in *Studies in Religious Fundamentalism*, Lionel Caplan, ed. (London: Macmillan Press, 1987), 33–4; Hiro, *Holy Wars*, 55–6.

41. John O. Voll, "Fundamentalism in the Sunni Arab World: Egypt and the Sudan," in *Fundamentalisms Observed*, Martin Marty and R. Scott Appleby, eds., 358–9.

42. Some scholars, such as Choueiri (*Islamic Fundamentalism*, 48–52) clas-

sify the Muslim Brotherhood as the final expression of reformism, but others argue that its militant opposition to political authority clearly places it within the framework of fundamentalism. See Zubaida, "Islamic Fundamentalism," 34–7; Hiro, *Holy Wars*, 60–9; Voll, "Fundamentalism in the Sunni Arab World," 360–72; Dekmejian, *Islam in Revolution*, 80–5.

43. Richard P. Mitchell, *The Society of the Muslim Brothers* (London: Oxford University Press, 1969), 7–16; Christina Phelps Harris, *Nationalism and Revolution in Egypt: The Role of the Muslim Brotherhood* (The Hague: Mouton and Co., 1964), 154–7, 177–81.

44. Mitchell, *The Society of the Muslim Brothers*, 29–30.

45. Harris, *Nationalism and Revolution in Egypt*, 159–60.

46. Mitchell, *The Society of the Muslim Brothers*, 133–62; Harris, *Nationalism and Revolution in Egypt*, 221–2.

47. Zubaida, "Islamic Fundamentalism in Egypt and Iran," 38–9.

48. Memtaz Ahmad, "Islamic Fundamentalism in South Asia: The Jamaat-i-Islami and the Tablighi Jamaat of South Asia," in *Fundamentalisms Observed*, Martin Marty and R. Scott Appleby, eds., 457–530; Graham Chapman, "Religious vs. Regional Determinism: Indian, Pakistan and Bangladesh as Inheritors of Empire," in *Shared Space: Divided Space*, Michael Chisholm and David M. Smith, eds. (London: Unwin Hyman, 1990), 106–34; Seyyed Vali Reza Nasr, *The Vanguard of the Islamic Revolution: The Jama'at-i Islami of Pakistan* (Berkeley: University of California Press, 1994), 3–10.

49. Nasr, *The Vanguard of the Islamic Revolution*, 9–27.

50. Ahmad, "Islamic Fundamentalism in South Asia," 503–6.

51. Nasr, *The Vanguard of the Islamic Revolution*, 141–6.

52. For a discussion of the geographical dimensions of India's religious pluralism, see A. K. Dutt and S. Davgun, "Religious Pattern of India with a Factoral Representation," *GeoJournal* 3, no. 2 (1979): 201–14.

53. Aziz Ahmad, *Studies in Islamic Culture in the Indian Environment* (Oxford: Clarendon Press, 1964), 140–66.

54. Peter van der Veer, "The Ruined Center: Religion and Mass Politics in India," *Journal of International Affairs* 50, no. 1 (Summer 1996): 254–77.

55. Robert Eric Frykenberg, "Fundamentalism and Revivalism in South Asia," in *Fundamentalism, Revivalists and Violence in South Asia*, James Warner Björkman, ed. (Riverdale, Md.: The Riverdale Company, 1988), 20–39.

56. Peter van der Veer, *Religious Nationalism: Hindus and Muslims in India* (Berkeley: University of California Press, 1994), 128–30; Ahmad, "Islamic Fundamentalism in South Asia," 510–24; Gilles Kepel, *The Revenge of God*, 34–5.

57. The first view is expressed in Ahmad, "Islamic Fundamentalism in South Asia," 458; the counter argument appears in Gabriel A. Almond, Emmanuel Sivan, and R. Scott Appleby, "Fundamentalism: Genus and Species," in *Fundamentalisms Comprehended*, Martin E. Marty and R. Scott Appleby, eds. (Chi-

cago: University of Chicago Press, 1995), 421. Also see Yahya Sadowski, "'Just' a Religion," *Brookings Review* 14, no. 3 (Summer 1996): 34–5.

58. van der Veer, *Religious Nationalism*, 53–6.

59. T. N. Madan, "The Double-Edged Sword: Fundamentalism and the Sikh Religious Tradition," in *Fundamentalisms Observed*, Martin Marty and R. Scott Appleby, eds., 602–7.

60. van der Veer, *Religious Nationalism*, 74.

61. A. S. Narang, *Storm over the Sutlej: The Akali Politics* (New Delhi: Gitanjali Publishing House, 1983), 51–2.

62. Donald Gold, "Organized Hinduisms: From Vedic Truth to Hindu Nation," in *Fundamentalisms Observed*, Martin Marty and R. Scott Appleby, eds., 536.

63. van der Veer, *Religious Nationalism*, 65.

64. Christophe Jaffrelot, *The Hindu Nationalist Movement in India* (New York: Columbia University Press, 1996), 13–17.

65. Gold, "Organized Hinduisms," 547–50; Jaffrelot, *The Hindu Nationalist Movement in India*, 28–31.

66. C. Ram-Prasad, "Hindutva Ideology: Extracting the Fundamentals," *Contemporary South Asia* 2, no 3 (1993): 285–309.

67. The purification of Hindu sacred places did become a major issue for fundamentalists, however, as discussed in chapters 3 and 4; but purification in this sense did not refer either to the Hindu community or to its beliefs and practices. Instead, it involved historical sites on which fundamentalists partially based their concept of Hindu identity.

68. Gold, "Organized Hinduisms," 542.

69. Jaffrelot, *The Hindu Nationalist Movement in India*, 35–8, 64–6.

70. Gold, "Organized Hinduisms," 548, 560.

71. J. A. Curran Jr., *Militant Hinduism in Indian Politics: A Study of the R.S.S.* (New York: Institute of Pacific Relations, 1951), 43.

72. Jaffrelot, *The Hindu Nationalist Movement in India*, 86–9.

73. Jaffrelot, *The Hindu Nationalist Movement in India*, 115.

74. Gold, "Organized Hinduisms," 535.

❸

GLOBAL VARIATIONS IN
CONTEMPORARY FUNDAMENTALISM

In recent decades, fundamentalist movements have emerged as significant cultural phenomena, with far-reaching effects, in various regions around the world. In the process, they have exhibited considerable diversity. Some, such as Christian fundamentalism in the United States, have emerged as mass movements, attracting a large and dispersed following. Others, such as Egypt's radical Islamic groups, operate as tightly knit elites outside the boundaries of conventional society. Similarly, some fundamentalist movements have created extensive institutional structures to advance their goals, including political parties, educational institutions, and social support systems. Groups like the Jamaat-e-Islami in Pakistan and the Rashtriya Swayamsevak Sangh in India exemplify this approach. In other cases, fundamentalist movements have been based more on an underlying sense of community than on formal organizations. Some strands of Christian fundamentalism follow this pattern, for example, as does much of the ultra-Orthodox Jewish community in Israel. Finally, as discussed in chapter 2, fundamentalist groups have focused on different types of threats to religious tradition and have addressed those threats in different ways. The complexity of forms manifested by fundamentalism thus represents an essential part of its character.

This chapter analyzes the nature of fundamentalism's diversity as a contemporary global phenomenon. The discussion focuses in particular on the varied ways in which fundamentalist groups relate to the geographical contexts in which they are located. Again, this approach derives from the thesis that fundamentalist movements are intrinsically contextual, responding to and acting upon specific, localized conditions. The manner in which a fundamentalist movement interacts with surrounding social and political structures represents a crucial element of its contextuality, providing important insights into the

group's motives and actions. The diversity within contemporary fundamentalism could be characterized in other ways, of course. The focus adopted here,
however, emphasizes the contextual sources and character of the diversity that
exists within fundamentalism. By investigating the varied interactions between
fundamentalists and the contexts that surround them, this approach clarifies
the meaning of fundamentalism as a global phenomenon, intrinsically tied to
particular settings.

In terms of the nature of their contextual interactions, fundamentalist movements can be divided into three major categories. The first includes groups
that dominate the context in which they are situated. Such groups have established their ideology as the guiding principle of an entire society or nation and
wield the power needed to enforce adherence to their religious principles.
Fundamentalists in this category assert that their ideological boundaries encompass all of society and in a sense are congruent with their society's political
boundaries. As a result, the "other" that the fundamentalists oppose exists by
definition outside their own society. Examples of this first category are relatively rare, but groups that do fit this category have a profound effect on the
social and political structures of their surrounding contexts. The most prominent examples of this category have developed in Iran since the Islamic Revolution of the late 1970s and in Afghanistan under the Taliban during the 1990s.
The fundamentalist regime established in Sudan in the 1980s fits this category
as well, but has had less success in enforcing conformity to its Islamic principles.

The second and third categories of fundamentalist groups include those that
have not established political or social control over the broader contexts in
which they are located. Most contemporary expressions of fundamentalism belong to these two categories, although for diverse reasons. Some groups are not
interested in exercising political or social control, often because the ideological
boundaries that they have created require their separation from the rest of
society. Other groups may hope ultimately to achieve a position of domination
but cannot under present conditions, either because they lack sufficient influence or because existing structural constraints, such as the legal separation of
church and state, prevent them from doing so. In any case, the groups associated with these two categories are situated in contexts where others holding
different beliefs also exert influence, a condition that inevitably generates tension between the fundamentalists and the surrounding society. For this reason,
these fundamentalist groups typically define themselves in opposition to some
"other" within the larger society in which they exist.

One category of nondominant groups includes fundamentalists who actively
participate in the larger society, even though they define themselves as a distinct element within it. In such situations, fundamentalists attempt to reform
society from within, using legitimate means to bring their surroundings into
conformity with their own beliefs. They often participate through the creation

of political parties and influence groups like the Bharatiya Janata Party in India and the Christian Coalition in the United States. They may also establish secular institutions or enterprises to promote their views, such as the cable television networks operated by Christian fundamentalists. In undertaking these efforts, the groups in this category see themselves as the authentic core of the larger society to which they belong. As a result, they do not consider the surrounding society or political state to be intrinsically evil, and they do not define themselves in opposition to it. Rather, they oppose the corrupting influences that threaten the larger society's moral integrity. Their objective, therefore, is to reassert the true moral foundations of society according to the certainties of their faith, a goal that often has strong nationalistic overtones. Until that goal is reached, they seek to extend their own ideological boundaries as broadly as possible within the larger society to which they belong.

The other category of fundamentalists not in control of their broader surroundings includes those who do not identify themselves as part of the larger society. They consider that society to be inherently corrupt or evil, and because they see it as a threat to their religious values, they seek to isolate themselves from it. They may continue to look for potential converts within the larger society, but they believe that its social and political structures are beyond redemption and must be rejected. Fundamentalists in this category use a variety of strategies to distance themselves from the larger society. In some cases they simply withdraw from the outside world, although the practical demands of daily life may make it impossible to achieve complete separation. Some Buddhist fundamentalists in Thailand follow this strategy, as do some of the haredim in Israel. Other groups limit their contacts with the larger society, but still try to influence secular authorities to adopt policies that conform to fundamentalist beliefs and goals. This approach has been widely used by many Jewish fundamentalists in Israel, who pressure the government to protect traditional Judaism even though they reject Israel's legitimacy as a political state. Some Christian fundamentalists in the United States follow a similar pattern, supporting traditional values in the domain of public policy while distancing themselves from certain public institutions, such as public schools.

Fundamentalist groups that isolate themselves from the outside world may also adopt a strategy of militant activism. Such groups represent the most radical expressions of religious fundamentalism. They respond to the threatening "other" by engaging in open conflict with it. Unlike other isolationists, groups that follow this strategy typically have substantial political aims, such as the overthrow of an existing ruler or the establishment of a new political state. Their ultimate goal is to redefine existing political and social boundaries to conform to their own ideological boundaries. Many such groups have engaged in armed conflict with the surrounding state, often in the form of terrorism. These fundamentalists are distinguished from other militants and revolutionaries, however, by their use of religious ideology in defining the boundaries of acceptable thought and action. Examples of groups following this strategy include the Islamic extremists in Egypt and Algeria who want to establish strict Islamic rule and militant Sikhs who have sought to create an independent homeland.

Together, these categories provide a useful framework for assessing global variations in the nature of fundamentalism and its interactions with the different contexts in which it has developed. Each category of groups defines its relationship to society at large in a distinctive manner, through patterns of domination, participation, or isolation, and each of the three categories encompasses a distinct set of goals, strategies, and impacts. Within a particular category, groups may differ significantly in terms of their specific objectives and methods. Such variations are most obvious among fundamentalists who isolate themselves from society, who may try to ignore, manipulate, or attack the "other" in society from their position of isolation; but the other two categories contain important variations as well. Nonetheless, the groups within each category share a common point of departure in defining their relationship to surrounding social and political structures, based on similar assumptions about the meaning of the ideological boundaries that they use to define themselves. The remainder of this chapter examines contemporary expressions of fundamentalism within each of these categories and the diverse ways in which they interact with their broader geographical contexts.

PATTERNS OF DOMINATION

Fundamentalists have achieved a position of domination in only a few countries, all located in the Islamic world. Groups belonging to other religious traditions have established fundamentalist communities at a more local scale, but none outside Islam has dominated an entire political state. Several factors account for this association between Islam and fundamentalist domination. Islamic fundamentalists believe that Islamic law governs all aspects of life, including economics, social customs, and politics as well as religion. Because they consider Islam to be a total way of life, they assert that in an authentic Islamic society religious authority and civil authority must be indivisible. They further believe that the prophet Muhammad founded the archetype of such a society in Medina during the seventh century and that their purpose is to recreate society based on that model. Their goal, then, is not simply to encourage individual piety; they want to reestablish Islam as the foundation of society and polity. The domination of society and the state by Islam represents the ultimate goal of Islamic fundamentalism. And this goal has been achievable, at least in theory, in regions where Islam is the dominant religion and fundamentalists have achieved the power necessary to maintain social and political control.

The primary example of fundamentalist domination emerged in Iran in

1979, when the Islamic Revolution led by Ayatollah Ruhollah Khomeini overthrew the regime of Shah Reza Pahlavi. The Islamic Revolution focused attention on the growth of fundamentalism in the Islamic world and provided a model for like-minded fundamentalists in other countries. Its success was grounded in conditions specific to Iran, however. One contributing factor was the predominance of Shiite Islam in Iran. For Shiites, the overthrow of the shah represented a crucial step in the realization of Islam's sacred history. According to Shiite belief, both political and religious leadership of the Islamic community were originally the responsibility of Imams descended from the prophet Muhammad, twelve of whom ruled through the tenth century A.D. Following that period, secular rulers seized control of temporal matters, leaving only religious affairs in the hands of Islamic jurists. Shiite Muslims believe that the period of secular rule will end with the return of the final Imam, the Mahdi (or messiah), who will reunite temporal and religious authority in a just Islamic state. Khomeini asserted that true believers should prepare for the return of the Imam by establishing such a state themselves. Although traditional Shiism taught that political power wielded by anyone other than the Imam was evil, by the twentieth century that teaching had given way to the belief that qualified Islamic jurists could serve as deputies of the last Imam and guide the community until the Mahdi's return. The creation of an Islamic republic under Khomeini's leadership thus conformed to the messianic beliefs of Iran's Shiite majority.[1]

The traditional autonomy of religious leaders in Iran also contributed to the revolution's success.[2] During the 1800s and early 1900s, the Kajar dynasty controlled Iran largely through alliances with local elites. Along with landowners and tribal leaders, prominent Muslim clerics (or mujtahids) wielded considerable power in this system. A mujtahid provided his local followers with spiritual guidance, while they supplied a constant source of revenue in the form of a religious tax. From this revenue, the mujtahid supported schools, charities, and other local religious institutions. The mujtahids thus controlled various social structures that reinforced their local power. When the Pahlavi dynasty came to power in the 1920s, the first shah sought to build a stronger central government and began to reduce the power of the local elites. In doing so, he tried to limit the mujtahids' authority, but they retained control of local religious institutions, including mosques, schools, and charities, and they continued to collect donations from their followers. As a result, they preserved an independent base of support. When popular discontent with the second shah emerged later in the century, Khomeini and other clerical leaders thus became the leading source of opposition, using the resources of their religious institutions to challenge the old regime.

A final factor in success of the Islamic Revolution was Khomeini's personal popularity. Although he lived in exile from 1964 to 1979, he had considerable influence over the Islamic clergy in Iran and maintained a large popular following. His appeal derived in part from the purity of his message. Essentially he argued that Islam could be authentically expressed only within a political state where Islamic law had been fully implemented. He further asserted that only a religious jurist (or faqih) with a thorough understanding of the sharia could legitimately rule in place of the Imam, an idea that he successfully linked to Shiite messianism. Khomeini's uncompromising opposition to the shah also strengthened his popular appeal. He regularly attacked policies imposed by the shah that promoted Westernization, weakened Islam, or increased Iran's dependence on foreign sources of aid (primarily the United States). He further declared that Iran's monarchical system was incompatible with Islam and had to be abolished. Khomeini's positions on these issues became especially popular during the 1970s as hostility toward the shah intensified throughout Iranian society. Liberals attacked the shah's autocratic system of rule, traditionalists condemned the shah's disregard for Islamic values, and urban workers and rural peasants criticized the shah for failing to improve living conditions among the poor. For this diverse coalition of groups, Khomeini's ideas offered what appeared to be a viable alternative to the status quo.[3]

By the late 1970s, the above-mentioned factors enabled Khomeini to launch the Islamic Revolution. In 1977, popular discontent produced a growing number of public demonstrations against the shah. At first these protests were organized primarily by secular activists, but the shah's hostility toward Khomeini and other religious leaders provoked the involvement of Muslim clerics. A published attack on Khomeini in 1978 led to major demonstrations by clerics and theology students in the holy city of Qom, during which security forces killed dozens of protesters. Religious leaders called for a national day of mourning on the fortieth day after the killings in Qom, and the government again used violence to suppress the protests, killing hundreds of dissidents in the city of Tabriz. These events solidified support for Khomeini within Iran's religious establishment, and the Islamic clergy became leaders in the effort to unseat the shah. They staged demonstrations across the country to mark the fortieth day of mourning after the killings in Tabriz, to which the government again responded with violence. As this cycle continued, the government imposed martial law; but the Islamic clergy continued to mobilize public demonstrations through their network of religious institutions. Ultimately the sheer size of these demonstrations, which on several occasions in late 1978 and early 1979 attracted over a million protesters in Tehran, undermined the Iranian army's support for the government (fig. 3.1). Without military support, the government fell. The shah left Iran early in 1979, and Khomeini returned from exile to lead the creation of an Islamic state.[4]

The anti-shah coalition contained considerable ideological diversity, but Khomeini's popular support ensured that his views prevailed in the formation of the new state. A new constitution established Iran as a Shiite Islamic republic, under the ultimate leadership of a faqih who ruled by divine authority.

Figure 3.1   A massive pro-Khomeini demonstration early in 1979. Such protests eventually undermined the Iranian army's support for the shah, allowing Khomeini to return from exile and establish an Islamic state. Tehran, Iran, 1979. *Source:* CORBIS/Bettmann.

Khomeini was recognized as the first faqih and given a lifetime term of office. The faqih's powers extended into all branches of government. Although the president was elected by popular vote, for example, the faqih had the power to disqualify presidential candidates and to remove an elected president from office. The constitution also required that all laws and institutions conform to Islamic principles. In essence, it defined a fundamentalist theocracy in Iran, in which Islam provided the rationale for all political and social structures.[5]

The fundamentalists also created several autonomous institutions to strengthen their control over Iranian society. The Revolutionary Committees provided a grassroots structure for implementing the fundamentalists' goals. The committees originated as neighborhood groups, often organized out of the local mosques that helped to organize demonstrations during the final year of the shah's regime. After the revolution, they became independent instruments of the state, charged with mobilizing local support for the government, implementing its programs, and maintaining public order. Their violent tactics eventually brought them under tighter central control, however. The fundamentalists also created a military force, the Revolutionary Guards. The constitution charged the guards with defending the Islamic Revolution, and membership in the group was open only to pious Muslims committed to the rule of the faqih. The guards played a major role in combating both the internal and external enemies of the fundamentalist regime and neutralized the potential threat of intervention by the regular armed forces, which before the revolution had supported the shah. A third institution, the Revolutionary Courts, served as an independent Islamic legal system overseen primarily by clerics. The Revolutionary Courts originally focused on bringing members of the old regime to trial and authorized the execution of hundreds of former government and military officials. The Revolutionary Courts also oversaw the prosecution of those accused of challenging the Islamic Revolution, and thus provided a means for fundamentalists to enforce their interpretation of the sharia.[6]

Through the Islamic constitution and the autonomous fundamentalist organizations, Khomeini and his followers transformed Iranian society. Adherence to the sharia eliminated many forms of entertainment, such as popular music, social dancing, and the consumption of alcohol, and the government banned movies and books considered to be incompatible with Islam. The legal system imposed traditional forms of corporal punishment, such as flogging and amputation. The banking system was reformed in accordance with Islamic law, which prohibited the payment or collection of interest. Arabic, the language of the Koran, became a mandatory subject in secondary schools. Universities required applicants to provide recommendations from their local clergy as proof of their commitment to Islam. The fundamentalists also placed many restrictions on women. Policies of gender segregation were imposed in schools and on public beaches; men were allowed to practice polygamy and to divorce their wives at will, and husbands had the right to prohibit their wives from working outside the home. Women also had fewer rights than men under the judicial system. In accordance with the Koran, the legal testimony of one man was equal in weight to the testimony of two women, and evidence given by women but not corroborated by men had no weight at all. By the early 1980s, all women were required to be properly veiled in public, facing harassment and public beatings if they violated this rule.[7]

Iran's redefinition as an Islamic republic also affected its relationships with other countries.[8] The fundamentalists believed that they had a duty to export the Islamic Revolution to other Muslim countries. The Islamic constitution in fact adopted the Koranic principle that all Muslims form a single nation and stated that Iran's policies should encourage worldwide Muslim unity. The fundamentalists did not propose to promote Islam by using military force against other countries, arguing that they would lead the Islamic world by example.[9] In practice, however, Iran provided support to various militant Shiite groups outside its borders and served as an important node in the informal network linking Islamic fundamentalists in different parts of Asia and Africa. Many Muslim leaders thus saw Iran's goal of exporting its revolution as a direct threat. Moreover, the militant Shiism espoused by Khomeini placed Iran at odds with Muslim states dominated by the Sunni branch of Islam, which does not accept Shiism's messianic beliefs. These factors, along with the presence of a large Shiite minority in Iraq sympathetic to Khomeini, are often cited as causes of the Iran-Iraq War that lasted through most of the 1980s.[10] The war produced massive casualties on both sides and ended in 1988 without a clear winner; but it did serve as a proving ground for Iran's Revolutionary Guards and significantly enhanced their prestige relative to the regular armed forces. In the decade following the revolution, Khomeini also condemned Muslim countries that maintained economic or political relations with the United States and its allies. This issue led to persistent tensions between Iran and countries along the Persian Gulf, such as Bahrain and Kuwait, but Khomeini directed his strongest criticisms at Saudi Arabia. The animosity between Iran and Saudi Arabia was further inflamed by conflicts between Iranian pilgrims and Saudi security forces in the late 1980s (see chapter 4).

Iran also adopted an aggressive stance toward the perceived enemies of Islam, particularly the United States and Israel, and to a lesser extent the Soviet Union. The United States was condemned as the shah's former ally, the source of corrupting cultural influences, and a political threat to the Islamic Revolution. Public demonstrations against the United States in 1979 culminated in an attack by militant students on the American embassy in Tehran. Following the attack, students held more than fifty Americans hostage in the embassy for over a year, an act that became the focus of hostility between the West and the new Islamic regime. Antagonism between the United States and Iran increased during the 1980s after Iraq received U.S. support in its war with Iran and again during the Gulf War in the 1990s when the United States sent a large military force to the region to repel Iraq's invasion of Kuwait. Iranian fundamentalists also maintained an uncompromising attitude toward Israel, which they viewed as a tool of the United States and a major threat to the Islamic world. Khomeini and his followers advocated the destruction of Israel and repeatedly called for universal Muslim support for the Palestinian cause. They also provided aid to Shiite militants in Lebanon and within the Palestinian community. Iran's interactions with the Soviet Union were less confrontational, and at various times each country sought to improve relations with the other. Nonetheless, Iran's leaders criticized the Soviet Union for its military aid to Iraq, its treatment of Muslims in central Asia, and its invasion of Afghanistan in 1979.

Since Khomeini's death in 1989, Iran has experienced an inevitable period of change.[11] The country's constitution has been amended to clarify the methods by which future faqihs will be chosen, for example. The government has also eased restrictions on the entertainment media and on the importation of foreign films. Government leaders took a significant step in 1997 when they distanced themselves from the death edict that Khomeini had issued in 1989 against author Salman Rushdie after finding him guilty of attacking Islam in his novel *The Satanic Verses*. Practical concerns have also undermined some specific fundamentalist policies. Private schools founded to provide an alternative to underfunded public education have ignored the rules on gender segregation, for example, employing male teachers to staff girls' classes in science and math.[12] Employment opportunities have also expanded for highly educated women.[13] In other respects, however, the ideological boundaries of Islamic fundamentalism continue to define Iranian society. Iran remains a vehement adversary of Israel, the legal status of women remains inferior to that of men, traditional Islamic punishments continue to be enforced, and the strict application of the sharia remains a priority of the courts. The autonomous judicial, military, and social institutions created after the revolution also continue to support the domination of Iranian society by fundamentalist principles.

A second example of fundamentalist domination developed in Afghanistan during the 1990s, but the movement that now controls most of that country differs in significant ways from Iran's Islamic Revolution. The fundamentalists that rule Afghanistan, like most of the country's inhabitants, are orthodox Sunni Muslims. They seek to enforce a strict interpretation of Islamic law, but unlike the Shiites in Iran they do not believe in the twelfth Imam's messianic return. The theological implications of creating an Islamic government in Afghanistan are thus less complex, as they do not involve identifying a leader to govern as the Imam's deputy. The fundamentalists in Iran and Afghanistan also achieved their dominant positions in different ways. In Iran, fundamentalists benefited from the preservation of clerical authority over local religious institutions, which provided them with an independent power base. In Afghanistan, on the other hand, the fundamentalist regime emerged in a power vacuum after the war against Soviet occupation and the resulting period of civil disorder had destroyed traditional sources of authority. The fundamentalist movement in Afghanistan developed in part out of the same hostility toward external forces that fueled Iran's Islamic Revolution, but the situation in Afghanistan has also been shaped by distinctive local factors.

Again, the war against Soviet occupation created the initial context out of which fundamentalism emerged in Afghanistan. The Soviets invaded Afghanistan in 1979 to sustain the Marxist government against which the country's Muslim tribes had rebelled. Resistance to the invasion was widespread but decentralized. Although most of the rebels identified themselves as Islamic mujahideen (holy warriors), ethnic differences among the Muslim tribes led to the formation of independent tribal guerrilla forces. The decentralization of the Afghan resistance was reinforced by Pakistan, the conduit for external aid to the rebels. For political reasons of its own, Pakistan did not want to encourage the development of a unified Afghan rebel force. It thus distributed aid among the various tribal factions, keeping each strong enough to operate on its own. After the withdrawal of the Soviets in 1989 and the defeat of the Marxist Afghan government in 1992, the persistence of this entrenched factionalism among the rebel forces led to civil war. Afghanistan became highly fragmented as local commanders fought to preserve control over their own pieces of terri-tory. The resulting anarchy, in which corruption and brutality became com-monplace, set the stage for the fundamentalist effort to reunify the country.

The hearth of that effort emerged in the Afghan refugee camps established in Pakistan during the war (fig. 3.2). By the late 1980s and early 1990s, these camps contained more than three million Afghans (while another two million had fled to Iran). The chaos and uncertainty of life in the camps led many refugees to reassert various Islamic practices and tribal customs as a means of restoring some sense of order to their lives. Traditional restrictions on women became more widely observed, for example. The reassertion of tradition also redefined the social environment of children raised in the camps. Children accounted for nearly half of the camps' residents, and many of them reached young adulthood as refugees. This experience had especially important impli-cations for the large number of boys who attended the traditional madrassas (or religious schools) set up in the refugee camps. The students in the madras-sas received a conservative religious education, which placed particular empha-sis on the proper observation of Islamic ritual. Having grown up believing that

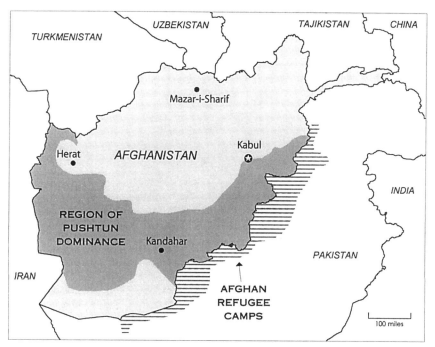

Figure 3.2   Key locations in the rise and spread of the Taliban's control over Afghanistan.

they would eventually return to Afghanistan, these students thus also came to expect that they would continue to lead a strict Islamic life after their return.

Within the above context, the Taliban movement emerged as a new expression of Islamic fundamentalism. The Farsi word *taliban* (seekers of religious truth) refers to students educated in a madrassa. It became associated with the new movement because most of the original members had been students in madrassas operating in the refugee camps, particularly those along Afghanistan's southeastern border.[14] In addition, many older members of the Taliban, and most of its leaders, had served with the rebel militias in the war against the Soviet occupation.[15] They were connected to the younger students in the refugee camps by their shared Pushtun ethnicity and their common origins in southeastern Afghanistan. After the war many of these rebels rejoined their families in the camps in Pakistan where the Taliban movement took shape, and some resumed their religious studies in the madrassas. The movement thus brought together a relatively young but experienced group of mujahideen and an even younger cohort of religious students, all of whom became committed to restoring order to Afghanistan through the creation of an Islamic society. Unlike fundamentalists in most other parts of the Islamic world, the Taliban were not driven primarily by the theoretical writings of an elite group of leaders. Their motivation came more directly out of the upheaval that Afghanistan had experienced during and after the Soviet occupation.

The Taliban movement initially moved into Afghanistan with the support of Pakistan's government. Pakistan viewed the chaos in Afghanistan with increasing concern during the early 1990s. One immediate problem was that the political anarchy disrupted transportation within Afghanistan and thus interfered with Pakistan's efforts to develop trade relations with the central Asian republics created when the Soviet Union collapsed in 1991. This issue reached critical proportions in 1994 when a local commander in southeastern Afghanistan seized a large convoy of Pakistani trucks en route to Turkmenistan. Pakistan could not take direct action against the commander without risking international repercussions, so instead it provided support for a group of several thousand Taliban to free the convoy. The group's leader, an experienced mujahid named Mohammad Omar, had already developed plans to take control of nearby Kandahar, Afghanistan's second-largest city and the original home of many Taliban, which had been devastated by fighting among competing local militias. Using weapons captured from a rebel arms dump inside Afghanistan, the Taliban combined the two missions and quickly accomplished both with little bloodshed.[16] Their swift defeat of the militias in and around Kandahar surprised even the group's own leaders, but was welcomed by the local population, who believed that the Taliban would restore peace and order to the region.

Their success in Kandahar strengthened the Taliban's identity as an organization. Thousands of additional students from the refugee camps traveled to

Kandahar to join the movement, which expanded its arsenal using arms and equipment captured from the local militias. The Taliban's leaders subsequently declared their intention to free all of Afghanistan from the corrupt militias and to restore order by establishing an authentic Islamic state. With growing popular support among their fellow Pushtuns, the Taliban quickly took control of several nearby provinces.[17] As they moved farther from Kandahar, however, the Taliban encountered greater resistance from other ethnic groups, residents of the larger cities, and Shiite Muslims. The Taliban also faced opposition from organized political factions, including the nominal government of Afghanistan. Nonetheless, they continued to expand their control, capturing the city of Herat in 1995 and the capital city of Kabul in 1996. An anti-Taliban coalition of former communists, Shiite Muslims, and ethnic Uzbeks, Tajiks, and Hazaras organized in northern Afghanistan, the only part of the country not under Taliban control. In 1998, however, the Taliban captured the leading northern city of Mazar-e-Sharif and cut the flow of supplies to the opposition from Iran, Uzbekistan, and Russia. The Taliban army also dealt brutally with those who had opposed them in the north, reportedly killing thousands of Shiite Hazara civilians after taking Mazar-e-Sharif.[18]

As they took over the country, the Taliban established new institutions to enforce their version of Islamic law. At first they established local councils to maintain order and administer Islamic justice. Later, after taking Kabul, they also formed a new national government and reconstituted Afghanistan as an Islamic state. The Taliban were not primarily interested in political affairs, however; their goals were to rid the country of corruption and atheism and to create a true Islamic society. They issued various edicts to move the country toward authentic Islam and set up the Department for the Propagation of Virtue and the Prohibition of Vice to ensure that those edicts were obeyed. The latter group, also known as the religious police, played a particularly important role in Kabul and Herat, the country's most liberal cities. Routinely using public beatings to enforce compliance, the religious police became a leading symbol of the Taliban's uncompromising rule. In recognition of their importance, the Taliban raised the religious police to the status of a government ministry in 1998.[19]

The policies imposed by the Taliban dramatically changed Afghan society. The system of justice became harsher as the Taliban instituted traditional penalties for criminal offenses: amputation for theft, stoning to death for adultery, live burial for homosexual activity, and public execution for murder. The Taliban also asserted tight control over many aspects of daily life. They restricted recreation, both to eliminate Western influences and to ensure that Afghans were not distracted from their Islamic duties. The Taliban thus banned television, movies, dancing, and popular music, and they prohibited the reading of foreign publications. Even the possession of caged songbirds and the playing of chess, both considered frivolous pastimes, were outlawed. Other laws required strict adherence to traditional Islamic standards of behavior and appearance. Men were required to pray regularly in their local mosques, for example, and the government required its male employees to grow full beards, later extending this rule to all men. The Taliban also banned long hair on men and the wearing of leather jackets.

Women were subjected to more severe restrictions. The government ordered that women be completely veiled when outside the home by wearing a traditional burka, a full-length veil that conceals the body's contours and obscures the eyes behind a small piece of mesh. Women who disregarded this rule faced public harassment and violence. The government also ordered that windows be painted over to prevent outsiders from seeing women unveiled at home and that cars and buses be equipped with curtains to hide female passengers from view. Women were not allowed to go out in public unless accompanied by a male relative and, with the exception of health workers, could not be employed outside the home. The Taliban also limited public services for women. Girls were not allowed to attend school, and male doctors were prohibited from treating female patients. The Taliban did establish separate hospitals for women, but they have been chronically understaffed and poorly equipped. These practices, along with the general restrictions on female mobility, prevented many women from receiving medical care of any kind. Finally, the government imposed penalties on taxi drivers and shopkeepers who provided services to women not properly veiled or not escorted by a male relative and punished the male relatives of women who violated the Taliban's rules.

In implementing their fundamentalist ideology, the Taliban drew a sharp boundary between their version of Islam and all other points of view. In doing so, they alienated Afghans who did not follow their strict interpretation of Sunni Islam, but they also antagonized neighboring countries, particularly Iran and Uzbekistan. Fearing the possibility of Taliban aggression, Uzbekistan maintained an armed force along its border with Afghanistan. It also provided considerable support to the anti-Taliban coalition operating in northern Afghanistan during the late 1990s. Iran did so as well, seeing the Taliban as a threat to Iran itself and to Afghan Shiites. The tension between Iran and the Taliban escalated in 1998 after Iran learned that Taliban forces had executed a group of Iranian diplomats in the battle for control of Mazar-e-Sharif. Iran responded by mobilizing its military along the border with Afghanistan, while the Taliban promised swift retaliation if Iran moved against them. Tensions between the two countries abated somewhat by the end of 1998, but Iran remained intensely suspicious of the Taliban.

The hostility of Iran and Uzbekistan reflected a more widespread uneasiness in the Islamic world regarding the Taliban. In their early rhetoric, the Taliban had espoused an expansionist philosophy, declaring their goal of spreading their ideology to other Islamic countries. They later stated that they had no intention of forcing other countries to accept their ideas, but many Muslim leaders saw the Taliban as a threat to stability in the region. Even in Pakistan, religious moderates and liberals worried about the movement's rapid growth. The Taliban's rigid fundamentalism has also raised concerns in non-Islamic countries. Russian leaders worry that the Taliban will promote Islamic activism among Muslims in the Central Asian republics.[20] India too opposes the development of an Islamic fundamentalist stronghold in the region. The United States has been more equivocal in its attitude toward the Taliban, who counter the influence of Iran and Russia in the region, but who at the same time provide refuge for Islamic terrorists.

The treatment of women in Afghanistan has also focused international criticism on the Taliban.[21] The Taliban assert that their restrictions on female behavior simply conform to Islamic principles and have been necessary to protect the dignity of women as social order has been reestablished. Feminists and human rights advocates respond that the Taliban's restrictions have been cruel and unjust. They note that under Taliban rule suicide rates among women have risen and that increasing numbers of women and children live in poverty, since women are not allowed to work. For many widows, begging provides the primary source of income. Economic hardships have further limited women's mobility because many cannot afford to buy a burka and so cannot go out in public. Most of the world's countries have refused to recognize the Taliban government until conditions for women improve and other human rights abuses end, and a number of international aid organizations have curtailed their activities in Afghanistan until conditions change. International pressure has not weakened the Taliban's commitment to their policies regarding women, but it has accentuated an important difference between the Taliban's values and those of the international community.

After the Taliban achieved dominance in Afghanistan, their ideology thus became the foundation for a new social order. The attitude of tolerance that had once been considered a key feature of Afghan culture gave way to a restrictive atmosphere defined by the Taliban's fundamentalist beliefs. In this way, the Taliban erected a religious boundary around Afghan society, which all Afghans were compelled to acknowledge. At the same time, that boundary isolated Afghanistan from the rest of the world. After the Taliban took control of Afghanistan, the "other" by which they felt threatened consequently shifted from the internal opposition to outside forces, particularly those perceived to be enemies of Islam, like Russia, and those perceived to practice Islam falsely, like the Shiites in Iran. The domination of the Taliban thus redefined the character of Afghanistan itself as well as its relations with other countries.

Along with Iran and Afghanistan, Sudan has often been characterized as an Islamic fundamentalist state. The Sudanese government has promoted the practice of Islam and has defined the sharia as the basis for Sudanese law. It has also established ties with Islamic fundamentalists in other countries and has been accused of providing refuge for Islamic terrorists. The Sudanese government enforces Islamic law less strictly than do the governments of Iran and Afghanistan, however. Women must be veiled in public, for example, but veils tend to be less concealing than those required in other fundamentalist states, and unveiled women are less likely to be punished. Similarly, although traditional Islamic punishments have been adopted for criminal offenses, they are rarely carried out. Sudan's leaders have promoted Islam more as a means of unifying their culturally diverse country than as a strategy for defending traditional values. Sudan thus provides a less definitive example of fundamentalist domination. Nonetheless, the establishment of an Islamic regime has had important consequences for Sudan, particularly in the area of international relations.

Sudan's branch of the Muslim Brotherhood started the modern movement to create an Islamic state during the late 1970s and early 1980s. In 1983, the Sudanese government initiated a policy of Islamization as a means of attracting popular support, but the enactment of laws based on the sharia generated strong opposition from secularists. These Islamic policies also heightened tensions between the northern two-thirds of Sudan, where Arab culture dominates, and the southern third, which has stronger cultural ties to tropical Africa. Following a period of economic decline, a military regime took control in 1989 intending to restore economic and social order along Islamic lines. It banned alcohol, required the veil for women, established traditional corporal punishments for criminal offenses, and created separate police units to monitor compliance with Islamic law. Many traditionalists welcomed the renewed emphasis on Islam, but these policies continued to be opposed by most southerners and by secularists throughout the country. In the absence of a widely recognized threat to essential traditions, moreover, the government found it difficult to inspire widespread popular support for the rigid application of Islamic law. Many Sudanese disobeyed the new rules, particularly in the south and in Khartoum, the nation's capital. The government subsequently acknowledged the impracticality of enforcing the new laws in non-Muslim communities and in the south has waived some of the more controversial measures. The Islamic regime has also received mixed support from students, a key group in the establishment of fundamentalist governments in Iran and Afghanistan.[22] Given these conditions, Sudan's fundamentalists have promulgated a relatively moderate version of Islamic rule.

Sudan's identity as a fundamentalist state has been strengthened by its foreign policy, however. By establishing ties with fundamentalists in other countries, Sudan's leaders underscored their Islamic principles and their opposition to Western influences. Sudan has cultivated an especially strong economic and military relationship with Iran. In addition, Sudan has become a refuge for Islamic radicals who oppose other governments in northern Africa and southwest Asia. Surrounding states have thus identified Sudan as a regional threat to peace. In 1995, for example, Egypt accused Sudan of harboring radicals connected to an attempt on the life of Egypt's president, and Ethiopian leaders claimed that Sudan itself had provided support for the failed assassination. In 1998, the United States used cruise missiles to destroy a pharmaceutical factory in Khartoum thought to be producing chemical weapons for Islamic terrorists. Such developments have defined an "other" that fundamentalists can cite as a threat to Sudan; but again, that threat did not motivate the fundamentalists' original rise to power, and it has not attracted widespread popular support for a strict Islamic order.

A pattern of fundamentalist domination has thus developed to some extent in Sudan, but less clearly than in Iran and Afghanistan. In the latter cases, Islamic fundamentalism has been established as the core ideology of society. Fundamentalists in both countries have sought to promote traditional religious belief—in Afghanistan the Sunni Islam of the rural southeast and in Iran messianic Shiism. In addition, they have confronted external forces that threaten their Islamic traditions, including Western culture and the political and economic power of the non-Islamic world. To pursue these goals, fundamentalists in Iran and Afghanistan have established rigid ideological boundaries that clearly isolate their countries from others. The fundamentalist domination of these societies has therefore had a profound influence on their inhabitants' daily lives, but it has also redefined their international relationships, thus affecting other societies as well. The fundamentalist domination of Sudan has been less complete, but has displayed some of the same elements. Most importantly, Sudan has isolated itself politically from most of its neighbors, from nonfundamentalist states in the Muslim world, and from the West.

PATTERNS OF PARTICIPATION

Most fundamentalist movements have not achieved social or political domination. Either they lack the strength to establish control over society, or existing social and political structures prevent them from doing so. As a result, such movements typically find themselves in conflict with other elements of the society in which they are situated. Such conflicts may develop around specific theological issues, but more typically they involve broader concerns regarding standards of individual behavior and sources of moral authority. In either case, a fundamentalist movement must come to terms with its social surroundings and develop strategies to protect its core beliefs from the "other" by which it feels threatened. In some cases, that "other" is not located solely within the group's own society. Islamic fundamentalists, for example, see Western hegemony as a threat, and so their attention focuses in part on interactions with forces originating outside their immediate social context. Invariably, though, fundamentalists who have not achieved a position of domination perceive sinister forces at work within their own society, and these forces become their first concern. Some fundamentalist groups respond to corruption within the sur-rounding society by isolating themselves from it, a pattern examined in detail in the following section of this chapter. Others respond by actively participating in existing social and political structures. By participating in the larger society, such groups attempt to render it more compatible with their fundamentalist beliefs.

A fundamentalist group's adoption of a strategy of participation derives from the nature of the group itself and of the society that surrounds it. Most impor-tantly, fundamentalists pursue this strategy when they believe that they have the means to transform society from within, a view often espoused by move-ments with a substantial following. The involvement of Christian fundamental-ist groups in American politics in recent decades, for example, in part arose from their conviction that they were large enough to become an important political force. But even a group that does not have a large membership may exert considerable influence and thus be convinced of its ability to bring about change. The Jamaat-e-Islami in Pakistan, for example, has had only modest success in electoral politics, but its insistent support for the creation of an Islamic state has repeatedly influenced government policies, and it represents an important voice in national political debates.

Fundamentalists who pursue a strategy of participation also typically see themselves as the moral keystone of the larger society to which they belong. They believe that they represent the religious concerns of a majority of the population or that they express their society's true religious values. Thus, they see themselves as the legitimate defenders of essential religious principles ig-nored by the rest of society. This characterization justifies the fundamentalists' efforts to bring about reform, but it also provides a rationale for their participa-tion in the larger society despite its corruption. Their goal in participating is not to destroy existing social or political structures but to make them conform to fundamental religious values. Indeed, such fundamentalists view that goal as a sacred responsibility. Participation, in other words, provides the means by which they can fulfill their obligation to return society to its proper moral path.

Fundamentalists can use this approach, however, only when the surround-ing society provides opportunities to participate legitimately in its structures and institutions. If the group's methods and objectives clash too strongly with established social and political mores, others will not tolerate its activities. The accommodation of fundamentalist activism may be ensured, for example, by democratic institutions that provide diverse groups with a political voice. The fundamentalist Bharatiya Janata Party operates freely as a political party within India's democratic system, for example, even though it denounces the secular character of the nation's constitution. In other cases, society accepts the partici-pation of fundamentalists because their beliefs arise out of a widely shared cultural heritage. Islamic political parties have thus thrived in Muslim states, even when they rigidly oppose the status quo, because they are firmly grounded in the country's underlying religious culture.

Fundamentalist participation in society at large most commonly takes the form of political action, either through direct involvement in electoral politics or by efforts to influence public policy. Many fundamentalist groups have established legitimate political parties, including the Jamaat-e-Islami in Pakistan and the Bharatiya Janata Party in India. Others have given their support to existing parties that agree with their views, or have formed advocacy groups to promote their agenda, like the Christian Coalition in the United States. Through such actions, fundamentalists in various settings have tried to use legislation, judicial decisions, and constitutional reform to impose their views on society. The political process has proven attractive to fundamentalists because, in societies where they do not dominate, it offers an authoritarian means of changing society. As the following discussion illustrates, however, fundamentalists have also adopted forms of participation to bring about change in a "bottom up" fashion, through individual persuasion. In the United States, for example, Christian fundamentalists have used the broadcast media to build support for their views among individual listeners. Fundamentalists have also established grassroots movements aimed at transforming society from below, including the Promise Keepers in North America and the Tablighi Jamaat in South Asia.

In attempting to reform society, fundamentalists establish ideological boundaries between themselves and others, defined by the religious basis of their concerns. These boundaries create a dilemma, however, because they make it more difficult for fundamentalists to influence the rest of society. Members of society who hold different beliefs are often wary of fundamentalists' efforts to effect reform. As a result, fundamentalist organizations trying to change society from within often express their immediate goals in more inclusive terms, so that they can draw support from outside the fundamentalist movement itself. During the 1980s, for example, American fundamentalists established the Moral Majority to promote their views on social issues such as abortion and homosexuality, but in doing so they sought support from other religious groups, including Roman Catholics and Orthodox Jews. Similarly, after the Bharatiya Janata Party achieved victory in the national elections in India in 1998, it tried to broaden its base of support in forming a coalition government by adopting more moderate positions on some issues. Attempts by fundamentalists to expand the appeal of their message cannot completely disguise its religious foundation, however. Fundamentalist participation in society thus inevitably generates some degree of conflict with those holding other points of view.

Finally, as suggested above, specific expressions of the fundamentalist strategy of participation necessarily reflect the nature of the larger social context in which they develop. Fundamentalists following such a strategy must adopt methods that are compatible with surrounding social and political structures. As a result, opportunities for participation differ from one context to the next. Islamic fundamentalists in Pakistan, which originated as an explicitly Muslim state, have thus developed patterns of participation different from those of Christian fundamentalists operating in the more pluralistic context of the United States. Because these fundamentalist movements have emerged in diverse locales, their approaches to participating in society have also varied.

Christian fundamentalists have made extensive use of political action to promote traditional biblical values and beliefs in U.S. society, to recreate the United States as a Christian nation (fig. 3.3). Despite their concern with politics, however, they have not formed a fundamentalist political party. The constitutional separation of church and state in the United States and the nation's entrenched two-party political system essentially preclude the formation of a new party with a narrowly defined religious identity. Christian fundamentalists have thus generally participated in politics within the context of the existing two-party system, aligning themselves primarily with the Republicans' conser-

Figure 3.3   The American flag flying in front of a conservative Protestant church. Protestant fundamentalists strongly emphasize the connections between Christian beliefs and "fundamental" American values, which in their view define the United States as a Christian nation. Kerrville, Texas, 1999. *Source:* the author.

vative wing. In addition, they have formed a variety of advocacy groups to advance their political goals. Some, like the Moral Majority and the Christian Coalition, have sought to influence national political trends and have addressed a broad range of issues from a fundamentalist perspective. Other fundamentalist advocacy groups have focused on specific policy issues, such as religion in the public schools and gay rights. Christian fundamentalists have also used the broadcast media to spread their political views and the religious beliefs on which they are based. And outside the realm of politics, they have founded a large network of voluntary associations, educational institutions, and the like, aimed at attracting new adherents as well as reinforcing the commitment of existing followers.

These contemporary patterns of participation began to materialize during the 1970s. Christian fundamentalists had in fact attempted to initiate reforms within U.S. society earlier in the century, but the debacle of the Scopes Monkey Trial caused them to abandon social activism for several decades. Instead, they concentrated on strengthening their own institutions, establishing schools and Bible institutes, independent churches and ministries, missionary organizations, and religious broadcasting systems. Through this institutional infrastructure, fundamentalists tried to protect their own religious culture, and especially their belief in biblical inerrancy, from the corrupting influences of modern society.[23] They began to adopt a less isolationist approach during the 1970s, however, as new communication technologies enabled conservative televangelists to reach much larger audiences. Transmitting their programs via satellite to local cable television systems, organizations like Pat Robertson's Christian Broadcasting Network and Jim Bakker's PTL (Praise the Lord) Satellite Network were able to disseminate their religious and political ideas to viewers across the country. This development provided fundamentalists with a powerful tool for advocating change within U.S. society.

A conservative turn in U.S. politics during the late 1970s furthered the resurgence of Christian fundamentalist participation in society at large. At that time, a broad conservative coalition emerged that was committed to reversing the liberal trends that had dominated U.S. society since the 1960s. Conservative politicians, principally in the Republican Party, saw Christian fundamentalists as natural allies in the formation of this coalition, as they shared the perception that U.S. society had entered a period of moral decline. Fundamentalists in turn saw the revival of conservatism as an opportunity to challenge the advancing threats of modernism and secularism. Within the new conservative milieu, they hoped to reshape U.S. society according to biblical principles. They pursued these goals by introducing a new social agenda into U.S. politics, intended to focus attention on issues of faith and morality. They were especially concerned with trends that challenged traditional religious beliefs or limited the role of religion in U.S. life (fig. 3.4). As a result, they became actively involved in the political debates surrounding a variety of controversial topics,

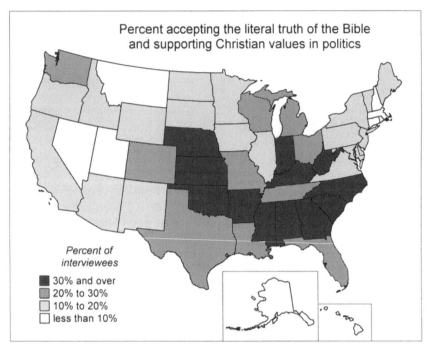

Figure 3.4 The percentage of respondents to a 1996 survey who expressed belief in the literal truth of the Bible and supported the application of traditional Christian values in politics. *Data source:* "God and Society in North America, 1996," conducted by the Angus Reid Group in conjunction with Queen's University's George Rawlyk Research Unit on Religion and Society; data provided by the American Religious Data Archive.

including abortion, gay rights, pornography, school prayer, the teaching of evolution, and equal rights for women.

A crucial event in the rekindling of political activity among fundamentalists was the formation of the Moral Majority in 1979. Led by Jerry Falwell, an influential Baptist minister and televangelist, the Moral Majority advocated the use of political means to restore traditional moral values in U.S. society. Specifically, conservative political strategists saw Falwell's organization as a vehicle for mobilizing fundamentalist voters. The organization's rapid growth, to over two million members by the national elections in 1980, made it an important factor in Ronald Reagan's successful bid for the presidency, and for the rest of the decade it helped to shape the Republicans' conservative social platform. As its influence grew, the Moral Majority also took up conservative positions on more secular issues, such as federal budget reform and defense spending. Falwell also tried to expand the group's membership to include other religious conservatives, including Roman Catholics, Mormons, and Orthodox Jews.

Nonetheless, the Moral Majority remained in essence an expression of the be-liefs and values of Protestant fundamentalists, and found it difficult to expand its membership beyond that community.

By the late 1980s, the Moral Majority's influence began to decline. The group faced substantial opposition from feminists, gay rights activists, and other liberals, and even some conservative Christians criticized its involvement in secular politics. Fundamentalist Pat Robertson's lack of success in the 1988 Republican presidential primary elections also signaled a decline in the politi-cal influence of religious conservatives at the national level. Falwell thus dis-banded the Moral Majority in 1989, claiming that it had achieved its goal of establishing a moral basis for the reform of U.S. society. The group left behind an important legacy, however. It had validated the strategy of participation by demonstrating that fundamentalists could influence the direction of U.S. poli-tics. In addition, its network of local chapters provided a framework for the continuing involvement of fundamentalists in local politics during the 1990s. Perhaps most importantly, the Moral Majority established a precedent for fur-ther fundamentalist activism by asserting the validity of religious belief as the foundation for public policy decisions.

The most visible successor to the Moral Majority was the Christian Coali-tion, founded in 1989 by Pat Robertson following his failure to win the Repub-lican presidential nomination. Robertson's Christian Broadcasting Network had contributed to the rapid growth in religious television during the 1970s, and his flagship program, the *700 Club*, attracted millions of viewers.[24] His failure in the Republican primary race convinced him, however, that the politi-cal success of Christian fundamentalists would require more effective organiza-tion at the grassroots level. The Christian Coalition thus concentrated at first on building strength through its local chapters. It quickly became the dominant force in a number of state Republican organizations and had considerable suc-cess in electing sympathetic local candidates in the early 1990s. By the middle of the decade, the Christian Coalition's grassroots strategy had also made it one of the leading conservative political advocacy groups, claiming nearly two million members. As a result of its growth, it began to exert increasing influ-ence nationally within the Republican Party, which it ultimately hoped to con-trol.

The Christian Coalition's political agenda closely resembled that of the Moral Majority. It took conservative stands on a wide variety of political issues and attempted to attract support from other conservatives outside the funda-mentalist movement. Its core concerns, however, remained focused on social issues tied to the goal of establishing biblical principles as the foundation of American society. Most importantly, its members sought to establish a central role for religion in the nation's public life. They supported a constitutional amendment to allow religious activities in tax-supported institutions like schools and town halls, and they favored public support for private schools run by religious organizations. They also proposed that taxpayers be allowed to redirect a portion of their taxes from public welfare programs to private charities and religious groups. More broadly, they opposed any threat to their conception of traditional biblical values and so fought against abortion, pornography, and gay rights. At the national level, the Christian Coalition lobbied against federal funding for the arts, which in its view supported the creation of morally offensive works, and it opposed distribution of free needles to drug addicts as a means of preventing the spread of AIDS. It also established a system of rating members of the Senate and House of Representatives according to their voting records on key issues and distributed the resulting "scorecards" as guides for conservative voters.

The Christian Coalition's participation in American politics created dissatisfaction among some fundamentalists, however. These critics argued that the organization made too many compromises in trying to broaden its support within the Republican Party and that it too often became involved with partisan issues not directly related to essential fundamentalist concerns. This tension led some fundamentalists to shift their support in the late 1990s to other organizations that maintained a more explicit commitment to the goals and ideals of Christian fundamentalism. Many such organizations had been established by conservative Christians, and together they became an even more important outlet for fundamentalist activism than the Christian Coalition. These groups tend to focus on a more specific set of issues than the Moral Majority and Christian Coalition, and many of them are more concerned with local issues and elections than with national politics. Nonetheless, their cumulative impact on American society has been substantial.

Focus on the Family and the Family Research Council, two closely linked groups that promote family values based on biblical principles, are representative of this type of organization. Both strongly oppose abortion, pornography, and the gay rights movement, and both seek to establish Christian values in public schools. They campaign against sex education that does not insist on abstinence before marriage, for example, and the Family Research Council advocates the return of school prayer. Homosexuality has been a major issue for these groups as well. The Family Research Council, for example, has taken stands against adoption by gay and lesbian couples, classroom discussions of homosexuality, and same-sex marriage. Their fundamentalist positions on such issues have also attracted substantial followings. By the late 1990s, Focus on the Family claimed over two million members—more than the Christian Coalition—and the membership of the Family Research Council exceeded half a million. Their membership growth and successful fund-raising in turn gave these groups increasing political influence within the Republican Party. An important sign of this rising influence was the announcement early in 1999 by Gary Bauer, the founder of the Family Research Council, that he would seek the Republican presidential nomination in the year 2000. The success of these two groups has also caused the Christian Coalition to reassert its own fundamentalist priorities as a means of retaining its influence.

The fundamentalist concern with family values has been expressed in similar fashion by many other groups, including the American Family Association, Concerned Women for America, and the Traditional Values Coalition. Other organizations such as Citizens for Excellence in Education (CEE) have focused more specifically on educational practices in public schools and their threat to traditional biblical values and beliefs. CEE rejects sex education that does not demand abstinence and attacks curricula that in its view promote tolerance of homosexuality and drug use. More broadly, CEE opposes the teaching of values and concepts that undermine students' religious beliefs. In this context, the teaching of evolution has resurfaced as a major issue. The CEE and other fundamentalists have recast the conflict over evolution, however, as a debate between Darwinian theory and creationism, a defense of the biblical account of creation presented in scientific terms. In addressing its various concerns, CEE's strategy of participation originally focused on electing fundamentalists to local school boards. The group claims that it helped to elect over twenty-five thousand Christians to school boards during the 1980s and 1990s, and in the southern and western states especially, these board members have had a significant impact on curricular policies and textbook selection. Nonetheless, CEE declared in 1998 that attempts to reform public schools were hopeless and that whenever possible true Christians should withdraw from the public schools, either by sending their children to Christian schools or by adopting the practice of home schooling. Even in this action, though, CEE sought to influence the larger society, asserting that public school systems would become mired in insoluble problems without a strong Christian presence and that their rapid decline would vindicate CEE's insistence on biblical values in education.

Participation in political parties and other public institutions is not the only form that fundamentalist activism has taken in the United States in recent years. Conservative Christians have also continued to build their own institutions, especially schools, to insulate themselves from secular influences, and some fundamentalists in fact oppose any type of formal association with those who do not share their beliefs. In addition, many fundamentalists concerned with reforming U.S. society have attempted to promote their agenda through nonpolitical means, such as personal evangelism. Fundamentalist broadcasting networks represent one important expression of this approach to Christianizing the United States. Fundamentalists also continue to use revival meetings and other public gatherings to spread their views, attempting to transform society by changing individual priorities and values.

During the 1990s, the latter strategy was best exemplified by the Promise Keepers, a Christian men's organization committed to establishing biblical family values as the foundation of U.S. society. In particular, the group stressed the need for men to fulfill their biblical obligation to provide strong leadership for their families. It has spread its message of male authority and responsibility through large outdoor rallies, often held in football stadiums, which have drawn tens of thousands of participants at a time (fig. 3.5). The organization has also established thousands of local support groups, through which trained leaders promote its fundamentalist beliefs. The Promise Keepers' name derives from their pledge to be active Christians, to lead their families according to biblical principles, to seek moral purity, and to associate with other men who have made the same pledge. The group has maintained close ties to politically active fundamentalists, however, and its leaders support the same conservative social agenda promoted by other fundamentalist groups. It has also been widely criticized by feminists, political moderates and liberals, and mainstream religious leaders for its idealization of the traditional patriarchal family, its opposition to abortion and gay rights, and its ambiguous stance on racial issues. Thus, while the Promise Keepers have adopted distinctive methods to promote their views, they clearly belong to the set of Christian fundamentalist groups that function as active participants in U.S. society.

The strategy of participation thus applies to various expressions of Christian fundamentalism in the United States. Again, a common feature of these fundamentalist groups is that they define themselves as the defenders of true Ameri-

Figure 3.5   A Promise Keepers rally at Veterans Stadium in Philadelphia. The Promise Keepers have held numerous rallies in football stadiums to spread their message of Christian renewal and male leadership of the family. Philadelphia, Pennsylvania, 1998. *Source:* Laurence Kesterson/Media Exchange International.

can values. Their participation in society arises from their conviction that they alone recognize the importance of biblical principles in traditional U.S. culture and that they have an obligation to see that those principles survive the threats of modernism and secularism. Fundamentalist participation in society is viewed with suspicion by many nonfundamentalists, and a number of liberal advocacy groups have developed strategies to counter fundamentalist attempts to introduce religious belief as the basis for government policies. The participation of fundamentalists in American society thus continues to generate controversy precisely because they see themselves as the nation's authentic core, a point of view not shared by those outside the fundamentalist movement.

Patterns of participation also appear in some forms of Jewish fundamentalism, but are complicated by the diverse nature of fundamentalist attitudes toward the state of Israel. As discussed in chapter 2, the haredi branch of Jewish fundamentalism originally opposed the creation of Israel as a human effort to preempt the divine redemption of the Jewish people. The haredim who migrated to Palestine thus remained separate from the Zionist society emerging there early in the twentieth century. By the 1930s, however, the haredi community had become divided over participation in the proposed state of Israel. Anti-Zionists remained firm in their opposition to a secular Jewish state. Others, primarily associated with Agudat Israel, saw the need for a Jewish homeland given the increasingly perilous conditions in Europe and gave their support to the idea of a unified Jewish society. They took a neutral position regarding the legitimacy of the state of Israel itself and held to the view of Jewish sacred history that asserted that the true Land of Israel could be realized only through divine action. Nonetheless, they believed that participation in Israeli society would provide a means of protecting their traditional beliefs and practices in the midst of a larger secular community. Agudat Israel thus participated in Israel's founding government and since independence has operated as one of several non-Zionist, ultra-Orthodox political parties.

The primary concerns of Agudat Israel and the other ultra-Orthodox parties have been religious issues and the welfare of their constituents. Immediately after independence their approach was mainly defensive, aimed at limiting secular intrusions on their communities. They fought against mandatory public education and compulsory military service for young women and yeshiva students. During the 1980s, however, they began to gain political influence, which allowed them to adopt a more aggressive stance. The roughly even balance between Israel's two dominant political coalitions, the Labor Party on the left and the Likud Party on the right, made it difficult for either to form a ruling coalition without the support of the smaller religious parties. This situation gave Agudat Israel and the other ultra-Orthodox parties considerable clout, and they used it to seek greater support from the government for their institutions and followers.[25] Government support for private religious schools increased, as did various subsidies for yeshiva students, and exemptions from military service were granted more routinely to ultra-Orthodox men and women. Partly in response to ultra-Orthodox demands, the government also eliminated operations by El Al, Israel's official airline, on the Sabbath. The ultra-Orthodox parties suffered a setback in the late 1990s when Israel's Supreme Court ruled against them on several key issues, such as military exemptions and the validity of conversions to Judaism performed outside Israel. Agudat Israel and the other parties remained committed to using the political system to seek redress, however, and continue to function as participants in the larger society.

The religious Zionist branch of Jewish fundamentalism has adopted a strategy of participation as well, but for very different reasons. Religious Zionists see the creation of the state of Israel as the first step in the divine redemption of the Jewish people. Unlike the anti-Zionists, they believe that Jews should advance the process of redemption through their own efforts rather than wait passively for divine action. Their primary objective is to begin reclaiming the Land of Israel, first by resettling it and then by forming a permanent bond between the land and the Jewish people. Through these actions, along with strict observance of Jewish law, they believe that they can initiate the coming of the Jewish Messiah. Religious Zionists thus have an inherent interest in participating in the development of the state of Israel, which in their view will play an important role in Jewish sacred history despite its organization as a secular state.

This branch of Jewish fundamentalism has been represented most vigorously by Gush Emunim ("Bloc of the Faithful"). This group was formed by the followers of Zvi Yehudah Kook, the son of Abraham Kook, the early leader of religious Zionism. Again, the Kooks taught that the return of Jews to Israel represented the beginning of the process of redemption and that observant Jews had the responsibility to move that process forward. The outcome of the Six-Day War in 1967 significantly strengthened the belief of the Kooks' followers in the imminent Jewish redemption. They saw Israel's decisive victory and its rapid occupation of the Sinai, the Gaza Strip, and the West Bank as an expression of a divine plan, reshaping the state of Israel to conform more closely to the boundaries of the biblical promised land. They thus identified 1967 as the beginning of the era of redemption. A subsequent conflict between Israel, Egypt, and Syria in 1973 raised new concerns, however. In a surprise invasion, Egypt and Syria had been able to reoccupy some of the territory they had lost in 1967. Israel promptly retook the disputed territory, but some Israelis saw the 1973 war as something of a defeat, since their defenses had briefly been overwhelmed. Kook's followers viewed the war with particular alarm, seeing it as a threat to continued Jewish possession of reclaimed portions of the Land of Israel. As a result, they asserted a new objective: to ensure that reclaimed portions of this sacred region remained under Jewish control.

To support this objective, Kook's followers officially formed Gush Emunim in 1974. The group's immediate goal was to establish Jewish settlements in the territories occupied by Israel in 1967, making Jewish possession of the occupied territories a fait accompli. Its members also hoped to pressure the Israeli government to undertake a policy of re-Judaization of the region, first through the formal annexation of the occupied territories and then by establishing a new state governed by the halakhah, or Jewish law. They believed that this process would gradually lead to the redemption. Gush Emunim attracted many religious Jews disaffected with the secular character of Israeli society and at the same time gained tacit support from additional nonmembers who held less radical versions of the group's views. Gush Emunim thus became an important political force during the 1970s, advocating full Israeli sovereignty over the biblical Land of Israel. They opposed any retreat from the occupied territories, where they became active in establishing new settlements. A few Israeli communities had already been organized in the occupied territories by the mid-1970s, but they generally lacked full support from the government. During the late 1970s, however, Gush Emunim acquired government backing for a number of new settlements, initiating a significant influx of Jewish settlers into these areas.

By the end of the 1970s, some members of Gush Emunim had become disaffected with the strategy of participation. A 1979 peace treaty between Egypt and Israel returned the Sinai to Egyptian control, a move opposed by Gush Emunim based on their belief that the biblical Land of Israel extended to the Nile River. Religious Zionists strongly protested the treaty, but to no avail. A small group of extremists within Gush Emunim began to assert that the reclamation of the Land of Israel was proceeding too slowly. They argued that the creation of settlements was not an effective strategy and advocated more aggressive measures. They thus initiated a terrorist campaign against Palestinian targets during the 1980s.[26] The extremists' actions culminated in an unsuccessful plot to destroy the Islamic shrines on the Temple Mount in Jerusalem. Gush radicals believed that this act would provoke a major war, from which Israel would emerge victorious and after which the Messiah would fulfill the redemption of the Jewish people. After the plot was discovered, however, the main body of Gush Emunim publicly disavowed support for the radicals. The group thus returned to its original goal of promoting settlement in the occupied territories, but its prestige declined sharply within Israeli society. In recent years, Gush Emunim has again become more vocal, protesting plans to give up portions of the occupied territories as part of a peace agreement with the Palestinians. Its influence has not returned to the levels of the 1970s, however.

Jewish fundamentalism has thus produced two patterns of participation in Israeli society. In both cases, an uneasy relationship exists between fundamentalists and the state of Israel, particularly with regard to territorial concerns. Agudat Israel finds fault with the state's secular character and its effort to create a Jewish homeland through human agency, while Gush Emunim opposes the state's unwillingness to establish permanent control over the occupied territories regardless of the political costs. Both groups believe, however, that their views represent the interests and true identity of the Jewish people and that participation within Israel's social and political structures offers the best strategy for advancing their particular goals.

In a number of contexts, Islamic fundamentalists also have justified their participation in existing social and political structures by claiming that they represent their society's true ideals. Again, such cases have developed where fundamentalists have been unable to achieve absolute domination but believe that they can bring about change through legitimate means. Islamic fundamentalists who have adopted a strategy of participation have typically focused on political action, often by forming political parties with the explicit goal of legally establishing Islam as the state's ultimate authority. Christian fundamentalists in the United States have an analogous goal, to establish biblical principles as the foundation of society, but they fall short of advocating the creation of a pure theocracy, an impossibility under the nation's Constitution. Christian fundamentalists thus tend to focus on specific moral issues, such as abortion or gay rights, through which they can promote their religious ideology indirectly. For Islamic fundamentalists, on the other hand, the totality of Islam requires the creation of an Islamic state in which civil law and religious law are united. The political organizations through which Islamic fundamentalists participate in society are therefore concerned with more than the promotion of Islamic values. They seek universal recognition of Islam as the ideological foundation of society and the political state. As a result, the Islamic fundamentalists that belong to these political parties tend to be more totalistic in their objectives than do their Christian counterparts.

Egypt's Muslim Brotherhood represents a key example of this approach to participation in society. Because of its opposition to the secular government, the Muslim Brotherhood was outlawed for much of the 1950s and 1960s. Many of its members were imprisoned, and a number of its leaders were executed. Changing political circumstances during the 1970s enabled the brotherhood to adopt a more participatory strategy, however. After Anwar Sadat became president in 1970, he initiated a new policy of tolerance toward the Muslim Brotherhood. Although by no means a fundamentalist, Sadat himself maintained a strong personal commitment to Islam, and he saw the brotherhood and other Islamic groups as potential allies in his effort to counter Marxist and socialist influences in Egypt. Sadat did not grant the Muslim Brotherhood legal status, but he released all of its members who were still imprisoned in 1971 and later allowed them to renew their activities in the nation's universities and to distribute popular publications. He also supported the new constitution, enacted in 1971, which made Islam the official religion of Egypt and declared the sharia to be a primary source of Egyptian law. As a result of these developments, the Muslim Brotherhood reestablished itself as a vital Islamic organization in Egypt.

The popular appeal of the Muslim Brotherhood was reinforced by an Islamic resurgence among the Egyptian people during the 1970s. That resurgence had begun after Egypt's swift defeat by Israel during the Six-Day War in 1967, which left the Egyptian people demoralized with their leaders and with the secular state they had established. Many Muslims interpreted Egypt's defeat as a divine punishment for turning away from Islam and so began to push for a revival of religion in daily life.[27] This renewed commitment to Islam manifested itself in numerous ways, including an increase in religious publishing, widespread use of the veil by Egyptian women, and celebrity status for popular preachers who spread their views via radio, television, and cassette recordings. As strict adherence to Islamic tradition became more commonplace, so did the belief that Islam offered the only viable means of addressing the nation's persistent economic problems and external political pressures. Within this context, the Muslim Brotherhood represented an important voice within Egyptian society, advocating the establishment of a pure Islamic state.

In promoting this goal, the Muslim Brotherhood no longer advocated the use of revolutionary tactics. Its leaders instead sought to reform Egyptian society gradually and peacefully, by building support among the masses, influencing government policies, and reshaping the legal system. They claimed that they wanted others to adopt their Islamic principles willingly and that they recognized that their goals could take decades to achieve. This position led many militant fundamentalists to leave the brotherhood and establish extremist organizations that operated outside the bounds of Egyptian society, as discussed later in this chapter. These extremists viewed Egypt and Egyptian society as "unbelieving" and thus incapable of supporting authentic Islam. The Muslim Brotherhood argued, on the other hand, that while Egypt's social, economic, and political problems reflected a lack of commitment to Islamic values, Egypt itself should not be considered un-Islamic. The brotherhood's leadership asserted that Egypt could be transformed from within, through legitimate means. By adopting this less extreme stance, the Muslim Brotherhood has been able to remain an active participant within Egyptian society. Again, the Egyptian government under both Sadat and his successor, Hosni Mubarak, has never formally legalized the brotherhood, but it has given it a degree of freedom in its operations.

To strengthen its political influence, the Muslim Brotherhood has adopted three principal strategies since the early 1970s. First, it has built support at the grassroots level by operating a vast network of social institutions, including schools, clinics, hospitals, and public charities. By providing services to the poor that frequently are not available from the government, the brotherhood has tried to demonstrate the effectiveness of its Islamic model in dealing with social problems. Following an earthquake that struck Cairo in 1992, for example, the brotherhood proved to be far more efficient than the government in providing assistance to residents of the city's hardest hit neighborhoods. The group's second strategy has focused on efforts to gain control over a number of influential professional associations in Egypt, representing doctors, lawyers, pharmacists, and engineers, among others. The brotherhood has used its control of these organizations to introduce Islamic principles into the professions involved and to support its charitable work. The brotherhood dominates the Egyptian Medical Syndicate, the country's leading association of doctors, for example, which in turn operates brotherhood-funded clinics.[28] These professional organizations also provide the brotherhood with a legitimate voice in public affairs.

The Muslim Brotherhood's third approach to extending its influence has been to participate in electoral politics. Because it is nominally a religious organization and has not been officially recognized by the government, the Muslim Brotherhood cannot support political candidates under its own name. Muslim brothers have thus run for Parliament either as independents or as members of another party. During the mid-1970s, a number of Muslim brothers were in fact elected to Parliament as members of Anwar Sadat's ruling party. Sadat accepted them in his party both to bolster his support among fundamentalist Muslims and to prevent them from establishing an independent political presence. Other Muslim brothers were elected as independent candidates, however, and cooperated with the government only to the extent that it supported their Islamic agenda. Sadat's assassination by Islamic extremists in 1981 resulted in his replacement by Hosni Mubarak, who was more hostile toward the Muslim Brotherhood. During the 1980s and 1990s, the brotherhood thus began to form alliances with various opposition political parties. In exchange for access to the brotherhood's base of popular support, these parties adopted the fundamentalists' call for a full implementation of the sharia. Using this strategy, several dozen members of the brotherhood were elected to Parliament in 1987, and the brotherhood became the leading opposition force in Egyptian politics.[29]

Growing conflict between the Egyptian government and Islamic extremists during the 1990s reinforced Mubarak's distrust of the brotherhood, however. The brotherhood repeatedly asserted that it opposed the use of violence to effect change, but by the early 1990s Mubarak no longer distinguished between the brotherhood's version of Islamic fundamentalism and the more extreme views espoused by terrorists. The government asserted that the brotherhood had provided support to various terrorist groups in Egypt and that because of its greater size the brotherhood in fact represented a bigger threat than the terrorists themselves. Prior to the parliamentary elections in 1995, Mubarak's regime arrested a number of Muslim brothers running for election and closed the group's headquarters in Cairo. The election itself was marred by violence and reports of government tampering, and Mubarak's party dominated the outcome. Despite growing conflict with the Mubarak regime, however, the Muslim Brotherhood remained publicly committed to its objective of creating an Islamic state through peaceful means.[30] The brotherhood thus continued its effort to pursue a strategy of participation in Egyptian society, even as the government made such participation more difficult.

The Jamaat-e-Islami in Pakistan has followed a similar strategy of participation, although its activities differ in significant ways from those of the Muslim Brotherhood. Most importantly, the Jamaat-e-Islami is not organized as a populist group. It asserts that social change can be achieved most effectively by an elite community of committed believers. As a result, the Jamaat maintains exacting rules of membership, and the size of the organization has remained rather small. From its original membership of seventy-five in the early 1940s, the Jamaat had grown to only around ten thousand full members by the mid-1990s (fewer than a thousand of whom were women). In the late 1990s, the Jamaat instituted a form of "associate" membership status as means of extending its popular influence, which brought more than two million additional Muslims into the organization. Most of the organization's work remains the responsibility of its full members, however.

The primary goal of the Jamaat is to use legitimate political means to establish an Islamic social order in Pakistan. According to the group's ideology, this social order must be rooted in individual religious commitment and cannot be realized through coercion. The Jamaat's members thus attempt to promote strict adherence to Islam in part by leading exemplary lives themselves, providing a model for other Muslims to follow. At the same time, the Jamaat sees Islam as more than just a codified set of practices and beliefs. In their view, Islam represents an integrated way of life encompassing all realms of human activity. As a result, the Jamaat recognizes the importance of creating social and political structures that will encourage the widespread observance of Islam. A key objective of the group has thus been to define Pakistan as a true Islamic state, with a constitution based on Islamic principles and a legal system based on the sharia. In the Jamaat's view, the official Islamization of Pakistan is mandated by the central role of Islam in defining the country's national identity, but it also offers the only meaningful solution to the country's problems and represents a necessary step in creating a context where authentic Islam can thrive.

In supporting the Islamization of Pakistan, the Jamaat-e-Islami has experienced a complex series of relationships with the country's rulers and political parties, reflecting its changing assessment of the major obstacles to the establishment of an Islamic order. During the military rule of the late 1960s and early 1970s, the Jamaat identified the leading opposition party, headed by Zulfikar Ali Bhutto, as the most serious threat to the creation of an Islamic state. Bhutto's party advocated the establishment of socialism in Pakistan. To the Jamaat, the socialists' desire to nationalize certain industries and institute land reform conflicted with the basic economic principles of Islam, which stressed the sanctity of private property. The Jamaat also feared that the socialists' policies would subvert the Islamic basis of Pakistan's national identity. The Jamaat thus supported the military regime and joined with a number of other rightist and centrist parties to challenge the socialists' ideas.

When elections were held in 1970, however, the Jamaat had little success in electing its own candidates to the national assembly, winning only four seats out of three hundred. The Jamaat thus began to revamp its strategy for promoting its Islamic goals. It made a concerted effort to incorporate populist issues regarding housing and employment into its political agenda, although its elitist organizational structure continued to prevent it from gaining a large popular following. In addition, it began to look for means other than electoral politics to influence the direction of the country. It became increasingly active in organizing street demonstrations, for example, which became an effective tool for bringing its views before the public. Similarly, it placed growing emphasis on its student wing, which had considerable success in taking control of student associations in Pakistan's universities. The Jamaat also developed coalitions with other political groups and tried to cultivate relationships with those in power.

During this time, the Jamaat specifically focused on two issues: the future of East Pakistan and the rewriting of the country's constitution. The Jamaat strongly opposed the independence movement in East Pakistan, arguing that the nation's Islamic identity should supersede regional or ethnic concerns. It fully supported the military in its efforts to retain control over East Pakistan, and many of its members fought in the ensuing civil war. This effort ended in failure with the creation of Bangladesh as an independent state in 1971, but it enhanced the Jamaat's credibility as a voice for national unity. The Jamaat's involvement in the writing of a new constitution in 1973 proved to be more successful. Using the experience its leaders had gained in negotiations involving the constitution enacted in 1956, the group successfully pushed for the inclusion of Islamic principles in the new document. The 1973 constitution thus declared Islam to be the state religion of Pakistan, and it retained the various Islamic provisions included in the 1956 constitution, including a proscription against laws that contradict Islamic principles. It also mandated that both the president and prime minister of Pakistan must be Muslims. The constitution fell short of establishing the sharia as the basis for civil law, but the Jamaat considered its ratification to be an important victory. After the constitution had been approved, moreover, the Jamaat began a new campaign supporting enforcement of the sharia.

In addition to its involvement with the above-mentioned issues, the Jamaat became a leading opponent of the socialist policies of the government elected in 1970, led by Prime Minister Bhutto. The Jamaat questioned Bhutto's interest in incorporating Islamic principles into his own programs and believed that

Bhutto himself showed little personal regard for Islamic values. Bhutto took steps to placate the group, closing casinos and nightclubs and banning gambling and the sale of alcohol, in accordance with Islamic law. These actions did not satisfy the growing opposition from other political parties and interests groups, however, and in 1977 a military coup led by General Mohammad Zia ul-Haq removed Bhutto from power. Although the Jamaat favored the concept of an elected government, it gave its support to Zia's regime because he promised to enact Islamic reforms. The Jamaat's leaders also began to place greater emphasis on the importance of enforcing the sharia than on the process through which such enforcement was achieved. This approach contradicted the Jamaat's traditionally democratic stance, but it conformed to their elitist strategy of initiating social change through leadership from above. Its support for Zia also enhanced the Jamaat's political influence. Several of its members served in Zia's cabinet during the early years of his regime, and Zia appointed several others to important government bodies concerned with the Islamization of Pakistani law.

Zia instituted a number of Islamic reforms, including the establishment of Islamic punishments for theft, adultery, and the use of alcohol, but the Jamaat eventually grew disillusioned with his regime. Some members of the Jamaat felt that the military government was moving too slowly in its policies of Islamization, that it was not effective in enforcing Islamic law, and that it had failed to promote true Islam among the masses. The Jamaat also grew impatient with Zia's refusal to hold open elections. It had opposed elections in the late 1970s, while Bhutto was still a potential threat; but after his execution in 1979, following his conviction for ordering the murder of a political rival, the Jamaat no longer supported Zia's decision to defer elections. Eventually, members of the Jamaat resigned from Zia's cabinet, and the group became increasingly critical of his regime. On some issues the Jamaat still agreed with Zia. Both favored giving aid to the Afghan rebels fighting against the Soviet occupation of Afghanistan in the 1980s, for example. But by the late 1980s, the Jamaat no longer considered Zia to be an effective ally in its effort to create an Islamic society in Pakistan.

In 1987, the newly chosen leader of the Jamaat, Qazi Hussain Ahmad, began to campaign actively against Zia. He argued that Zia had failed to bring about genuine change and that his ineffectual policy of Islamization did not justify the continued postponement of democratic elections. The Jamaat also criticized Zia's support for a 1988 law that replaced the existing legal code with the sharia. Although the group's members had at one time favored such a law, they now opposed it because they believed that it enforced merely a superficial adherence to Islamic practice rather than a genuine commitment to Islamic principles. In the absence of government efforts to promote authentic Islam, the new law had no meaning in the Jamaat's view. The Jamaat further charged that Zia had instituted Islamic policies to advance his own political goals rather than to promote the welfare of society, and they claimed that his use of those policies to justify the existence of his military regime had in fact hindered the Islamic cause. The Jamaat's opposition to Zia's policies became a moot point in 1988, however, after he was killed in an airplane explosion over eastern Pakistan.

Elections held later that year brought about a new period of democratic rule, but the Jamaat-e-Islami again had little success in electing its members to national office. Moreover, it has repeatedly found itself at odds with the political parties that have governed Pakistan since the late 1980s. Leadership of the country has passed back and forth several times between Benazir Bhutto, daughter of the former prime minister, and Nawaz Sharif, a former supporter of General Zia. When Bhutto has been in power, the Jamaat has opposed her liberal political agenda and in 1996 led a vigorous protest campaign to remove her from office, based on charges of government corruption. The Jamaat has been little happier with Sharif, however. Sharif tried to appease the fundamentalists in 1998 by proposing a constitutional amendment that would establish the sharia as Pakistan's legal code, but the Jamaat accused Sharif of using Islam solely for political purposes and argued that his proposal would not in itself make Pakistan a true Islamic state. The Jamaat also faulted Sharif for not providing adequate support to Muslim separatists in Kashmir seeking independence from Indian rule, a struggle that the Jamaat defined as a jihad, or holy war.

The Jamaat-e-Islami has thus followed a distinctive pattern of participation in trying to establish an Islamic social order in Pakistan. Although it has had little success in electoral politics, the Jamaat has maintained a powerful political voice through its adept use of political alliances and its ability to organize massive public demonstrations. It has also succeeded in establishing itself as a legitimate representative of Islam, a crucial function given Islam's importance as a source of national unity and identity in Pakistan. The Islamic clergy in Pakistan also serve this function, but they have been less successful than the Jamaat in establishing their credibility as an effective political force. Much of the Jamaat's political authority derives from its uncompromising vision of a totally Islamic society. This vision has repeatedly placed the group in opposition to the nation's political leaders and has even led the group to oppose ostensibly pro-Islamic policies that it considers to be incomplete or insincere. At the same time, by pursuing the creation of a true Islamic order through legitimate means the Jamaat has defined itself as an integral force within Pakistani society. Moreover, the group had tried to use its distinct identity within Pakistani politics to expand its base of popular support in recent years. The Jamaat thus remains committed to a strategy of participation, through political action as well as through the example that its members set for other Muslims.

Islamic fundamentalists in Malaysia have also used the issue of national identity to justify a strategy of participation. In Malaysia, however, the connections between religion and national identity are confounded by the country's complex racial and ethnic composition. Ethnic Malays, almost all of whom are Muslims, are the largest ethnic group, but account for less than 60 percent of the total population. Over a fourth of all Malaysians are ethnic Chinese, largely descended from nineteenth-century migrants, and another 7 percent are descended from predominantly Hindu migrants from India. Indigenous peoples, largely concentrated on the island of Borneo, account for most of the rest of the population. Within this diverse ethnic mixture, Muslims account for only slightly more than half of Malaysia's inhabitants. Fundamentalists seeking to redefine Malaysia as an Islamic state thus face considerable opposition from other groups.

The process of decolonization at first appeared to support Muslim interests in Malaysia. After Britain granted independence in 1957 to Malaysia's predecessor, the federation of Malaya, the country's new constitution established Islam as the official religion. Malay nationalists insisted on this provision as part of their plan to ensure that Malaya would be primarily a Malay state. The constitution also made Malay the official language, and the country's first government, dominated by the leading Malay political party, the United Malays National Organization (UMNO), enacted various policies to promote economic opportunities for ethnic Malays.[31] When the country was reorganized as Malaysia in 1963, with the addition of Singapore and portions of Borneo, Islam remained the official religion, and Malay, the official language.[32]

Even before independence was achieved, however, disagreements emerged over Islam's role in the new state. Most Malay nationalists did not want to create a strict Islamic state at the time of independence, believing that Malaysia's large non-Muslim minority would oppose such an effort. Instead, these secular nationalists were primarily concerned with achieving economic parity between Malays and the wealthier Chinese minority. For most nationalists, including UMNO, Islam's status as the official religion was intended to be merely symbolic. Indeed, the constitution guaranteed the rights of other religious communities, and Islamic laws concerning marriage and divorce applied only to Muslims. Some Malay Muslims, however, believed that the symbolic interpretation of Islam's social role would weaken their religion's influence and ultimately erode the status of the Malay majority. They argued that the new state should be genuinely Islamic and that Islamic principles should be fully integrated into its institutions, economy, and legal system. To promote this view, conservative Muslims founded the Pan Malayan Islamic Party in the early 1950s. Later this group became known as the Parti Islam SeMalaysia ("Islamic Party of Malaysia," or PAS). After independence, PAS became the country's principal Islamic party and a leading proponent of fundamentalist ideas.[33]

PAS developed a strong following in the predominantly Malay states located in the northern third of peninsular Malaysia, particularly in the state of Kelantan (fig. 3.6). In the country's first elections, held in 1959, PAS won control of

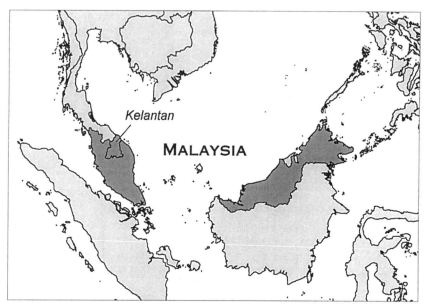

Figure 3.6 The state of Kelantan represents the hearth of the Islamic fundamentalist movement in Malaysia.

the state governments in Kelantan and neighboring Trengganu, and it remained in power in Kelantan continuously until 1977. This regional base of support established PAS as an important political voice and introduced a geographical dimension into the conflict between the fundamentalists and other national political parties. UMNO tried to resolve this conflict by co-opting PAS, based on both groups' support for Malay nationalism. Throughout the 1960s, the government had developed policies to expand economic opportunity for Malays. Tensions between the Malay and Chinese communities resulting from these policies erupted in ethnic riots in 1969. When, in the aftermath of the riots, the government renewed its efforts to promote Malay economic interests, PAS gave its support to this new initiative and in 1973 joined the political coalition led by UMNO. The participation of PAS in the ruling coalition ended in 1977, however, when UMNO tried to unseat Kelantan's PAS government. Declaring a state of emergency in Kelantan, the central government dismissed the elected state government and appointed an administrator to run the state until new elections were held. The government then banned public rallies during the election campaign, eliminating the primary vehicle by which PAS communicated with voters. With a sophisticated network of radio, television, and print media at its disposal, UMNO had much greater success in spreading its views, and it won control of the state government in a decisive electoral victory. In response to these actions, PAS withdrew from UMNO's political coalition.

The government's removal of PAS from power in Kelantan had important political ramifications. In addition to reviving antagonism between PAS and UMNO, this episode strengthened contacts between PAS and Angkatan Belia Islam Malaysia ("Malaysian Islamic Youth Movement," or ABIM). ABIM had been formed in the early 1970s during a resurgence of Islamic sentiment and had been particularly influential in Malaysia's universities. The group had ideological ties to fundamentalist organizations in other countries, such as the Muslim Brotherhood and Jamaat-e-Islami, and it became an increasingly important voice of Malaysian fundamentalism during the 1970s. Its members asserted that Malaysia should be reorganized as an authentic Islamic state based on a full implementation of the sharia. They favored creation of a new Islamic bank, in which the un-Islamic practice of charging interest would be eliminated, and an Islamic university, which would promote genuine Islamic belief. Although ABIM's agenda resembled that of PAS, it criticized PAS for participating in the ruling coalition of the mid-1970s, and opposed the Malay nationalism that PAS espoused. ABIM's members believed that ethnic nationalism was incompatible with the universality of Islam, and they argued that Islam should be the sole basis for Malaysian identity.

When PAS withdrew from the ruling coalition to protest the central government's actions in Kelantan, however, ABIM's leaders decided to lend their support to PAS. Despite their past differences, ABIM saw PAS as a potential ally in the cause of promoting Islam and assisted in PAS's electoral campaigns in Kelantan in 1977. PAS again had little success in the Kelantan elections and lost control of the state government, but the process of cooperation established important connections between PAS and ABIM. Many ABIM members subsequently left their organization to join PAS in the late 1970s and early 1980s. As they did so, this "new guard" of former ABIM members began to reshape PAS's ideology. They called for PAS to abandon its connections to Malay nationalism and devote itself more exclusively to the promotion of Islam. Motivated in part by the success of the Islamic Revolution in Iran, this "new guard" also demanded that PAS leaders adhere more strictly to Islamic customs and abandon all Western practices.

Two developments in 1982 dramatically changed the relationship between PAS and ABIM. First, ABIM's leader at the time accepted an invitation to join UMNO, which had been working on its own Islamization program to counter the fundamentalists' influence. Many fundamentalists objected to this compromise with the establishment, and a new wave of ABIM members joined PAS, in which ABIM's original views were becoming more widely accepted. As a result, ABIM itself declined in importance as an expression of fundamentalism. In a second key development, young PAS leaders who had largely begun their fundamentalist careers in ABIM officially took control of PAS in 1982 and established their more rigid ideology as the party's official doctrine. This shift in power reinvigorated PAS, and during the 1980s it resumed its public criticism of the government. It argued that UMNO's largely symbolic policy of Islamization did not reflect genuine religious commitment and did too little to integrate Islamic principles into Malaysian society. PAS also increased its attacks on the political uses of ethnic chauvinism by the parties in power.

In elections held in 1990, PAS regained control of the state assembly in Kelantan, which it dominated for the rest of the decade. This victory enabled the Islamic fundamentalist movement in Malaysia to reestablish a regional base from which to advance its goal of creating an Islamic state. Within Kelantan itself, PAS leaders have tried to initiate this process by promoting strict Islamic practices. The PAS government banned gambling, for example, and outlawed the consumption of alcohol by Muslims. It has also banned various forms of public entertainment, including public dancing, carnival rides, theater, and even the performance of traditional Malayan folk music. According to PAS leaders, these activities are un-Islamic because they promote immoral behavior and inappropriate contact between the sexes. At the few public concerts that they do permit, the authorities require separate seating areas for men and women. PAS has prohibited the performance of traditional shadow puppet theater, an important indigenous art form, because the stories that it depicts are based on the Hindu epic *Ramayana*. PAS has also tried to incorporate traditional Islamic attitudes toward women into Kelantan society. The government has erected billboards instructing women on the proper way to dress and has tried to discourage the use of Western-style cosmetics. Women depicted in public advertisements, such as on billboards, must have their hair veiled. To prevent inappropriate contacts between men and women, the state government has also discouraged women from working at night, and in the state capital men and women are required to use separate checkout lines in supermarkets.[34]

PAS ultimately intends to establish the sharia as the legal code for all Muslims in Kelantan and eventually throughout Malaysia, but in pursuing this goal it has faced stiff opposition from the nation's central government. In 1996, Kelantan's state assembly approved a measure that would institute traditional Islamic corporal punishments for criminal offenses. The state government did not implement this measure, however, after national leaders stated that they would take steps to prevent such punishments from being carried out. PAS leaders interpreted this to mean that the national government would declare a state of emergency in Kelantan, as it had in the late 1970s, and remove PAS from power. Not wanting to provoke a confrontation, PAS yielded on this issue.[35] Nonetheless, it remains committed to the creation of an authentic Islamic order as the only legitimate means of ensuring justice and morality in Malaysia. PAS's strategy of participation in Malaysian society thus continues to reflect its view that it represents the nation's core values and true identity.

In various settings, then, Islamic fundamentalists have justified a strategy of participation by defining themselves as the defenders of society's religious ideals. In claiming this role, they establish the moral basis for their interactions with society at large and legitimate their participation in political processes. Some Islamic fundamentalists participate in society through means other than political action, such as missionary activity and charitable work. Throughout South Asia, for example, the Tablighi Jamaat avoids involvement in politics and concentrates instead on promoting authentic Islamic practice among individuals. But for most Islamic fundamentalist groups, the responsibility of participating in society derives from the sacred ideal of the Islamic state and demands a commitment to political action. Following the model established by Muhammad, the creation of an Islamic state involves the acceptance of Islam as a total way of life. As a result, the organization of such a state requires the complete transformation of society. The fundamentalist groups adopting a strategy of participation believe, moreover, that this transformation cannot be imposed or coerced, but must be accepted by choice. For these groups, political participation thus provides a means of fulfilling their responsibility to promote acceptance of an authentic Islamic order.

Hindu fundamentalists have adopted a strategy of participation based on their conviction that they stand for the essential core of Indian culture. Unlike their Muslim counterparts, however, Hindu fundamentalists do not focus their efforts on creating a political state based on a sacred model. They also do not seek to establish a specific body of religious law, since Hinduism does not possess a universal legal code. Instead, Hindu fundamentalists are primarily concerned with matters of identity, and in particular with the recognition of *Hindutva*, or Hinduness, as the essence of Indian culture. This concern finds its clearest expression in the concept of *Hindu Rashtra*, or Hindu nation, the idea that a single national identity based on *Hindutva* encompasses all of the people whose cultural and religious traditions originated in the Indian subcontinent.[36] In promoting the concepts of *Hindutva* and *Hindu Rashtra*, the fundamentalists seek to ensure that this sense of Hindu identity remains undiluted by secularism, pluralism, and Westernization. Hindu fundamentalists have also expressed the goal of creating a utopian Hindu state, Ram Rajya (the Kingdom of Ram, the central Hindu deity for most fundamentalists), but they consider the legitimation of *Hindutva* as the source of India's identity to be a more pressing issue.

By claiming to represent the authentic character of Indian society, Hindu fundamentalists have made a strategy of participation an intrinsic part of their ideology. The primary vehicle for that strategy is the Sangh Parivar, their network of social, political, and religious organizations. The central group in the Sangh Parivar is the Rashtriya Swayamsevak Sangh, or RSS, the association of young activists formed in the 1920s. The main function of the RSS is to build a community of committed followers, primarily through the creation of local groups of volunteers united by their shared experiences of indoctrination and paramilitary training. The RSS asserts that Hinduism lies at the heart of Indian nationalism, that it is superior to other religions, and that Hindus must aggressively protect their cultural identity. This ideology continues to attract a large following, and by the late 1990s the group claimed roughly four million members. The exclusive and even secretive nature of the RSS has limited its effectiveness as an agent of change outside the fundamentalist community, however. To promote their ideology within Indian society at large, fundamentalists have thus formed various other organizations, each with a distinct mission. The most prominent of these groups have been the Vishwa Hindu Parishad ("World Hindu Society," or VHP) and the Bharatiya Janata Party ("Indian People's Party," or BJP).

The VHP originated in 1964 as a missionary society responsible for promoting the practice of Hinduism throughout India and in Indian communities overseas. It defines Hinduism in broad terms as the religion of the Hindu nation, and so it encourages the adoption of a Hindu identity by all Indians. Within India, one of the group's central objectives has been to counter the spread of Islam and Christianity, both considered to be undesirable foreign influences. Much of this effort has focused on reestablishing the Hindu affiliation of untouchables who have converted to another faith. Members of the untouchable castes are considered to be spiritually unclean in Hindu society and have traditionally faced severe discrimination. Both Islam and Christianity have thus offered a means of escaping the pariah status into which they were born. In some instances, entire untouchable communities have gone through the conversion process together. The VHP has tried to attract these converts back to Hinduism by advocating an end to the concept of untouchability. In addition, it has vigorously opposed Christian and Muslim missionary work among the untouchables and has advocated laws limiting proselytization. The VHP has also tried to block the spread of Islam and Christianity among the tribal groups in India that practice local animistic religions. According to VHP thought, these tribal groups are members of the Hindu nation since they are indigenous to the region, but because of their traditional isolation they require direction in becoming full participants in the larger Hindu culture. In addition to these concerns, the VHP has promoted the idea that Hindu identity includes other indigenous religious traditions, including Jainism, Buddhism, and Sikhism. Finally, the VHP has attempted to encourage Hindu practice among secularized Hindus. In all of these efforts, then, the VHP's approach to participation in society has been to strengthen the Hindu nation by extending the boundaries of *Hindutva*.[37]

Hindu fundamentalists have also influenced Indian society through political participation. The VHP has been involved in such efforts, particularly through large public processions that it began to organize in the 1980s, often with the help of the RSS. These processions have lasted for days or even weeks, traversed large areas of the country, and attracted millions of spectators and participants, and they provided the VHP with an effective means of spreading its message of Hindu unity and identity.[38] Hindu fundamentalists have promoted their political agenda more directly, though, by forming political parties, beginning with the Jana Sangh in 1951. This group remained active into the 1970s, although it had difficulty reaching beyond its original constituency of Hindi speakers in northern and central India. In the late 1970s it briefly merged with a coalition of other political groups to form the Janata Party, which governed India from 1977 to 1980. Jana Sangh leaders had hoped that this move would expand their base of popular support, but conflicts with secular elements in the Janata Party and weakening support for the coalition led the fundamentalists to reorganize as a separate group, the Bharatiya Janata Party, in 1980. The BJP tried to broaden its appeal by incorporating a stronger populist component into its platform, emphasizing the need to restore moral principles to government and eliminate social inequalities. At the same time, the BJP remained committed to the concepts of *Hindutva* and Hindu nationalism and attacked the ruling government's secularist policies as a threat to Hindu culture.[39]

Since 1980, the BJP has become increasingly influential in Indian politics. It began as a regional party in the so-called Hindi Belt of north-central India (fig. 3.7) and won only two seats in the national parliamentary elections held in 1984. As the BJP advanced its platform of Hindu nationalism and economic development, however, increasing numbers of Hindus saw it as an alternative to the Congress Party that had dominated Indian politics since independence. The BJP also benefited from growing conflict between Hindu and Muslim interests in India during the late 1980s and early 1990s. The symbolic focus of that conflict was the controversy surrounding the Babri Mosque in the northern city of Ayodhya. Hindu fundamentalists claimed that this mosque, built in the early 1500s, was situated on the birthplace of the Hindu deity Ram and the site of a former Hindu temple. They demanded the removal of the mosque so that a temple to Ram could be erected there. The federal government opposed any attempt to destroy the mosque, leading the fundamentalists to charge that the government's policies favored minority religious groups and threatened Hinduism's status as the essence of Indian national identity. The BJP's support for the fundamentalist position increased its following within the Hindu community as tensions over the issue rose. With the assistance of the other organizations in the Sangh Parivar, the BJP consequently achieved its first major electoral victories in 1990, when it won control of two state governments in northern and central India and joined with the Janata Party to form a coalition government in two others. The following year, the BJP won control of a fifth northern state, Uttar Pradesh, India's most populous province.[40] In national elections held in 1991 the BJP emerged as the second largest party in India's parliament.

The BJP suffered a temporary reversal in its political fortunes in 1992, after a demonstration organized in Ayodhya by the BJP, RSS, and VHP and attended by BJP president L. K. Advani resulted in the destruction of the Babri Mosque.

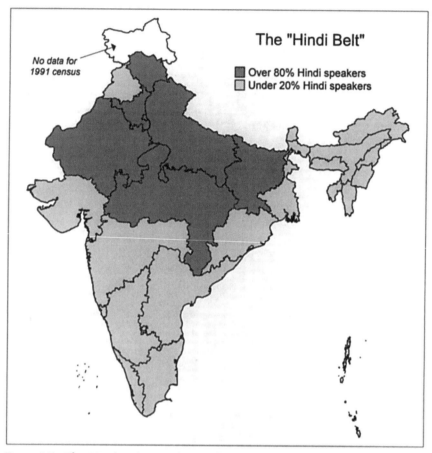

Figure 3.7   The "Hindi Belt" in India. Hindi speakers dominate most of the northern states of India but represent a small proportion of the population elsewhere in the country. Hindi speakers account for slightly more than 60 percent of the population of the union territory of Chandigarh, which is too small to appear on this map (cf. figure 4.11). *Data source:* Census of India, 1991.

The federal government responded by dismissing four of the state governments that the BJP controlled, installing temporary federal administrations in their place. In elections held in 1993, the BJP regained control in only two of the states that it had previously governed. As a result, the BJP began to modify its platform somewhat, emphasizing its support for Hindu nationalism rather than Hinduism itself. It subsequently won control of two more northern states in 1994 and 1995. Growing dissatisfaction with the ruling Congress Party also contributed to greater success for the BJP in national politics. In elections held in 1996, the BJP won a plurality of the seats in India's national parliament, but opposition to its Hindu nationalist ideology prevented it from organizing other parties into a ruling coalition. In elections held in 1998, however, the BJP won an even larger plurality of the seats in parliament, despite its fundamentalist platform. The BJP still attracted its highest levels of support in its hearth in north-central India, but its nationwide constituency had also continued to grow (fig. 3.8). The BJP thus succeeded in creating a coalition government, and Atal Bihari Vajpayee, one of the founders of the BJP and a long-time member of the RSS, became prime minister.

Opponents of the BJP criticized its fundamentalist connections, and particularly its ties to the militant RSS, whose members had campaigned for BJP candidates. In forming the coalition of political parties required to achieve a parliamentary majority, the BJP thus had to adopt a more moderate public stance on some issues. Prior to the 1998 elections, for example, the BJP had promised that it would initiate construction of a temple to Ram on the site of the demolished Babri Mosque in Ayodhya, but after the election these plans were postponed. The BJP also appeared to drop its campaign to establish a uniform civil code throughout India, which would have eliminated separate laws for the Muslim community governing marriage and property rites. Nonetheless, the BJP maintained its commitment to the concept of *Hindutva* as the ethos of Indian culture, and many of its leaders continued to declare their support for the RSS and its concept of Hindu nationalism. Mirroring a key concern of the RSS, the BJP has also initiated policies aimed at building India's national strength. One major goal has been to promote greater economic self-sufficiency by restricting some types of foreign competition. A far more controversial effort has focused on the development of nuclear weapons, a goal long espoused by the BJP as a necessary step in protecting the Hindu nation from external threats, and in particular from Pakistan. As part of this effort, the government tested a series of nuclear devices in 1998 and announced its intention of eventually supplying the Indian military with nuclear weaponry. The nuclear tests sparked widespread international criticism and provoked Pakistan into carrying out similar tests to demonstrate its own nuclear capability. International opinion had little impact on the BJP's leadership, however, which insisted on its right to protect India's national interests.

The BJP has thus achieved substantially greater electoral success than have most Islamic fundamentalist parties. The greater success of the BJP in part reflects the different nature of its agenda. Unlike the Islamic fundamentalist parties, which have emphasized the establishment of a strict code of Islamic law, Hindu fundamentalists have used political action primarily to promote an inclusive and somewhat abstract interpretation of Hindu identity. Critics have argued that the concept of *Hindutva* is not as inclusive as the fundamentalists claim. Nonetheless, the focus on identity has enabled Hindu fundamentalists

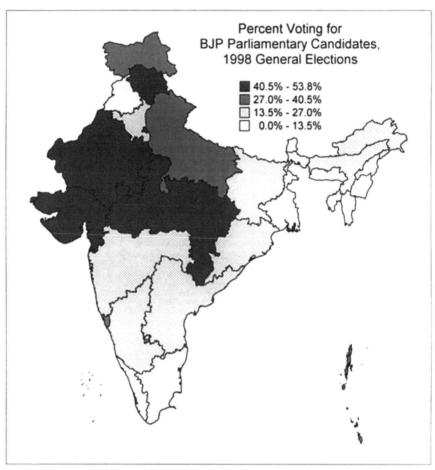

Figure 3.8   Electoral support for parliamentary candidates belonging to the Bharatiya Janata Party in India's 1998 General Election. *Data source:* Election Commission of India.

to attract a large and diverse following within the Hindu community and at the same time to look for support among other religious groups encompassed by the concept of *Hindutva*. The BJP has not entirely ignored matters of law, of course. After taking control of the state government in Delhi in 1994, for example, it passed the nation's strictest cow protection law, banning the slaughter of cows and the sale or possession of beef, prohibitions based on the cow's sacred status in Hinduism. Similarly, the BJP has repeatedly called for the elimination of special civil laws for Muslims. Such efforts do not take on the same significance that the goal of enacting the sharia does for Muslims, however. For Hindu fundamentalists, the central purpose of their strategy of participation is to promote a sense of national identity that preserves the cultural and religious traditions that have evolved within the homeland of the Hindu nation.

Other fundamentalist movements in South Asia have also pursued strategies of participation based on issues of identity. In Sri Lanka, fundamentalists among the dominant ethnic group, the Sinhalese, have focused on the role of Buddhism in defining their national identity. Some scholars argue that Sinhalese Buddhist activists are not true fundamentalists, as they are not primarily concerned with doctrinal issues.[41] Using the criteria outlined in chapter 1, however, these activists clearly display fundamentalist traits.[42] They are strongly motivated by the belief that external forces threaten their religious traditions and that they must respond to those threats to protect their religious identity. Early manifestations of Buddhist fundamentalism addressed the impacts of Western imperialism, which undermined the status of Buddhism when Sri Lanka was a British colony. More recently, Buddhist activists have focused on the pluralistic nature of Sri Lankan society, asserting that the country's Tamil Hindus and other minorities threaten the Sinhalese-Buddhist basis of Sri Lanka's national identity. In defining these threats, Buddhist fundamentalists also adhere to an idealized understanding of Sri Lanka's past, in which Buddhism defines the core of the national culture. That understanding largely derives from the *Mahavamsa*, a fifth-century chronicle that describes the origins of the Sinhalese people and the coming of Buddhism to Sri Lanka. This work depicts Sri Lanka as a sacred land, destined to become the stronghold of Buddhism in its purest form.[43] From the fundamentalist perspective, the *Mahavamsa* defines Buddhism as the foundation of Sinhalese identity and an essential component of Sri Lankan culture.

These beliefs have motivated Buddhist fundamentalists to promote their ideology through a strategy of participation within Sri Lankan society. That strategy originated in the efforts of Anagarika Dharmapala, a Buddhist revivalist active in the late nineteenth and early twentieth centuries. Dharmapala espoused a purification of Buddhist practice through the elimination of syncretistic elements derived from Hinduism, and he emphasized adherence to Buddhist standards of moral behavior. Most importantly, he advocated a concept of Sinhalese nationalism based on Sri Lanka's Buddhist heritage and supported the creation of an independent Buddhist state. Dharmapala's ideas strongly influenced the thinking of S. W. R. D. Bandaranaike, an important political leader during the early years of Sri Lankan independence. Bandaranaike had formed a Sinhalese Buddhist political group, the Sinhala Maha Sabha, in 1937, which reorganized as the Sri Lanka Freedom Party (SLFP) in 1951. The SLFP sought to advance the cause of Sinhalese nationalism and adopted the fundamentalist position that the Sinhalese represented a select group within Sri Lanka that would lead the country to an authentic Buddhist order. Its platform called for the establishment of Sinhalese as the national language and Buddhism as the state religion. The SLFP's agenda also received vigorous support from the United Monks' Front, an organization of Buddhist monks founded in 1956 to advance Buddhism's political interests. Growing nationalist sentiment and economic discontent brought the SLFP to power in 1956, resulting in Bandaranaike's election to the position of prime minister.[44]

Bandaranaike's government promptly made Sinhalese the country's official language and undertook various efforts to promote the status of Buddhism as the country's dominant religion. These measures met with considerable resistance, however, particularly from Sri Lanka's Tamil minority. Tamil opposition to the language law resulted in violent rioting in the nation's capital in 1957. Following the language riots, moreover, the more extreme elements within the Buddhist fundamentalist movement became increasingly unhappy with Bandaranaike's inability to secure Sinhalese Buddhist hegemony in Sri Lanka. Rising animosity toward Bandaranaike ultimately led to his assassination in 1959 by a member of the United Monks' Front. This act contributed to a decline in the influence of the latter group, but the SLFP continued to support the cause of Sinhalese Buddhist nationalism under the leadership of Sirimavo Bandaranaike, the former prime minister's widow.[45] Other political parties also began to support Sinhalese Buddhist interests, including the United National Party (or UNP), the SLFP's chief rival. A new national constitution established in 1972 thus preserved the status of Sinhalese as the official language and gave special recognition to Buddhism as the country's foremost religion.

The continuing efforts of Sinhalese Buddhists to protect their hegemony in Sri Lanka led to increasing discontent among the Tamil Hindu minority during the 1970s. Tamil activists sought greater political autonomy for the areas that they dominated, primarily in the northern and eastern parts of the island, and they wanted Tamil to be adopted as a second official language. During the late 1970s the UNP-led government made some concessions to the Tamils, but militants within the group were not satisfied. Moreover, many Sinhalese vigorously opposed the concessions. In response to anti-Tamil rioting in the early 1980s, civil war broke out as Tamil rebels began to engage in terrorism and guerrilla warfare to force the creation of an independent Tamil state. This conflict provoked a dramatic resurgence of Sinhalese Buddhist fundamentalism during the 1980s. To the fundamentalists, the Tamil independence movement posed a grave threat to Sri Lanka's Buddhist identity and to the dominant status of the Sinhalese. As a result, they opposed any government compromise with the Tamil militants. Fundamentalist sentiments intensified after a government agreement with India brought an Indian peacekeeping force to Sri Lanka from 1987 to 1990. The resumption of the civil war in the 1990s after the departure of the peacekeeping force further strengthened the fundamentalists' opposition to negotiation with the Tamils.

The fundamentalist resurgence that began during the 1980s again found expression in the positions adopted by Sinhalese political parties, which reasserted their determination to protect Buddhist interests.[46] The UNP-led government strongly supported the concept of Sri Lanka as a Buddhist state and established a separate government agency to promote Buddhist interests. Fundamentalist rejection of a negotiated settlement to the civil war, which would inevitably give the Tamils greater autonomy, has also influenced UNP policy. The UNP lost control of the government in 1994, when the daughter of the Bandaranaikes, Chandrika Kumaratunga, was elected president as a member of the People's Alliance Party on a platform of national reconciliation. As the leading opposition group, however, the UNP has been able to block Kumaratunga's efforts to enact constitutional changes designed to give the Tamils greater autonomy. In 1997, Sri Lanka's Buddhist clergy formed a commission to study the government's proposal to increase Tamil autonomy, which also concluded that adoption of the proposal would threaten the integrity of Sri Lanka and should be opposed.

During the civil war, Buddhist fundamentalists have thus used a strategy of participation to promote their view of Sri Lanka's national identity. According to that view, Sri Lanka is a Buddhist nation. The fundamentalists believe that any action that undermines Sri Lanka's Buddhist identity represents a threat both to the country and to its Sinhalese majority. Because they believe that Sri Lanka's sacred history has destined it to be a homeland for authentic Buddhism, they also see attacks on the state's religious identity as a threat to Buddhism itself. As a result, the Buddhist fundamentalists in Sri Lanka have maintained an uncompromising position regarding the resolution of the civil war, which has persisted throughout the 1990s.

The strategy of participation adopted by Sikh fundamentalists has been complicated by the Sikhs' status as a regionally based minority within India. As the majority group within the state of Punjab, Sikh fundamentalists recognize an essential bond between their religion and the region that they inhabit, and they define themselves as the defenders of the region's core values. As a result, they believe that they have a key role to play within the Sikh's regional society. Within India as a whole, on the other hand, the Sikhs are a small minority (accounting for roughly 2 percent of the population), and most Sikh fundamentalists do not identify strongly with India at large. They have sought to participate in Indian society and politics primarily to protect their own interests as a religious minority. Their efforts to create an autonomous Sikh state have also placed them in direct conflict with Indian society, leading some fundamentalists to abandon their strategy of participation at the national scale, as described later in this chapter. The nature of Sikh fundamentalist activism has thus been shaped by different factors within its regional and national contexts, based on the contrasting status of the Sikhs in India and in their Punjab homeland.

In defending their interests, Sikh fundamentalists have focused heavily on the issue of identity. They believe that the structure of Indian society poses a significant threat to the integrity of their religious traditions and to the survival of their distinctive culture. This threat differs from the threats perceived by the Hindu and Buddhist fundamentalist movements described previously, however. The latter groups fear that the connections between religious tradition and national identity will be diluted by the pluralistic nature of the societies in which they live and by the implementation of secularist government policies. The Sikhs, on the other hand, fear that ultimately they will be absorbed into India's dominant Hindu culture and that their distinct traditions and identity will be lost altogether. Sikh fundamentalists have thus been concerned primarily with establishing structures to protect their religious culture from the pressures of assimilation and accommodation. Their success during the 1920s in transferring control of Sikh temples from their hereditary custodians to the Shiromani Gurdwara Prabandhak Committee (SGPC) represented an important move in this direction. Later, their efforts focused more directly on increasing Sikh political authority over their regional homeland, a goal that continues to motivate the Sikh fundamentalist movement today.

Sikh fundamentalists originally pursued the expansion of Sikh political power through a strategy of participation, primarily through the vehicle of the Akali Dal, the Sikh political party. During the 1950s, the fundamentalists sought to establish a province within India where Sikhs would be the majority. At the time, the region dominated by the Sikhs was part of a larger state (also called Punjab) in which Hindus were in fact the majority. The Sikhs believed that this situation threatened their cultural integrity and economic interests. The Akali Dal thus asserted that the political boundaries of the region should be redrawn to give the Sikhs their own province. Hindus in the region resisted the idea of defining a new state in religious terms, however. As a result, the Akalis modified their strategy and proposed that a separate state be created for speakers of Punjabi, the language of the Sikh community. State boundaries had been revised in other parts of India to correspond to the distributions of language groups, and so the Akalis' proposal was politically feasible. Nonetheless, the government commission responsible for boundary revisions did not find the case for a separate Punjabi state to be compelling and declined to take action.[47]

The Akali Dal remained committed to the idea of a separate Punjabi province, however, and continued to pursue this objective into the 1960s. The Indian government remained opposed to the idea, seeing it as a threat to national unity and a potential source of religious conflict. Attitudes toward the Sikhs' political aspirations changed during the mid-1960s, however, following a brief war between India and Pakistan concentrated along the Punjab border. Sikh support of India's war effort convinced national leaders that the creation of Punjabi state would not endanger the nation. In 1966, the government thus divided the existing state of Punjab into three parts: a new, smaller Punjab, dominated by Punjabi speakers; the state of Haryana, dominated by Hindi speakers; and a shared capital city in Chandigarh. Within the redefined state of Punjab, Sikhs now accounted for a majority of the population.

The redrawing of Punjab's borders reinforced the fundamentalists' strategy of participation during the 1960s and 1970s. Although the Akali Dal was not the dominant political party in Punjab during this period, even among Sikhs, it did play an important role in Punjabi politics. On several occasions the Akali Dal joined with other parties to form ruling coalitions in the state, and it continued to provide a legitimate political voice for fundamentalist concerns. During the 1970s, it also expanded its involvement with secular issues, calling for new policies to promote economic development among the predominantly rural Sikhs and to increase access to the water resources that Punjab shared with surrounding states. At the same time, the Akalis grew increasingly critical of the concentration of power in the hands of India's central government and demanded greater provincial autonomy in the areas of economics and social and religious affairs.[48]

The growing conflict between Sikh fundamentalists and India's central government during the early 1980s eventually made it more difficult for the Akali Dal to maintain its participatory approach. During this time, radical Sikh fundamentalists began to advocate secession from India as the only way to resolve Sikh concerns. They asserted that the Sikhs represented a distinct nationality and claimed that Sikhs would be at a disadvantage economically, politically, and culturally as long as they remained part of India. Support for the creation of a fully independent Sikh political state, to be known as Khalistan, grew rapidly within the fundamentalist movement, but it also contributed to the factionalization of the Akali Dal. Although some Akalis supported the cause of Sikh independence, moderates in the party held to the view that Punjab should seek greater autonomy but still remain a part of India. Various leaders tried to bring the party together in demanding concessions from India's central government, but internal disagreements over the issue of Khalistan led to a growing split between Akali extremists and moderates, weakening the party's effectiveness.

The Akali Dal's influence was further challenged by the rise of a new fundamentalist leader, Jarnail Singh Bhindranwale, during the late 1970s. Bhindranwale's involvement in Sikh politics had in fact been encouraged by the Akalis' main rival, the Congress Party, in an effort to undermine support for the Akali Dal within the Sikh community. Bhindranwale turned out to be a more radical fundamentalist than most members of the Akali Dal, however, and he developed a large popular following, particularly among those who supported the idea of Sikh independence. As will be discussed later in this chapter, he had little use for the participatory strategy that the moderates in the Akali Dal had followed. In the early 1980s he began to advise Sikhs to acquire weapons to protect themselves against the Indian government, and his followers became involved in terrorist attacks against Hindus and Sikh moderates.[49] In 1982, Bhindranwale and a group of armed supporters took sanctuary in the Golden

Temple compound in Amritsar and made it their headquarters in their increasingly militant conflict with the Indian government. The central government responded by dismissing Punjab's state government in 1983 and establishing direct control over Punjabi affairs. The following year, the Indian military carried out an armed assault on the Golden Temple, killing Bhindranwale and many of his supporters.

These events severely hindered the Akali Dal's ability to maintain its strategy of participation, at least in the short term. The dismissal of the state government in 1983, for example, temporarily eliminated the Akalis' primary political forum. Moreover, moderates in the party continued to face violent opposition from radical fundamentalists who insisted that the creation of Khalistan should remain the Sikhs' top priority. A moderate Akali Dal government was elected to lead the state in 1985, but continuing violence in Punjab forced the central government to resume direct control of the state in 1987. When elections were again held in Punjab in 1992, the Akali Dal resumed its participation in the state government, but by this time moderates in the party had adopted a new approach emphasizing Punjabi rather than Sikh interests. In 1997, this regionalist approach in fact led to an alliance between the Akali Dal and Punjab's branch of the Bharatiya Janata Party, which together formed a ruling coalition in the state government. The connections between the Akali Dal and the Sikh fundamentalist movement have thus weakened in recent years. Some Akali leaders have criticized the party's decision to place less emphasis on religious concerns, however, and have argued that the Akali platform should explicitly address Sikh interests. This position was most forcefully advanced early in 1999 by Gurcharan Singh Tohra, president of the SGPC, the organization responsible for the supervision of Sikh temples. Tohra asserted that the current Akali leadership had abandoned Sikh interests to pursue its own political advancement and declared his intention to restore Sikh interests to the Akali Dal's agenda.

The Sikh fundamentalist strategy of participation has thus gone through various stages as conditions within India and the Sikh community have changed. The fundamentalist character of this strategy appears to have been weakened in the 1990s by the Akali Dal's pursuit of a more moderate course. Nonetheless, the potential still exists for the party to return to a more fundamentalist stance, or for some other group to take its place as the primary vehicle for legitimate fundamentalist activism. Many Sikhs remain committed to the fundamentalist goal of protecting their religious and cultural traditions and continue to see Hindu hegemony in India as a threat to their distinct identity. At the same time, most Sikh fundamentalists believe that change at both the regional and national levels should be achieved through participation rather than through violent conflict. The campaign of violence carried out by Sikh extremists in the 1980s and early 1990s, which resulted in the deaths of tens of thousands of Sikhs and Hindus, left lasting scars on the Sikh community, and

most fundamentalists adamantly dissociate themselves from the extremists' destructive tactics. In general, the Sikh fundamentalist movement thus continues
to see participation as an effective strategy for strengthening its own influence
within Sikh society and for protecting Sikh culture and identity from external
pressures.

In the various cases described, fundamentalist groups have adopted strategies of participation because they believe that their religious traditions embody
the core values of the larger society to which they belong. Fundamentalist
action in defense of those traditions serves to realize the larger society's true
character. This interpretation by fundamentalists of their social role depends
on the recognition of two distinct boundaries. The first boundary defines the
fundamentalist group itself and is based on adherence to a specific set of religious beliefs and practices. The second boundary defines the larger society to
which the fundamentalist group is linked and generally derives from a common
national history or culture. The fundamentalists recognize a connection between the meanings of these two boundaries and through a strategy of participation seek to make that connection explicit in the larger social order. In many
instances, this effort focuses on clarifying the relationship between the fundamentalists' religious identity and a more widely held sense of national identity.
Such efforts have an inherent potential for producing social conflict, since nonfundamentalists reject the fundamentalists' claim that they represent society's
true values. Fundamentalists believe that they cannot legitimately abandon this
social role, however. Even if they have little chance of bringing about change,
they believe that they have a sacred obligation to preserve the authentic character of the larger society and restore its proper moral order. This sense of obligation is central to the identity of the fundamentalist groups pursuing a strategy
of participation.

The ways in which fundamentalist groups have addressed this obligation
vary, reflecting differences in their particular beliefs and in the nature of their
surrounding contexts. Christian fundamentalists in the United States believe
that they must ensure that biblical values are integrated into the structure of
U.S. society. In their view, this goal conforms to the original intention of the
country's founders and must be realized for the United States to function as a
moral society. For Islamic fundamentalists following a strategy of participation,
social obligation centers on the creation of an Islamic state. This goal mirrors
the prophet Muhammad's founding of an ideal society and provides a means of
establishing an authentic Islamic community within a modern political context.
Some Muslim groups, like the Tablighi Jamaat, concentrate instead on reinforcing personal piety, but most Islamic fundamentalists believe that the totality of Islam requires the complete transformation of the social and political
order. Finally, in various contexts within South Asia, fundamentalists have defined their obligation to society in terms of the protection of group identity.
Matters of identity are particularly important in South Asia because of the

region's great religious diversity and because of the complex relationships that exist among its various religious traditions. Hindu and Buddhist fundamentalists specifically believe that they must protect the religious identity of their national culture from the debilitating effects of pluralism and secularism. Among Sikh fundamentalists, on the other hand, the sense of obligation focuses on a smaller regional community and its protection from the forces of assimilation.

PATTERNS OF ISOLATION

The patterns of domination and participation described in this chapter reflect the assumption by many fundamentalists that they have a moral responsibility to the rest of society. That sense of responsibility leads them to remain legitimately engaged with the larger society, even if segments of it reject their ideology. Some fundamentalist groups believe, however, that they cannot rightly maintain ties to the society in which they are situated. They consider society to be hostile and corrupt, its values inherently incompatible with their religious beliefs, and its institutions beyond redemption. Such groups often treat society at large as their enemy, the "other" that threatens their religious traditions. Fundamentalist groups in this category thus adopt strategies of isolation with respect to the surrounding society. They define themselves through the use of ideological boundaries that tend to be both exclusive and absolute, precluding routine connections with the outside world. In their view, this approach offers the only viable means of protecting their threatened beliefs and preserving their distinct identity.

Fundamentalist groups have implemented strategies of isolation in diverse ways, based on different ways of interacting with the world beyond their own boundaries. Some view the surrounding society as a potential vehicle for promoting their own goals, despite its moral corruption, and so attempt to manipulate it from outside. Such groups must moderate their degree of isolation, but they do so solely with the intention of strengthening their own fundamentalist community. Other groups have attempted to achieve a more complete withdrawal from society, concentrating on their own religious communities and ignoring events in the outside world. Groups adopting this approach see any formal contact with the larger society as intrinsically corrupting and keep such contacts to a minimum. Finally, a third type of isolationist group rejects these defensive approaches and instead mounts a direct attack on the hostile external society. Groups of this type believe that to preserve their traditions and identity, they must destroy the external forces that threaten them. All fundamentalist groups that adopt a strategy of isolation thus define the surrounding society as a threat, but they have dealt with that threat in quite different ways.

The anti-Zionist branch of haredi Jewish fundamentalism represents a key example of the isolationist strategy. The haredim initiated such a strategy in Eastern Europe in the late 1800s to avoid corruption by modernist and secularist elements in Jewish society, and those who migrated to Palestine maintained this strategy in the midst of the larger Zionist society there. The strategy of isolation took on a new religious significance for the haredim in Palestine, however, based on their conviction that the idea of a Zionist state contradicted the principles of Jewish sacred history. They believed that while awaiting divine redemption they were destined to remain in a state of exile and were obliged to refrain from political action. They thus saw participation in the creation of a Jewish state as a violation of their religious beliefs.[50] As discussed previously, many haredim later abandoned their opposition to Zionist society, adopting a strategy of participation based on an attitude of neutrality toward the legitimacy of a Jewish state. This non-Zionist attitude, most closely associated with Agudat Israel, reflected a belief among more moderate haredim that the Jewish community encompassed liberal and secular Jews as well as the Orthodox. The anti-Zionist core of haredi fundamentalism rejected that idea, however. In their view, Jewish migration to Palestine had created two distinct and irreconcilable societies, one composed of authentic Jews and the other dominated by secular Zionists.[51] The anti-Zionists asserted that any contact with nonbelievers would diminish the truly religious rather than improve the surrounding society. As a result, organized as the Edah Haredit and Neturei Karta, they continued to isolate themselves from Zionist society. After independence, they refused to recognize the legitimacy of the state of Israel, and since then, they have taken various steps to remain separate from it. They generally do not to vote in public elections, for example, and use religious exemptions to avoid compulsory military service.

In implementing their strategy of isolation, the anti-Zionist haredim have physically separated themselves from Israeli society. Most live in highly segregated neighborhoods, primarily located in Jerusalem and Bnei Brak. They leave their neighborhoods as infrequently as possible, and often pressure nonharedi residents to move out.[52] High birthrates among the haredim have led to their continued expansion into new residential areas, increasing conflict with others over neighborhood control. Within their neighborhoods, they have also established their own institutional structures. Their schools are designed to protect haredi children from the corrupting influences of the outside world. Haredi schools stress the ideological gulf that separates the anti-Zionists from Israeli society, encouraging students to avoid participating in secular institutions and to reject the legitimacy of Israeli statehood.[53] The haredim have also established yeshivas where young men devote themselves to Torah study, often well into adulthood. Finally, the haredim have sought to create a separate "kosher" economy that conforms to religious law. Haredi food stores of course sell only kosher items, and meat is marked with the name of the rabbi that certified it. Haredi stores enforce strict rules of behavior among their customers, requiring that women be modestly dressed. The stores contain no elaborate displays, and their furnishings tend to be austere. Some provide makeshift synagogues so customers will not miss afternoon or evening prayers. As a service to the haredi community, some stores are organized as cooperatives or nonprofit businesses and sell their goods at lower prices than other stores. Others keep prices low by reducing profit margins or by paying their employees lower wages.[54]

The creation of separate haredi institutions has led to divisions within the anti-Zionist community, however. The Edah Haredit, the anti-Zionists' largest formal organization, has attempted to provide institutions and services to serve its constituents' needs. As a result, this group has had to maintain some contacts with the surrounding society, in officially registering marriages and divorces, procuring food from nonharedi sources, and acquiring licenses for slaughter-houses.[55] The less formally organized Neturei Karta criticizes such concessions. Its leaders assert that cooperation with the state is theologically unacceptable and therefore advocate complete withdrawal from Israeli society. Moreover, they oppose any form of legislation regarding religious matters, arguing that merely the discussion of such matters by the secular government desecrates Judaism. Opposition to the state of Israel is so strong among the most radical members of Neturei Karta that they have even made symbolic gestures of sup-port for the state's enemies, such as the Palestinian Liberation Organization.[56]

Despite their efforts to isolate themselves, however, members of the Edah Haredit and the Neturei Karta do not completely ignore Israeli society. They have vigorously protested certain government policies and patterns of public behavior and have demanded government action to remedy conditions that threaten their ability to practice traditional Judaism. A major concern of the haredim has been Israeli society's disregard for the religious prohibition against secular activity during the Sabbath. The haredim have repeatedly called for the government to close streets in or near their neighborhoods on the Sabbath, asserting that the traffic disturbs their Sabbath observances and offends their religious values.[57] Similarly, they have protested against movies and sporting events on the Sabbath. To protect traditional Jewish standards of behavior, they have lobbied the government to establish gender segregation on the bus routes running through their neighborhoods, as discussed at the start of chapter 1. The haredim have also objected to the intrusion of secular values into their world, demanding that the government remove billboards and public advertise-ments that display immodestly dressed female models.

Because they generally do not vote, the anti-Zionists have had to use other methods to express their positions on these issues. Most often, they have used street demonstrations (fig. 3.9). Public protests directed at traffic on roads near their neighborhoods have become a regular occurrence on the Sabbath, for example. Occasionally these protests have led to violence, such as throwing rocks at passing cars, although the rabbinical leadership of the Edah Haredit has condemned such actions. Haredi militants have also set fire to public adver-

Figure 3.9   Haredim rally against Israel's Supreme Court. Although they isolate themselves from Israeli society, the haredim have often tried to influence government policies. This rally was held in response to a series of court rulings allowing shopping on the Sabbath, restricting exemptions from military service for yeshiva students, and limiting ultra-Orthodox control over conversions to Judaism. In keeping with their belief in public gender segregation, the haredim used long cloth barriers to keep male and female demonstrators apart. Jerusalem, Israel, 1999. *Source:* Media Exchange International.

tisements that they consider to be offensive and have harassed nonharedi women whose clothing does not conform to their standards of modesty. The Edah Haredit has exerted influence through more formal channels as well. Several members of the organization sat on the government-appointed committee that recommended gender segregation on certain bus lines, for example.[58]

These attempts to manipulate government policy and public behavior signify a degree of interaction with society at large, but the haredim pursue these efforts from a position of isolation. They do not act as participants in society, and their intention is not to reform the state of Israel, whose existence they do not acknowledge. Rather, they react against surrounding conditions to declare and protect their own identity and to challenge the legitimacy of the state. Their protests against activity near their neighborhoods on the Sabbath, for example, are intended to strengthen their isolation from secular influences and proclaim their outrage at violations of Jewish law. The haredim's manifestation of ideological boundaries that separate them from other Israelis also contributes to group solidarity among them and reinforces the socialization of young people into their community.[59] Their interactions with the surrounding state thus serve to promote their strategy of isolation and maintain the ideological boundaries that they have defined.

A somewhat different pattern of isolation characterizes the Santi Asoke movement, an expression of Buddhist fundamentalism that emerged in Thailand during the 1970s.[60] The movement's founder, Rak Rakpong, had been a media celebrity in Thailand during the 1960s, working as a movie producer, songwriter, and television host. In 1970 he underwent a conversion experience, was ordained as a Buddhist monk, and became known as Phra Bodhirak (the title "Phra" denoting his status as a monk). During the early 1970s, Bodhirak became increasingly critical of the role of Buddhism in Thai society. Buddhism has in fact been the state religion throughout the modern history of Thailand, but as such it has taken on some of the characteristics of a "civil religion," serving as one element of a larger national identity. This trend has been reinforced by the strong ties between the government and the Sangha, the monastic order officially responsible for overseeing Buddhist practices in Thailand. In Bodhirak's view, the Sangha had become preoccupied with superficial concerns and paid too little attention to the essential meanings of Buddhism. He argued that because the Sangha did not effectively promote Buddhism, Thai society had been corrupted by secular popular culture, materialistic values, and the vices associated with them, such as drug and alcohol use, gambling, and prostitution. Bodhirak asserted that these trends had undermined the influence of traditional Buddhist values.

To counter this moral decline, Bodhirak founded the Asoke movement in 1975.[61] In doing so, he did not intend to reform society through direct action, which he claimed was not feasible. Instead, he sought to create an alternative to the corrupt secular world, which would serve as an example to others. The purpose of the movement was thus to establish a society whose structure would reflect Buddhist principles. To achieve that goal, Bodhirak proposed that the new society would function more or less in isolation from the outside world. He believed that it should be located in a rural setting, to protect its members from corrupting secular influences and to enable them to lead a simple, self-sufficient way of life. He further believed that the new society should reject traditional social distinctions and thus asserted that it should contain monks as well as lay people and that it should not practice gender segregation. Bodhirak also emphasized the importance of religious study and discussion as means of building a unified moral community. His vision of the perfect society thus focused less on abstract issues of religious belief than on strategies for integrating a Buddhist ideology into everyday life. According to Bodhirak, authentic Buddhism could be preserved in Thailand only through the creation of such a society.

Bodhirak and his followers established a network of small agricultural communities. The first, Santi Asoke, was founded near the capital city of Bangkok in 1976. Two others, Sisa Asoke and Sali Asoke, were established the same year in nearby provinces in central and eastern Thailand, and several more have been created since then. The Asoke communities follow strict rules of behavior. Their residents are vegetarians and do not consume alcohol, coffee, or tea. They live in simple dwellings, wear plain clothing, and most do not wear shoes. They also reject the idea of personal possessions. Their economic life focuses on the goal of self-sufficiency. Most members work on communal organic farms, and the group mills its own rice and produces its own cloth. The group also operates a number of stores and restaurants, where it sells whatever surplus it produces. The revenue from these operations pays for items that the group cannot manufacture itself. Some members also work outside the rural communities, to help generate income for the group. In terms of their religious practices, the Asoke fundamentalists reject many traditions associated with Thai folk Buddhism, such as belief in magic. They also criticize the use of many traditional rituals and have banned images of Buddha from the assembly halls where they worship. The movement focuses solely on what it considers to be the authentic spiritual essence of Buddhism.

The austere way of life in the Asoke communities has kept them fairly small, and permanent residents number only in the thousands. The group has attracted a broader number of sympathizers, however, perhaps as many as one hundred thousand. Because these supporters continue to live within the mainstream of Thai society, they have been able to generate influence for the Asoke movement in the outside world. One key supporter has been Chamlong Srimuang, a former governor of Bangkok and general in the Thai army. Drawing on his popularity as a politician known for his high ethical standards, Chamlong founded the Palang Dharma ("Power of Virtue") Party in 1988 to promote traditional moral values, and under his leadership the party received the fundamentalists' support and provided a forum for their views. The party is not officially associated with the Asoke movement, however, and many of its leaders have no ties to the fundamentalists. Moreover, while such connections allow the movement's views to be more widely disseminated, the Asoke movement continues to define itself as being separate from the mainstream of Thai society.

The ideological boundaries created by the Asoke movement have in turn led to persistent tensions with Thai authorities. Bodhirak's condemnation of the Buddhist establishment drew sharp criticism from the government and the Sangha. Because of his distinctive views, the Sangha Council in 1989 ordered Bodhirak to renounce his claim of being a Buddhist monk and to stop his unauthorized ordination of others as monks. Bodhirak refused and was eventually arrested and charged with violating Buddhist discipline and distorting Buddhist teachings. Bodhirak then declared the Asoke movement to be an independent group, not under the Sangha's jurisdiction. Although freedom of religion is guaranteed in Thailand's constitution, the courts ruled that as a Buddhist Bodhirak was legally bound to recognize the authority of the Sangha Council. Bodhirak was thus convicted of the charges against him in 1995 and received a sentence of six years in prison (subsequently reduced to a two-year suspended sentence). In addition, seventy-nine followers whom he had unlawfully ordained received short sentences for impersonating a monk. After his conviction, Bodhirak asserted that the Asoke movement would continue, despite government opposition.

The strategy of isolation pursued by the Asoke movement thus has not resulted in its complete separation from Thai society. Its oppositional stance, particularly regarding the Buddhist establishment embodied in the Sangha, has led to conflict with Thai authorities. At the same time, supporters operating within the mainstream of society have helped to extend the influence of the movement's beliefs beyond its core membership. Ultimately, though, the Asoke movement remains isolationist in character. Its conviction that Thai society has been corrupted by modernism and secularism establishes a distinct ideological boundary between the group and its surroundings, and that boundary is reinforced in everyday practice by the self-sufficient isolation of the Asoke communities.

The isolationist strategies of the anti-Zionist haredim and the followers of the Santi Asoke movement reflect their belief that to create an authentic religious community they must first separate themselves from the surrounding social order. A corollary of this belief is that the creation of such a community does not require the moral or political transformation of the larger society, only isolation from it. In this sense, the groups discussed above exhibit an inner-directed focus, concentrating primarily on perfecting their own community. Other fundamentalist groups have used strategies of isolation to pursue a radically different type of objective. The latter groups see their isolation from the rest of society as an interim step, not as a final goal. They ultimately seek to create an ideal religious community but believe that to do so they must bring about a moral or political restructuring of the surrounding society. For such groups, strategies of isolation serve to define a context from which they can launch an ideological assault against society at large. These groups thus maintain an outer-directed focus, aimed at effecting change beyond their own ideological boundaries. Because their goals place them in direct conflict with the surrounding social or political order, these more aggressive isolationists have repeatedly resorted to violence in trying to advance their cause.

A number of Islamic fundamentalist groups in Egypt have adopted this more militant approach since the 1970s. Many of the early leaders of these groups were Muslim brothers who rejected the strategy of participation adopted by the brotherhood during Sadat's regime. They considered the surrounding society to be incapable of genuine reform and defined themselves in opposition to it. These radicals were strongly influenced by the ideas of Sayyid Qutb, the militant Muslim brother who advocated the destruction of Egypt's secular government during the late 1950s and early 1960s. Qutb argued that the restoration of an authentic Islamic order offered the only means of curing society's problems, which derived from the moral bankruptcy of the state. He thus proposed that, like the prophet Muhammad, true believers should isolate themselves from the unbelieving society that surrounds them and initiate a holy war to establish the rule of Islam. Such ideas strongly appealed to Egyptian militants during the Islamic resurgence of the early 1970s and laid the ideological groundwork for the formation of new fundamentalist groups.

The most isolationist of these new groups was the Jamaat al-Muslimin ("Society of Muslims"), founded by Shukri Mustafa, a former Muslim brother.[62] The members of this group considered themselves to be the only true Muslims; in their view, the rest of Egyptian society was corrupt and unbelieving and had to be completely rebuilt to conform to Islamic principles. Following Muhammad's model, they prepared for jihad against the surrounding society by separating themselves from it. Most of the group's members lived in low-income residential areas in Cairo's outer suburbs, isolated from mainstream social and religious institutions. They prayed at home rather than in the official mosques, removed their children from state schools, and refused military service. Other members abandoned mainstream society entirely and relocated to the mountainous regions of Upper Egypt. The group's strategy during the early 1970s focused primarily on building its numerical strength, which grew to several thousand members by the middle of the decade. As it grew, the group became more aggressive, however, and began to attack bars and movie theaters. After some of its members were arrested for such actions, the group retaliated in 1977 by kidnapping and executing a government official. The government responded by imprisoning hundreds of members and executing the group's leaders, including Mustafa. The group subsequently declined in importance as a fundamentalist organization, although it did not disappear completely.

Another important radical movement, al-Jihad ("Holy War"), arose during the late 1970s and early 1980s through the merger of several smaller groups committed to overthrowing Egypt's secular government.[63] Unlike the Jamaat a-Muslimin, al-Jihad did not consider the majority of Egyptians to be unbelievers. Its leading ideologue, Muhammad Abdul Salam Faraj, argued that the main enemy of authentic Islam was the secular state, not society in general. He further asserted that jihad should focus on destroying the existing political structure by violent means, since no other approach would prove effective. These views became the foundation of al-Jihad's ideology. It thus isolated itself from its surrounding context politically rather than socially and defined itself as the enemy of the state, but not of the Egyptian people. Indeed, al-Jihad's leaders believed that their violent opposition to the government would eventually inspire a mass uprising against Sadat's government. To further this end, a group of Egyptian soldiers with ties to al-Jihad assassinated Sadat in 1981. This action did not instigate the popular uprising that al-Jihad had anticipated, instead provoking an armed confrontation with Egyptian security forces in the city of Asyut, a major al-Jihad stronghold. Over a hundred militants were killed, and thousands were jailed. Government suppression of the group limited its impact over the next decade. It became increasingly active during the 1990s, however, and has been tied to a number of bombings in Egypt and other Muslim countries.

As it has resumed its violent tactics, al-Jihad has been closely linked to another militant organization, Jamaa al-Islamiyya, also known as the Islamic Group. The Islamic Group originated amid the mixture of groups that originally made up al-Jihad and after Sadat's assassination became Egypt's leading militant group. It has undertaken a broader range of activities than al-Jihad and seeks to build a larger popular following.[64] In other ways, though, the two groups are quite similar. Like al-Jihad, the Islamic Group has a loose organizational structure, and independent cells within the group operate more or less autonomously. The group follows the teachings of Omar Abdel Rahman, a former religious leader of al-Jihad, who advocates the violent overthrow of Egypt's secular government. Both the Islamic Group and al-Jihad have received assistance from Iran and other Islamic militants outside Egypt, which they have used to support a campaign of violence against government officials, the police, Egyptian Coptic Christians, and secularists. In the early 1990s, the Islamic Group also began to target foreign tourists in Egypt. These attacks have been motivated in part by the fundamentalists' conviction that tourism has corrupted Egyptian society, but they also seek to weaken the government by threatening a major source of foreign income. They staged their deadliest attack in 1997 at an ancient temple in Luxor, killing fifty-eight tourists and four Egyptian guards. Both the Islamic Group and Talaeh al-Fath ("Vanguards of Conquest"), an offshoot of al-Jihad, claimed responsibility for the massacre. Together, al-Jihad and the Islamic Group have killed over twelve hundred people in Egypt since the early 1990s. They have also committed terrorist acts in other countries, including al-Jihad's 1995 bombing of an Egyptian embassy in Pakistan and the Islamic Group's attack on the World Trade Center in New York City in 1993. Rahman, who came to the United States in 1990 to escape house arrest in Egypt, was convicted of planning the latter attack, and in 1996 received a life sentence.

The Islamic Group and al-Jihad have thus developed a strategy of isolation different from that of the Jamaat al-Muslimin. While the latter group was completely alienated from Egyptian society, the Islamic Group and al-Jihad do not challenge the Islamic character of the Egyptian masses. Rather, they reject the legitimacy of the Egyptian state and are committed to its destruction. As a result, their sense of isolation is defined against the surrounding political order, and they carry out their jihad against the government as underground movements. This approach has not physically separated them from the rest of society, but it has clearly isolated them in an ideological sense.

Militant Islamic fundamentalists in Algeria have adopted a strategy closer to that of the Jamaat al-Muslimin. Fundamentalist activity first became visible in Algeria during the early 1980s, partly in response to the success of Iran's Islamic Revolution. Activists demonstrated in favor of incorporating the sharia into Algerian law, and radicals waged a limited guerrilla war against the government. Algeria's ruling party, the National Liberation Front (FLN), vigorously suppressed these early militants but made various concessions to the rise of Islamic sentiments within Algeria as a whole. These actions minimized the impact of fundamentalism on Algerian society until the late 1980s, when government corruption and economic decline heightened popular opposition to the FLN. The government subsequently instituted democratic reforms that legalized the formation of new political parties and provided for open elections. The largest of the new parties was the Islamic Salvation Front (FIS), a fundamentalist group that sought to create an Islamic state based on the sharia. Their more immediate goals included a ban on alcohol and stricter gender segregation in public. The FIS enjoyed considerable success in local elections held in 1990, and in the first round of national elections in 1991 it led all other parties by a significant margin. Fearing a fundamentalist takeover, the Algerian military installed an emergency government early in 1992, which invalidated the recent elections, outlawed the FIS, and imprisoned some of the party's leaders. Some FIS members remained committed to the goal of changing Algeria's political order from within, but the more militant fundamentalists abandoned this strategy and began a prolonged campaign of violence. Many of these militants had fought with the mujahideen in Afghanistan's war against Soviet occupation and so had extensive training in guerrilla warfare.

During the 1990s, the Armed Islamic Group (GIA) emerged as the most powerful of the guerrilla organizations, and it adopted a strict strategy of isolation. Influenced by the ideas of Sayyid Qutb, the GIA saw itself as a revolutionary vanguard distinct from the rest of Algerian society and the only true representative of Islam. Its goal was to create an Islamic state through the violent overthrow of Algeria's secular government and the destruction of its un-Islamic society. The group considered moderate Muslims to be infidels and thus legitimate targets of violence. Based on these convictions, the GIA and other radicals waged a brutal guerrilla war against Algerian society throughout the 1990s, reinforced by a continual flow of young recruits alienated by government repression and economic hopelessness. At first the GIA targeted those associated with the mainstream establishment, including government officials, the police, journalists, and intellectuals. It also attacked foreigners, both to rid the country of external influences and to undermine the country's tourist economy. Algerians who did not follow the sharia eventually became targets as well. The radicals were accused of carrying out drive-by shootings of unveiled women in the mid-1990s, for example. As the guerrilla war continued, the GIA became increasingly indiscriminate in its use of violence as a means of destabilizing society and demonstrating the government's inability to maintain order. The radicals staged random attacks on ordinary citizens and by the late 1990s had massacred entire villages. The government has tried to suppress the rebel militants, but it has not been able to bring the violence to an end. By the late 1990s, human rights groups estimated that as many as 150 thousand people had been killed during this conflict. Many Islamic fundamentalists in Algeria reject the extreme violence of the GIA. Some of those who advocate the use of violence against the state object to indiscriminate attacks on civilians. Others, such as the FIS, favor a more moderate approach based on political negotiation. The GIA and other radical groups became the dominant force in Algerian fundamentalism during the 1990s, however, and defined the conflict between militant Islam and Algerian society in violent, oppositional terms.

Sikh extremists have also engaged in violent aggression against society from a position of ideological isolation. As discussed previously, Sikh fundamentalists have generally tried to bring about change through strategies of participation. During the late 1970s and early 1980s, however, a group of Sikh radicals forcefully rejected the participatory approach. This radical movement developed around the teachings of Jarnail Singh Bhindranwale. Bhindranwale, a Sikh preacher, had originally been encouraged to enter politics by secular politicians, who hoped that he would weaken the influence of the Akali Dal. Bhindranwale quickly became the most radical leader in the Sikh community, however. In fighting the threats to Sikh unity and identity, Bhindranwale specifically advocated a return to the Sikhs' militaristic traditions and their emphasis on armed action. An important focus of his ideology was the traditional Sikh concept of the "two swords," representing temporal and spiritual authority. In the late 1600s and early 1700s, Sikh leaders had asserted that the two swords must function as one in the fight against Muslim oppression, since the political and religious repercussions of that conflict were inseparable. Military action in defense of the Sikh community thus took on the character of a religious obligation. Bhindranwale argued that contemporary Sikhs must respond to the threats that they faced in a similar manner, by recognizing the essential connections between militant political action and religious duty.

As Bhindrinwale's radicalism intensified during the 1980s, he became increasingly committed to a strategy of isolation. This strategy had two components, reflecting the Sikhs' position as a regionally based religious minority within India. The primary component involved separation from Indian society, as expressed in the demand for an independent political state, Khalistan. Bhindranwale and his followers did not consider themselves to be part of India. They saw themselves as a separate ethnoreligious community with distinct interests. As a result, they believed that the surrounding Hindu majority represented a continuing threat to the Sikhs, religiously, economically, and politically. They were particularly antagonistic toward the Hindu fundamentalists who argued that the Sikhs belonged to a larger Hindu nation. As part of this component of his strategy of isolation, Bhindrinwale advocated armed resistance to the Indian government and to the state government that he felt had betrayed Sikh interests. His followers began to attack Hindus living in Punjab, killing local Hindu leaders as well as ordinary citizens. The second component of Bhindranwale's isolationist strategy involved the relationship between the radicals and the larger Sikh community. Bhindranwale asserted that the Sikh community was indivisible and that all of its members should fight for the same goals. Nonetheless, he condemned those who did not adhere to his interpretation of Sikhism and considered Sikhs who had adopted secular ways or who opposed the creation of Khalistan to be enemies of his cause. In practice, then, the ideological boundaries that defined his movement did not include the entire Sikh population. Indeed, after the radicals began to use terrorist tactics against their enemies, they occasionally chose moderate Sikhs as targets.

The radicals became more violent as the 1980s progressed, hoping that conflict with the Indian state would unify the Sikh community and build support for an independent Khalistan. Eventually the increase in violence led Bhindranwale and his followers to isolate themselves physically, and in 1982 they took sanctuary in the Golden Temple compound in Amritsar to protect themselves from the Indian authorities. The compound housed both the Golden Temple and the Akal Takht, the two most important Sikh shrines. A nearby complex contained the offices of the Akali Dal and the SGPC. Many Sikhs also lived in the temple compound's residential quarters, including the moderate leader of the Akali Dal. Bhindranwale turned the compound into an armed camp, however, amassing a large arsenal and establishing fortifications. Sikh radicals continued to move into the compound, including many wanted for murder and other terrorist acts. In response to this radical buildup, the government installed security forces around the temple compound, which engaged the radicals in several gun battles early in 1984. As tensions mounted many of the more moderate Sikhs living in the compound surrendered, but Bhindranwale and about five hundred followers remained firmly entrenched. The government decided to remove the radicals by force and in June 1984 staged a commando assault on the temple compound. Hundred of Sikh radicals were killed in the attack, including Bhindranwale himself. Many unarmed Sikh pilgrims to the Golden Temple were also killed, as were a smaller number of Indian soldiers. The entire Sikh community was outraged by the attack on the temple compound. Surviving radicals responded with a new wave of terrorism, and Sikhs across northern India engaged in violent protests. As a result of their strong martial heritage, Sikhs were significantly overrepresented in the Indian armed forces at that time, and many chose to desert after the attack on the temple compound. Later in the year the nation's prime minister, Indira Gandhi, was assassinated by two Sikhs in her personal bodyguard. Hindus subsequently retaliated, killing thousands of Sikhs in riots throughout the country.

These events increased the sense of threat felt by fundamentalist Sikhs, and they continued to advocate the creation of an independent Khalistan, by force if necessary. The militants escalated the terrorist campaign that they had initiated in the early 1980s, ultimately resulting in over twenty-five thousand deaths. In the years immediately following the attack on the temple compound, moreover, radical groups like the Khalistan Liberation Force had little difficulty in recruiting members. During the early 1990s, the radicals also exerted increasing control over daily life in Punjab, posting decrees banning the consumption of alcohol and other unacceptable behavior and threatening to kill those who voted in public elections. The government responded with increasing brutality, however, killing or imprisoning most of the radicals' leaders.

The cumulative effects of a decade of destruction and violence, as well as the return of elected government in Punjab in 1992, significantly weakened support for the radicals within the Sikh community. By 1993, the government had nearly eliminated the radical Sikhs' presence in Punjab.[65] Sporadic bombings and assassinations did continue throughout the 1990s, often directed by radicals living in exile, particularly in Canada and the United Kingdom. Nonetheless, most Sikh fundamentalists abandoned the radicals' strategy of isolation during the 1990s and renewed their efforts to promote Sikh interests through legitimate political participation. Many Sikhs still hoped to achieve greater political autonomy, or even an independent Sikh state, but through democratic means.

The various examples previously discussed illustrate that the strategy of isolation does not preclude interactions between fundamentalists and the surrounding society. Groups adopting this strategy are isolated in the sense that they define themselves as being ideologically separate from the society in which they are situated. The group's dissociation from society derives primarily from its religious ideology, but it may be reinforced through spatial segregation. Even physically isolated fundamentalists cannot avoid some form of interaction with the surrounding society, however. By definition, fundamentalism cannot exist in a social vacuum. It necessarily involves a reaction against a perceived threat. Interaction with some threatening context thus represents an essential part of all fundamentalist strategies. Isolationist groups differ from those using other approaches in that they do not act primarily out of a sense of responsibility to larger social structures. They are instead concerned with demonstrating their own distinctiveness and preserving their beliefs and values. Isolationist fundamentalists have used various means to achieve these ends, from political lobbying to street demonstrations to terrorist violence. All of these forms of activism provoke hostility toward the group, because they are seen as attempts by self-defined outsiders to dictate how society should operate. The attitude of the larger society toward isolationist groups thus also generates interactions between them, even while reinforcing the fundamentalists' ideological isolation.

CONCLUSIONS

The cases examined in this chapter illustrate the diversity of fundamentalism as a global phenomenon. All of the fundamentalist groups discussed in this
chapter have tried to protect certain religious traditions from perceived threats,
but their specific goals and methods have varied considerably. In large part,
such variations reflect the different ways in which fundamentalist groups relate
to the larger context in which they are situated. A few groups in the Islamic
world have been able to assert complete authority over the surrounding society
or political state and have thus controlled a wide range of institutions and social
structures. A much larger number of groups maintain that they represent the
core values of the surrounding society or state, even though they do not control
it. Such groups seek to restore those core values by actively participating in the
larger society, although they also may develop exclusive institutions to serve the
immediate needs of their own members. Finally, some groups do not consider
themselves to be part of the larger society and attempt to isolate themselves
from it, at least in terms of their own self-identity. From this position of isolation they may simply try to minimize contact with the larger society, or they
may engage in active conflict with it.

The three broad strategies examined in this chapter provide a useful taxo-
nomic framework for characterizing the nature of different fundamentalist
groups, the ideologies that motivate them, and their impacts on the contexts in
which they are situated. Like all such frameworks, however, these strategies do
not fully capture the complexity of the phenomena to which they are applied.
Although most fundamentalist groups have a clear association with one of the
three strategies, their actions may also incorporate elements of the other two.
Dominant fundamentalist groups have clearly followed strategies of isolation
in the context of international relations, for example, since their fundamentalist
policies inevitably alienate them from other countries. Similarly, fundamentalists pursuing a strategy of participation have in some cases achieved a position
of domination at a local or regional scale, as have isolationists within the context
of their own separate communities. Moreover, groups sharing the same general
strategy—of domination, participation, or isolation—differ significantly in
terms of their specific goals and the methods that they use to achieve them.
Such differences necessarily derive from the contextual nature of fundamentalism as a form of religious expression. Despite their conceptual similarities, individual fundamentalist movements are shaped primarily by the specific
characteristics of particular groups and the places they inhabit: the beliefs held
by the group in question, the cultural history of the place in which it emerged,
the group's relationship to surrounding social and political structures, and the
individual actions and ideas of its members. The diverse nature of the groups
encompassed by each of the broad strategies outlined in this chapter thus rep-

resents a manifestation of fundamentalism's inherent contextuality, as well as a key element of its complexity as a global phenomenon.

NOTES

1. Abdulaziz A. Sachedina, "Activist Shi'ism in Iran, Iraq and Lebanon," in *Fundamentalisms Observed*, Martin E. Marty and R. Scott Appleby, eds. (Chicago: University of Chicago Press, 1991), 403–56.

2. Sami Zubaida, "The Quest for the Islamic State: Fundamentalism in Egypt and Iran," in *Studies in Religious Fundamentalism*, Lionel Caplan, ed. (London: Macmillan Press, 1987), 42–8.

3. Dilip Hiro, *Holy Wars: The Rise of Islamic Fundamentalism* (New York: Routledge, 1989), 158–69; Youssef M. Choueiri, *Islamic Fundamentalism* (London: Pinter Publishers, 1990), 154–60.

4. Parviz Daneshvar, *Revolution in Iran* (London: Macmillan, 1996), 94–109; Asaf Hussain, *Islamic Iran: Revolution and Counter-Revolution* (London: Frances Pinter, 1985), 123–30.

5. Mohsen M. Milani, *The Making of Iran's Islamic Revolution* (Boulder, Colo.: Westview Press, 1988), 263–6; Daneshvar, *Revolution in Iran*, 143–5; Hussain, *Islamic Iran*, 137–9.

6. Milani, *The Making of Iran's Islamic Revolution*, 255–60; Hussain, *Islamic Iran*, 142–7; Daneshvar, *Revolution in Iran*, 133–5.

7. Milani, *The Making of Iran's Islamic Revolution*, 308–10; Homa Omid, *Islam and the Post-Revolutionary State in Iran* (New York: St. Martin's Press, 1994), 181–6.

8. Hiro, *Holy Wars*, 207–26.

9. Hussain, *Islamic Iran*, 187.

10. Daneshvar, *Revolution in Iran*, 153–6.

11. Shireen T. Hunter, *Iran after Khomeini* (New York: Praeger, 1992), 24–32, 95–6.

12. Omid, *Islam and the Post-Revolutionary State in Iran*, 177.

13. Azadeh Kian, "Gendered Occupation and Women's Status in Post-Revolutionary Iran," *Middle Eastern Studies*, 31, no. 3 (July 1995): 407–21.

14. Ahmed Rashid, "Pakistan and the Taliban," in *Fundamentalism Reborn? Afghanistan and the Taliban*, William Maley, ed. (New York: New York University Press, 1998), 72–3.

15. William Maley, "Introduction: Interpreting the Taliban," in *Fundamentalism Reborn? Afghanistan and the Taliban*, William Maley, ed., 15.

16. Rashid, "Pakistan and the Taliban," 80–1.

17. Anthony Davis, "How the Taliban Became a Military Force," in *Fundamentalism Reborn? Afghanistan and the Taliban*, William Maley, ed., 43–71.

18. Kenneth J. Cooper, "Taliban Massacre Based on Ethnicity," *Washington Post*, November 28, 1998, 1(A).

19. Suzanne Goldenberg, "Heart of Darkness," *The Guardian (London)*, October 13, 1998, 2.

20. Anthony Hyman, "Russia, Central Asia and the Taliban," in *Fundamentalism Reborn? Afghanistan and the Taliban*, William Maley, ed., 104–16.

21. Nancy Hatch Dupree, "Afghan Women under the Taliban," in *Fundamentalism Reborn? Afghanistan and the Taliban*, William Maley, ed., 145–66.

22. Milton Viorst, "Sudan's Islamic Experiment," *Foreign Affairs* 74, no. 3 (May/June 1995): 45–58.

23. Steve Bruce, "The Moral Majority: The Politics of Fundamentalism in Secular Society," in *Studies in Religious Fundamentalism*, Caplan, ed., 177–94.

24. The exact size of the audience for the *700 Club* and other religious programs has been subject to various interpretations, as discussed in Steve Bruce, *Pray TV: Televangelism in America* (London: Routledge, 1990), 96–109.

25. Gilles Kepel, *The Revenge of God: The Resurgence of Islam, Christianity and Judaism in the Modern World* (University Park: Pennsylvania State University Press, 1994), 178–80.

26. Ehud Sprinzak, "Three Models of Jewish Religious Violence: The Case of Jewish Fundamentalism in Israel," in *Fundamentalism and the State*, Martin E. Marty and R. Scott Appleby, eds. (Chicago: University of Chicago Press, 1993), 469–77.

27. John O. Voll, "Fundamentalism in the Sunni Arab World: Egypt and the Sudan," in *Fundamentalisms Observed*, Martin Marty and R. Scott Appleby, eds., 376–81.

28. David Kelly, "Illegal Muslim Group Building Power in Egypt," *San Francisco Chronicle*, May 21, 1993, 10(A).

29. Hiro, *Holy Wars*, 82–7.

30. Muhammad M. El-Hodaiby, "Upholding Islam," *Harvard International Review* 19, no. 2 (Spring 1997): 20–4.

31. Sven Cederroth, "Islamism in Multireligious Societies: The Experience of Malaysia and Indonesia," in *Questioning the Secular State: The Worldwide Resurgence of Religion in Politics*, David Westerlund, ed. (New York: St. Martin's Press, 1996), 365–6.

32. Singapore subsequently withdrew from Malaysia in 1965 to become an independent republic.

33. Manning Nash, "Islamic Resurgence in Malaysia and Indonesia," in *Fundamentalisms Observed*, Martin Marty and R. Scott Appleby, eds., 703–5; K. S. Jomo and Ahmad Shabery Cheek, "Malaysia's Islamic Movements," in *Fragmented Vision: Culture and Politics in Contemporary Malaysia*, Joel S. Kahn and Francis Loh Kok Wah, eds. (Honolulu: University of Hawaii Press, 1992), 79–106.

34. "Kelantan Govt Bans 'Un-Islamic Performances," *The Straits Times* *(Singapore)*, July 6, 1995, 18; "No Public Singing and Dancing, Decrees Kelantan Government," *The Straits Times (Singapore)*, October 7, 1995, 21; "Paying for Your Groceries? Ladies, Queue Here," *The Straits Times (Singapore)*, January 9, 1996, 20; Nick Cumming-Bruce, "Malay Party on Lonely Crusade for Islam," *The Guardian (London)*, May 14, 1996, 11.

35. Brendan Pereira, "No Islamic Laws for Kelantan . . . for Now," *The Straits Times (Singapore)*, October 5, 1996, 2.

36. Yogendra K. Malik and V. B. Singh, *Hindu Nationalists in India: The Rise of the Bharatiya Janata Party* (Boulder, Colo.: Westview Press, 1994), 13–5.

37. Peter van der Veer, *Religious Nationalism: Hindus and Muslims in India* (Berkeley: University of California Press, 1994), 130–7.

38. Ibid., 124–6.

39. Christophe Jaffrelot, *The Hindu Nationalist Movement in India* (New York: Columbia University Press, 1996), 315–9; Malik and Singh, *Hindu Nationalists in India*, 31–8.

40. Robert G. Wirsing and Debolina Mukherjee, "The Saffron Surge in Indian Politics: Nationalism and the Future of Secularism," *Asian Affairs: An American Review* 22, no. 3 (Fall 1995): 181–206.

41. Bruce Matthews, "Buddhist Activism in Sri Lanka," in *Questioning the Secular State*, David Westerlund, ed., 284–96.

42. Also see Donald K. Swearer, "Fundamentalistic Movements in Theravada Buddhism," in *Fundamentalisms Observed*, Martin Marty and R. Scott Appleby, eds., 647–8; Tessa J. Bartholomeusz and Chandra R. de Silva, "Buddhist Fundamentalism and Identity in Sri Lanka," in *Buddhist Fundamentalism and Minority Identities in Sri Lanka*, Tessa J. Bartholomeusz and Chandra R. de Silva, eds. (Albany: State University of New York Press, 1998), 1–35.

43. Gananath Obeyesekere, "Buddhism, Nationhood, and Cultural Identity: A Question of Fundamentals," in *Fundamentalisms Comprehended*, Martin E. Marty and R. Scott Appleby, eds. (Chicago: University of Chicago Press, 1995), 234–6.

44. Swearer, "Fundamentalistic Movements in Theravada Buddhism," 636–41.

45. Kingsley M. de Silva, "Buddhist Revivalism, Nationalism and Politics in Modern Sri Lanka," in *Fundamentalism, Revivalists and Violence in South Asia*, James Warner Björkman, ed. (Riverdale, Md.: Riverdale Company, 1988), 146–7.

46. Matthews, "Buddhist Activism in Sri Lanka," 292; George D. Bond, "Conflicts of Identity and Interpretation in Buddhism: The Clash between the Sarvodaya Shramadana Movement and the Government of President Premadasa," in *Buddhist Fundamentalism and Minority Identities in Sri Lanka*, Tessa Bartholomeusz and Chandra de Silva, eds., 41–4.

47. Ishtiaq Ahmed, "Religious Nationalism and Sikhism," in *Questioning the Secular State*, David Westerlund, ed., 269–70.

48. Ahmed, "Religious Nationalism and Sikhism," 271–4; T. N. Madan, "The Double-Edged Sword: Fundamentalism and the Sikh Religious Tradition," in *Fundamentalisms Observed*, Martin Marty and R. Scott Appleby, eds., 611; Emile Sahliyeh, "Religious Fundamentalisms Compared: Palestinian Islamists, Militant Lebanese Shi'ites, and Radical Sikhs," in *Fundamentalisms Comprehended*, Martin E. Marty and R. Scott Appleby, eds. (Chicago: University of Chicago Press, 1995), 138.

49. Paul Wallace, "The Dilemma of Sikh Revivalism: Identity versus Political Power," in *Fundamentalism, Revivalists and Violence in South Asia*, James Warner Björkman, ed., 69.

50. Aviezer Ravitzky, *Messianism, Zionism and Jewish Religious Radicalism* (Chicago; University of Chicago Press, 1996), 68–9.

51. Gerald Cromer, "Withdrawal and Conquest: Two Aspects of the Haredi Response to Modernity," in *Jewish Fundamentalism in Comparative Perspective: Religion, Ideology and the Crisis of Modernity*, Laurence J. Silberstein, ed. (New York: New York University Press, 1993), 177.

52. Samuel C. Heilman and Menachem Friedman, "Religious Fundamentalism and Religious Jews: The Case of the Haredim," in *Fundamentalisms Observed*, Martin Marty and R. Scott Appleby, eds., 239.

53. Jackson Diehl, "Jerusalem Children Moving to Religious Schools," *Washington Post*, September 26, 1989, 21(A).

54. Dina Shiloh, "Shopping Religiously," *Jerusalem Post*, July 30, 1997, 7.

55. Menachem Friedman, "Jewish Zealots: Conservative Versus Innovative," in *Fundamentalism in Comparative Perspective*, Lawrence Kaplan, ed. (Amherst: University of Massachusetts Press, 1992), 162–3.

56. Ravitzky, *Messianism, Zionism and Jewish Religious Radicalism*, 70, 76–7.

57. Joel Greenberg, "Jerusalem Road Is Secular-Religious Battleground," *New York Times*, July 15, 1996, 3(A).

58. Haim Shapiro, "Separate Seating Buses to Run in Bnei Brak and Jerusalem," *Jerusalem Post*, July 10, 1997, 1.

59. Cromer, "Withdrawal and Conquest," 177; Ravitzky, *Messianism, Zionism and Jewish Religious Radicalism*, 70–3.

60. Swearer, "Fundamentalistic Movements in Theravada Buddhism," 667–77.

61. Marja-Leena Heikkila-Horn, "Two Paths to Revivalism in Thai Buddhism: The Dhammakaya and Santi Asoke Movements," *Temenos* 32 (1996): 93–111.

62. Zubaida, "The Quest for the Islamic State," 39–42; Voll, "Fundamentalism in the Sunni Arab World," 381–3; Hiro, *Holy Wars*, 72–3.

63. Voll, "Fundamentalism in the Sunni Arab World," 383–4; R. Hrair Dek-

mejian, *Islam in Revolution: Fundamentalism in the Arab World* (Syracuse, N.Y.: Syracuse University Press, 1985), 97–101; Abdel Azim Ramadan, "Fundamentalist Influence in Egypt: The Strategies of the Muslim Brotherhood and the Takfir Groups," in *Fundamentalism and the State,* Martin Marty and R. Scott Appleby, eds., 152–83.

64. Chris Hedges, "Egypt Fears More Violent 'Holy War' by Militants," *New York Times*, December 19, 1993, 3(1).

65. "Peace at Last in Punjab," *Economist* (May 22, 1993): 45.

4

GEOGRAPHICAL DIMENSIONS OF
FUNDAMENTALISM

The preceding chapters have surveyed the basic concerns of a variety of fundamentalist movements and their diverse interactions with the larger social contexts in which they are situated. Throughout these discussions, the ideologies
and objectives espoused by fundamentalist groups have repeatedly exhibited
important geographical dimensions. Hindu fundamentalists seek to reclaim the
supposed site of Lord Ram's birth in Ayodhya so that they can build a new
temple there. Haredi Jews continue to demand that roads in and around their
residential enclaves in Jerusalem be closed to traffic on the Sabbath, to prevent
their exposure to irreligious behavior. In Afghanistan, the Taliban have imposed rigid limitations on the spatial mobility of women, effectively confining
many to their homes. Fundamentalists in Pakistan strive to create an authentic
Islamic state in which the sharia serves as the basis of the country's legal system. Christian fundamentalists in the United States have boycotted the Disney
Company to protest its accommodation of activities sponsored by gay and lesbian organizations in its theme parks. These examples obviously involve many
different beliefs and strategies, but together they clearly illustrate the importance of issues of space and place in fundamentalist thought and action.

The prevalence of such issues reflects the inherently geographical character
of essential fundamentalist concerns. Fundamentalists typically respond to
threats against their religious traditions through expressions of territoriality, by
attempting to control the meaning or use of the geographical space that they
inhabit. The territorial strategies employed by fundamentalists take various
forms but often concentrate on enforcing adherence to traditional religious
practices or on separating the group from the "other" by which it is threatened.
Similarly, the fundamentalist conviction that all realms of human activity must
conform to religious principles inevitably produces distinctive spatialities, or

spatial constructions of social order.[1] The insistence on public segregation of
the sexes in Jewish and Islamic fundamentalism represents an obvious instance
of the incorporation of religious belief into the spatial structuring of social
forms and relations. The geographical concept of place, defined as a location
to which a culturally defined meaning has been attached, also figures prominently in fundamentalist concerns.[2] In defending the integrity of a sacred site,
establishing a distinct religious community, or advocating loyalty to a traditional
religious homeland, fundamentalists implicitly use place-based meanings to define the religious significance of the locations involved. In sum, geographical
issues are central to the defining concerns of fundamentalist movements and
yield important insights into fundamentalism's motives and objectives.

The purpose of this chapter is to examine the nature and impacts of the
principal geographical dimensions of contemporary fundamentalism. The geographical concerns of different fundamentalist movements are again quite varied in their details, reflecting the diverse contexts and traditions from which
different movements have arisen. In general terms, however, these concerns
revolve around three basic themes: the control of sacred places and sacred
space, the use of religious principles to govern secular space, and the intercon-
nectedness of religious and territorial identity. Each of these themes reflects
ideological concerns essential to fundamentalism. The attention given to sacred
places and sacred space derives most commonly from the belief that a holy
site associated with the group's sacred history is threatened by some form of
desecration and must be protected to ensure the survival of the group's traditions. Some fundamentalists also focus on the role of particular places in fulfilling the sacred destiny of their group, such as the creation of a messianic
religious utopia. Fundamentalist efforts to control secular space reflect the
conviction that corrupting influences threaten the integrity of the traditional
moral order, which must be upheld through adherence to authentic beliefs and
practices in all aspects of life. Efforts to enforce adherence to their values
typically result in the creation of a distinct spatial expression of the fundamentalists' sense of moral community. Such expressions take various forms, from
religiously segregated neighborhoods to theocratic political states, but they all
involve some type of territorial control. Finally, the fundamentalist concern
with matters of religious identity, essential in differentiating between true believers and the "other," often contains a significant geographical component.
That component may be based on the group's attachment to an area having
crucial historical or symbolic associations with their religious traditions, or it
may arise from the desire to establish an effective territorial base for promoting
the group's interests. In either case, the assertion of a territorial identity represents a crucial part of the group's response to perceived threats.

The geographical themes outlined above represent an essential component
of contemporary fundamentalism. They have been the primary focus of fundamentalist activism in varied settings and have generated considerable conflict

between fundamentalists and their opponents. Fundamentalist responses to these themes have not followed a uniform pattern, however. These themes encompass a wide variety of particular concerns, which have been expressed in distinctive ways by different groups. Indeed, these themes are crucial in understanding the intrinsically contextual nature of fundamentalism, since in effect they define the specific concerns that tie fundamentalist movements to their surroundings. The remainder of this chapter thus looks at the various ways in which these themes have been expressed by different groups, both to elaborate on the geographical nature of fundamentalist concerns and to consider the impacts of those concerns in diverse contexts.

THE CONTROL OF SACRED SPACE

The belief that particular locations are endowed with sacred qualities appears in many forms within the world's various religions.[3] The perceived sanctity of a place in some cases derives from its specific religious function, for example as a ritual point of contact between the human and the divine or as the seat of religious authority. Sacred places are also defined by their associations with crucial events in the founding or development of a religion and by their prophesied role in the fulfillment of a religion's sacred history. Whatever the source of their sacred character, because such locations figure prominently in traditional religious beliefs and practices, they are of central importance to fundamentalists. In particular, fundamentalist groups are intensely concerned with establishing or maintaining control over sacred locations as part of their defense of religious tradition. Such concerns commonly lead to conflict with outside forces, since fundamentalists rarely have undisputed command of these sacred locations. As a result, the desire to control sacred space represents a principle motive of fundamentalist activism in many different contexts.

Fundamentalist concerns with this issue derive primarily from the belief that a sacred location is being desecrated or endangered in some way. Typically the perceived threat to the site arises from the larger processes or forces in opposition to which a fundamentalist movement has defined itself. In some cases this threat involves the encroachment of secular influences on sacred space, but it can also grow out of religious conflicts. Such conflicts may develop when a fundamentalist group and other adherents of the same religion disagree over the proper care and use of a sacred place. Haredi fundamentalists in Jerusalem, for example, have protested the attempts of less traditional Jews to pray at the sacred Western Wall in groups of mixed gender, in violation of traditional practice. Conflicts over sacred space also arise when groups from different religious traditions have assigned sacred meaning to the same location, as in the controversy between Jews and Muslims concerning the Temple Mount in Jerusalem. In struggles over a contested sacred place that they already control, fundamentalists generally adopt a defensive strategy and may try to isolate the site physically or at least limit access to it. In cases where fundamentalists have attempted to reclaim sites that are controlled by others, however, they have used more aggressive approaches, as in the destruction of the Babri Mosque in Ayodhya by Hindu fundamentalists.

Fundamentalist concerns with sacred locations do not focus solely on the threat of desecration. Some groups also believe that they must take action to ensure that the religiously ordained roles of their sacred places are properly fulfilled. Such efforts may reflect a basic incompatibility between the beliefs of fundamentalists and of other members of the same religion who control a sacred site. Saudi attempts to suppress political activity among Iranian Muslims on pilgrimage in Mecca, for example, have led fundamentalist leaders in Iran to condemn the management of holy sites in Saudi Arabia by that country's Muslim monarchs. Concerns over the fulfillment of a place's religious purpose also arise when fundamentalists assign a special status to the place in their beliefs, particularly in matters concerning the culmination of their religious history. Religious Zionists, for example, want to maintain control over biblical lands occupied by Israel as a means of advancing the ultimate redemption of the Jewish people through their return to their promised land. These kinds of concerns with sacred places do not always have intrinsic fundamentalist overtones, since they are not necessarily tied to the perception of a threat against the group and its beliefs. Nonetheless, because they may involve disputes over the use and control of space, they too have the potential to produce conflict and have on occasion become a key issue for fundamentalist groups seeking to assert the legitimacy of their traditional beliefs.

Fundamentalist concerns with sacred space are often interpreted by outsiders to be largely symbolic, but this view ignores the spiritual immediacy attributed to holy sites by religious traditionalists. Fundamentalists do not try to protect a sacred place from desecration simply as a means of symbolizing their larger struggle against some threatening force. The sacred places that they defend perform routine but vital functions in their religious lives, serving as concrete manifestations of religious tradition and authority. The defense of such places takes on a genuine sense of urgency for fundamentalists. Similarly, efforts to control locations associated with the fulfillment of sacred history are grounded in the belief that the group's actions will contribute directly to the actualization of divinely inspired events. The desire to control sacred space thus derives from issues of profound importance to fundamentalists and underlies some of the most intense conflicts involving fundamentalist groups in recent years.

A notable example of the fundamentalist concern with sacred space appears in the ongoing disputes between Jews and Muslims over the Temple Mount in Jerusalem (fig. 4.1). For both groups, this site has significant associations with the sacred past. According to Jewish belief, the Temple Mount contains the

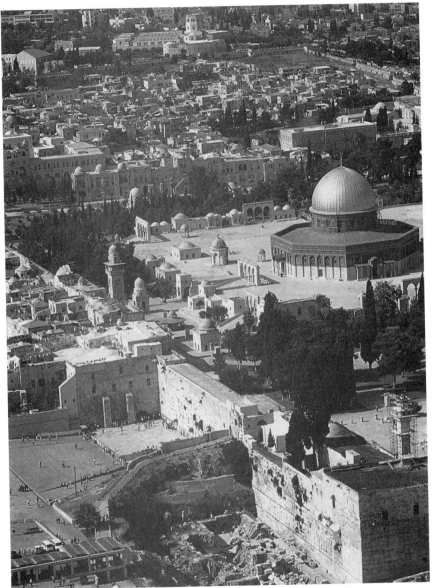

Figure 4.1 The Temple Mount in Jerusalem. Both Jewish and Islamic fundamentalist emphasize the sacred meaning of this site. To Jews, it encompasses the location of Jerusalem's second Temple, including the surviving Western Wall, located in the center of the photograph. Several important Muslim shrines occupy the top of the Temple Mount, including the Dome of the Rock (in the upper right of the picture), which according to Muslim belief houses the rock from which Muhammad ascended on a trip to heaven. *Source:* Corel. Copyright 2000, Rowman & Littlefield Publishers, Inc. and its licensors. All rights reserved.

biblical location where Abraham constructed the altar on which he was to sacri-fice his son Isaac. This location later became the site of the first and second Jewish Temples in Jerusalem. The first Temple, completed in 957 B.C., housed the Ark of the Covenant and became ancient Judaism's preeminent religious shrine. After successive desecrations of the first Temple by other groups, con-struction of the second Temple began at the same site in 20 B.C. The new Temple again became the center of Jewish religious life but was destroyed in A.D. 70 by Roman forces suppressing a Jewish rebellion. Only a fragment of the second Temple remained intact: the Western Wall (also known as the Wail-ing Wall), which runs alongside a portion of the Temple Mount. The Western Wall thus represents Judaism's most sacred site and serves as a major pilgrim-age center and place of prayer.

The Temple Mount has also considerable importance as an Islamic holy place, however. Like Jews, Muslims consider Abraham (or Ibrahim) to be their ancestral patriarch, and so his association with the location gives it a sacred character. Moreover, most of the Temple Mount lies within an enclosure known in Arabic as Haram al-Sharif ("Noble Sanctuary"), which contains two of Islam's oldest and most important shrines: the Dome of the Rock, built between A.D. 685 and 691 and distinguished by its octagonal layout and golden dome, and al-Aqsa Mosque, originally completed in A.D. 705. According to Muslim belief, the first of these structures contains the rock from which Mu-hammad ascended on a miraculous journey from Jerusalem to heaven and back to Mecca. Al-Aqsa Mosque also commemorates that journey, but was built as a congregational mosque to accommodate large numbers of worshippers. It was only the second such mosque to be built, the first being in Mecca. After the holy cities of Mecca and Medina, Haram al-Sharif represents Islam's third most sacred place.

The importance of this site to both Jews and Muslims has led to persistent controversies over issues of access and control, which have been exacerbated in recent decades by the broader conflict between Israelis and Palestinians. Prior to 1967 Jordan controlled the Old City of Jerusalem, where the Temple Mount is located, but Israel occupied the Old City during the Six-Day War and has held on to it ever since. Muslims have retained authority over Haram al-Sharif itself, but have become increasingly concerned with perceived threats to the sacred site from Israel's secular society and from Jewish militants. At the same time, some Jewish militants have asserted their intention to reclaim possession of the Temple Mount, to protect it from desecration and to ensure their access to it. Other Jewish fundamentalists, who believe that the Temple Mount can be reclaimed only through divine action, concentrate on preventing improper ritual behavior at the Western Wall. This contested sacred site has thus become a primary focus of fundamentalist activism among both Jews and Muslims in Jerusalem and has generated a variety of conflicts involving the two religious communities.

The religious Zionist branch of Jewish fundamentalism has made repeated attempts to reclaim control of the Temple Mount, as a means of advancing the redemption of the Jewish people. During the early 1980s, a number of militant activists devised plans to take over the Temple Mount or attack the Muslim shrines there.[4] The most elaborate of these plots, carefully drawn up over a period of several years by a small cadre of Gush Emunim members, proposed to destroy the Dome of the Rock and al-Aqsa Mosque using explosives that the group had stockpiled.[5] The militants responsible for this plan believed that the Muslim shrines desecrated the Temple Mount and that their destruction was a necessary step in preparing for the return of the Messiah. The Israeli authorities arrested the conspirators in 1984, before the plan was carried out. Efforts by religious Zionist fundamentalists to reclaim the Temple Mount have continued, however. The Temple Mount Faithful, an activist group with close ties to Gush Emunim, has undertaken an especially persistent campaign over the past two decades to end Muslim control of the site.

The activities of the Temple Mount Faithful have revolved around two key issues: their desire to hold prayers on the Temple Mount and their ultimate goal of building a third Temple on the site of the earlier two. The first of these issues has created controversy even within the Jewish community. Israel's Chief Rabbinate has prohibited Jews from praying on the Temple Mount because in doing so they could accidentally violate the location of the Holy of Holies, the inner sanctuary of the first Temple where the Ark of the Covenant had been kept in ancient times. The Israeli government also prohibits Jews from praying on the Temple Mount, in keeping with the 1967 agreement to allow Muslims to retain authority over the site, and on numerous occasions the police have arrested members of the Temple Mount Faithful who tried to force their way into the Muslim compound on Jewish holy days. Nonetheless, the group's members continue their efforts to hold prayers on the Temple Mount.

They have also continued to assert their goal of building the third Temple. In their demonstrations near the Temple Mount during the 1990s, they have repeatedly displayed a massive block of stone, transported by truck and weighing over four tons, which they have dedicated as the cornerstone of the new Temple. These actions have provoked great concern among Muslims in Jerusalem, but they have also been opposed by haredi fundamentalists who believe the new Temple cannot be built until after the return of the Messiah. The religious Zionists' goal of building a third Temple on the Temple Mount has also attracted the attention of some Christian fundamentalists in the United States, who believe that the Jewish people must be restored to the land of Israel and their Temple reconstructed before the Second Coming of Christ can occur. A number of wealthy Christian fundamentalists have, in fact, made significant donations to the Temple Mount Faithful and related groups to help achieve this end.[6]

The haredi branch of Jewish fundamentalism has been strongly critical of the religious Zionists' strategies concerning the Temple Mount. Although the haredim do not accept the authority of Israel's Chief Rabbinate, they believe that the religious Zionists should obey the prohibition against prayer on the Temple Mount and avoid any action that might inadvertently contaminate the Holy of Holies, the precise location of which is not known. Moreover, because they reject the idea that human actions can affect the progress of Jewish sacred history, they believe that the faithful should make no effort to rebuild the Temple before the Messiah has arrived and reclaimed the Temple Mount. The haredim thus have not been concerned with asserting immediate control over the entire sacred site or with destroying the Muslim shrines. Instead, they are primarily interested in protecting the site from desecration by the improper actions of other Jews. Again, they have condemned the goals and actions of the Temple Mount Faithful, which they view as heretical. In addition, haredi fundamentalists have denounced Jews who fail to observe traditional practices when praying at the Western Wall. Based on biblical tradition and Jewish law, the haredim believe that men and women praying at the Western Wall must be physically segregated from one another, that women's voices must not be audible to men engaged in prayer, and that only men may read from the Torah or wear prayer shawls (fig. 4.2). In defense of these beliefs, they have persistently demonstrated against Conservative and Reform Jews (largely from the United States) who have tried to pray at the Western Wall in groups composed of both men and women.[7] The haredim have also opposed attempts by Jewish women to assert their right to pray aloud and read from the Torah at the Western Wall. A group known as Women of the Wall has tried since the late 1980s to convince authorities to allow them to worship at the sacred site as they see fit, but the Israeli courts have generally sided with the haredim in enforcing traditional practices.[8]

Among Islamic fundamentalists, the controversy surrounding control of the Temple Mount has produced an overriding concern with the defense of the Muslim shrines there. They see the efforts of religious Zionists to reclaim the Temple Mount not only as a challenge to Muslim control of the sacred site but as a threat to the very core of their religious traditions. Even the holding of prayers on the Temple Mount by religious Jews would endanger the sanctity of the place, from the Muslim point of view. This defensive stance emerged after Israel captured the Old City of Jerusalem during the Six-Day War and was strongly reinforced by the plots to attack Haram al-Sharif in the early 1980s. Subsequent efforts by the Temple Mount Faithful and similar groups to reclaim the Temple Mount further heightened the concerns of Islamic fundamentalists, who saw the defense of their holy sites as a sacred responsibility. In response to perceived threats against Haram al-Sharif, Muslim activists staged violent demonstrations outside al-Aqsa Mosque on various occasions during the late 1980s and 1990s, often hurling rocks from their compound on the Temple Mount onto Jews praying at the Western Wall directly below.

Figure 4.2   Gender segregation at the Western Wall. In support of the traditional prohibition against men and women praying together, a gender barrier divides the open space in front of Jerusalem's Western Wall. The area at right is reserved for women; a larger area to the left is reserved for men. Jerusalem, 1995. *Source:* CORBIS/Annie Griffiths Belt.

The most notable of these protests took place in 1990, when fundamentalist preachers urged worshippers at al-Aqsa Mosque to prepare to defend Haram al-Sharif against the Temple Mount Faithful, which was reportedly planning to lay the cornerstone for the third Jewish Temple inside the Muslim compound several days later. On the appointed day, a riot erupted among several thousand Muslims gathered outside al-Aqsa Mosque, who began to throw rocks down on a crowd of over twenty thousand Jews celebrating the Succoth holiday at the Western Wall, injuring more than twenty people. Israeli police stormed Haram al-Sharif and in the ensuing fighting killed at least nineteen of the Muslim protesters and wounded well more than a hundred (fig. 4.3). The violence provoked a series of Palestinian attacks against Israeli police and civilians in the following weeks. In 1996 a new threat to Haram al-Sharif sparked violence between Israeli police and Islamic fundamentalists: the opening of a tunnel connecting a series of archaeological sites excavated beneath the Temple Mount. Muslim activists vigorously opposed the tunnel's opening, claiming that it violated Islamic sacred space, that it would undermine the shrines atop the Temple Mount, and that it would enable Jewish extremists to plant explosives

Figure 4.3 Bloody handprints on the Temple Mount. In 1990, Israeli police used violent force to quell a Muslim protest on the Temple Mount, killing nearly twenty protesters and wounding over a hundred. As evidence of the conflict, Muslim fundamentalists soaked their hands in the blood of the wounded and left bloody handprints on a wall inside the Haram al-Sharif compound. Jerusalem, Israel, 1990. *Source:* CORBIS/David H. Wells.

beneath the shrines. During a demonstration against the tunnel's opening, Israeli police stormed the Muslim compound, killing three Palestinians and wounding several dozen.

During the late 1990s, Islamic fundamentalist concerns intensified, as support for the reclamation of the Temple Mount became more widespread within the Jewish community. Members of the ruling political coalition in Israel began to support the idea that Jews should have the right to pray on the Temple Mount, for example. In addition, reports surfaced in 1998 that Jewish extremists were developing new plans to destroy the Muslim shrines inside Haram al-Sharif, causing the Israeli government to increase security to prevent such attacks from occurring. The impending arrival of the new millennium in the Christian calendar also raised the possibility that Christian fanatics might target the Temple Mount as a means of bringing about Armageddon and the Second Coming of Christ. Early in 1999, Israeli police arrested fourteen members of an extreme Christian cult from the United States on charges that they planned to carry out such a plan. Islamic fundamentalists have responded to these various threats by asserting that they will protect Haram al-Sharif at any cost.

Perceived threats against their holy sites have thus been a major focus of activism among Israel's Islamic fundamentalists. This concern has encompassed sacred places outside of Jerusalem as well. A fundamentalist group known as the Islamic Movement has mapped all of the Muslim holy sites in Israel and has sought to restore them and return them to the custody of Muslim authorities.[9] Of particular concern are mosques taken over by the Israelis during their War of Independence in 1948, which have since remained under government control and have often been closed to Muslims as places of worship.[10] Controversy has also developed around the Tomb of the Patriarchs, in Hebron. Jews and Muslims both believe that this site contains the tombs of Abraham, his wife, Sarah, his son Isaac and grandson Jacob, and their wives, Rebecca and Leah. The tombs themselves are believed to lie in a cave beneath al-Ibrahimi Mosque, a medieval Muslim structure. After Israel captured Hebron during the Six-Day War, Jewish settlers began moving into the predominantly Palestinian city and demanded access to the holy site. The tomb was thus opened to both Jews and Muslims, leading to persistent friction between the two groups. After a Jewish settler massacred twenty-nine Muslims praying at the site in 1994, authorities installed permanent partitions separating the areas open to Jews and Muslims. Muslims objected to the partitions, claiming that they desecrated a site that for centuries had been used exclusively by followers of Islam. In recent years, as the Israelis and Palestinians have tried to work out a peace agreement that would include the return of Hebron to Palestinian control, access to the site has become an important issue. Islamic fundamentalists eventually want to prohibit Jews from worshipping at the site, but Jewish fundamentalists reject this possibility and insist on maintaining a Jewish settlement near the tomb. As at the Temple Mount, the overlapping traditions of the two groups have thus created a contested space in which both have an abiding interest.

The reluctance of Jewish fundamentalists to give up Hebron also relates to the broader concern of religious Zionists with maintaining control over *Eretz Israel*, the sacred Land of Israel. The concept of *Eretz Israel* refers to the promised land in which the Jewish people once lived in accordance with divine law and to which they will be restored by the Messiah. For Gush Emunim and other religious Zionists, the reclamation of *Eretz Israel* signifies an essential step in the fulfillment of Jewish sacred history, and unlike the haredi fundamentalists, members of Gush Emunim believe that this step can be advanced through human action. The exact boundaries of *Eretz Israel* are not precisely defined, but Gush Emunim interprets them in very broad terms, reaching from the Euphrates River in Iraq to the Nile Delta.[11] The group's immediate concern, however, is to maintain control over the West Bank region captured from Jordan during the Six-Day War, historically a major portion of the Palestinians' homeland but also the site of the biblical regions of Judaea and Samaria. To achieve that goal, the Gush actively worked to establish Jewish settlements throughout the West Bank, starting in the mid-1970s.[12] Since then it has created dozens of such settlements, containing as many as twenty-five thousand Gush followers. Although an additional one hundred thousand Israelis have settled in the occupied territories, members of Gush Emunim represent an especially significant force because they attach explicit religious significance to the preservation of their settlements. They see the Palestinians as intruders in Judaism's sacred territory and believe that giving up political control of any portion of *Eretz Israel* would be blasphemous.[13] Palestinian demands for greater autonomy in the region have thus generated a new sense of threat among the religious Zionists and have strengthened their fundamentalist commitment to *Eretz Israel*. The resulting tensions on the West Bank between religious Zionists and Palestinians have become a major obstacle to peace.

The various conflicts over sacred space in Israel and the occupied territories have had important political implications for the region. In their efforts to protect their sacred sites, Jewish and Islamic fundamentalists have both infused contemporary events with religious meanings not easily reconciled to processes of political compromise. An analogous situation exists in India, where the geographical intersection of Hindu and Muslim traditions has also led to religious and political controversy. The primary focus of that controversy is the city of Ayodhya, where a long-standing dispute over control of the Babri Mosque emerged in the 1980s as a defining concern of the Hindu fundamentalist movement. As the fundamentalists' political power has grown during the 1990s, their commitment to building a Hindu temple on the site of the demolished mosque has become an increasingly volatile issue within Indian politics, generating opposition from secular Hindus as well as the Muslim community.

The roots of the controversy can be traced back to the early 1500s, when the Mogul emperor Babar ordered the construction of a mosque in Ayodhya, which subsequently bore his name. According to Hindu tradition, the mosque was built on the site of an older temple, which had marked the birthplace of Lord Ram, an incarnation of the Hindu god Vishnu and hero of the *Ramayana* epic. Scholars have found little evidence of the existence of such a temple, but the Moguls apparently did build mosques on existing religious sites as a means of asserting their authority during their conquest of India. In any case, Hindus continued to pray at the mosque, and Ayodhya remained an important Hindu pilgrimage site under Muslim rule. After the British took control of the region in the nineteenth century, they tried to prevent religious conflict by prohibiting Hindu pilgrims from entering the mosque compound; but Hindu reverence for the site led to persistent conflicts over the issues of control and access. In 1949, shortly after India gained its independence, Hindu militants took over the mosque and declared that an idol of Ram had miraculously appeared there. This event provoked widespread rioting among Hindus and Muslims and caused the Indian government to close the mosque to members of both religious communities. Thus after 1949, the mosque was no longer used as a place for Muslim worship. Hindus and Muslims continued to dispute control of the site, however. Although the mosque itself did not have unusual religious significance, Muslims opposed giving up the site for fear that other mosques in northern India would also be taken from them. This fear was reinforced by Hindu claims that other mosques also stood on the sites of former temples and should be removed.

During the 1980s, the Hindu fundamentalist movement took up the reclamation of Ram's birthplace at Ayodhya as one of its central goals. In 1984, the Vishwa Hindu Parishad organized a campaign to regain access to the sacred site, and two years later a state court granted Hindu worshippers the right to enter the mosque compound, a decision that sparked violent Muslim protests. In the late 1980s, tensions increased as the Bharatiya Janata Party joined with the VHP in calling for the destruction of the Babri Mosque and its replacement with a temple to Ram, actions that the Indian government opposed.[14] The Hindu fundamentalists' growing determination to reclaim the holy site in Ayodhya at this time had several motivations. As a product of the period of Mogul conquest, the Babri Mosque represented a challenge to Hindus' hegemony in the region and a symbol of their historical subjugation to Muslim rule. The government's refusal to allow the replacement of the mosque with a Hindu temple, on the other hand, reinforced the fundamentalists' concern that contemporary secularist policies threatened the integrity of Hindu traditions. Most importantly, the fundamentalists believed that reclaiming the birthplace of Ram, the Hindu deity of greatest significance to them, would be a crucial step in strengthening the Hindu nation and that it would lay the groundwork for the future realization of Ram Rajya, the Kingdom of Ram, throughout India. The controversy surrounding the holy site in Ayodhya thus encompassed the major threats perceived by the fundamentalists as well as their ultimate religious aspirations. In addition, the BJP's position brought it considerable support from the Hindu community and helped to expand its role in Indian politics.

As support grew for the fundamentalists' goal of reclaiming Ram's birthplace, they adopted increasingly aggressive tactics. The VHP called on Hindu communities throughout India to begin consecrating bricks to be used in constructing the temple to Ram and in 1989 laid a ceremonial foundation for the new temple a short distance from the mosque itself, a ritual that brought hundreds of thousands of Hindus to Ayodhya.[15] In the weeks leading up to the laying of the foundation, Hindu processions carrying consecrated bricks for the temple had provoked violence in a number of Indian cities, and after the foundation was laid, rioting across India resulted in the deaths of hundreds of Hindus and Muslims (fig. 4.4). The following year, hundreds of thousands of Hindu fundamentalists marched on Ayodhya with the purpose of destroying the mosque and starting construction on the temple. The government arrested more than 100 thousand people trying to get to Ayodhya, but thousands of the

Figure 4.4 Consecrated foundation bricks for the proposed Ram temple at Ayodhya. Hindu fundamentalists brought the bricks to Ayodhya from across India in 1989, as part of the VHP's campaign to remove a mosque constructed on Ram's alleged birthplace. Ayodhya, India, 1989. *Source:* CORBIS/Zen Icknow.

fundamentalists entered the city and stormed the contested site. Before being driven off by a massive police force, they succeeded in planting several saffron Hindu flags atop the mosque and doing minor damage to the structure. The fundamentalists suffered numerous casualties in the assault, and the event again sparked massive rioting across India, leaving hundreds more dead.

The fundamentalists staged another march on Ayodhya in 1992, with more lasting consequences. Organizers from the VHP, the BJP, and the Rashtriya Swayamsevak Sangh assembled several hundred thousand followers in the city in early December. Their original goal had been to start construction of the Ram temple, but India's Supreme Court issued an order prohibiting damage to the mosque or construction of the Hindu temple. BJP leaders assured the government that the marchers would obey the court's decision and would simply conduct a mass prayer ritual. As a result the government provided only a small police force to maintain order. On the morning of the march, the fundamentalists assembled near the sacred site and began to pray, but some of them eventually broke through barriers surrounding the mosque and began to demolish it. Using only hand tools, they completely destroyed the mosque by the end of the day. In its place they set up a small shrine to Ram.[16] Marchers also tore down roughly half of the other mosques in Ayodhya as well as the homes of many Muslim residents of the city. The destruction in Ayodhya immediately produced Hindu-Muslim riots across India, the most extensive since independence, and thousands of people were killed in the following weeks. Protests also spread to other Islamic countries, and in neighboring Pakistan demonstrators attacked or destroyed more than thirty Hindu temples in retaliation. The Indian government responded by arresting a number of Hindu fundamentalist leaders, temporarily outlawing the VHP, and dismissing the BJP-run government of Uttar Pradesh, where Ayodhya is located. Police also retook control of the disputed site to prevent further action by the fundamentalists.

Despite efforts by the Indian government in the early 1990s to devise a compromise solution, the conflict over the holy site in Ayodhya persisted throughout the rest of the decade. The conflict has in fact taken on a new complexity in recent years, following the success of the BJP in national elections held in 1998. In preparing for these elections, the BJP had clearly stated that if it controlled the government the construction of the Ram temple in Ayodhya would be one of its top priorities. This position contributed to support for the BJP within the traditional Hindu community, which in turn enabled the BJP to become the leading party in India's parliament. In forming a functioning government, however, the BJP had to postpone action on the temple to ensure the cooperation of other political parties in its ruling coalition as well as to lessen discontent within the Muslim community. At the same time, though, the VHP has continued to make preparations for the temple's construction. It has established workshops near Ayodhya and elsewhere in northern India where stone carvers are producing the ornate pillars that will form the temple's structural framework.[17] Other parts of the temple are also being prefabricated, so that the structure can be readily assembled when construction begins. BJP leaders have stated that the temple will not be built before India's Supreme Court has resolved the Ayodhya conflict, and early in 1999 the VHP declared that it would postpone construction for at least two years, to help sustain the BJP's ruling coalition. Nonetheless, the VHP continues to assert that the temple will eventually be built on the contested site. In addition, it has claimed that mosques in the northern Indian cities of Mathura and Varanasi were also established on the sites of demolished Hindu shrines and that it will replace those mosques with temples as well.

The determination of Hindu fundamentalists to build a temple to Ram in Ayodhya reveals their underlying regard for the sacred meaning of place. As in the disputes over sacred places in Israel, the fundamentalists' concern with the site in Ayodhya reflects their conviction that its occupation by another religious group threatens the integrity of their own religious beliefs. In their view, their effort to revive and unite the Hindu nation cannot succeed while the sacred nature of this site, as they have defined it, remains unrealized. As a result, they seek to reclaim the site not just by taking possession of it but by giving material expression to its traditional sacred significance, in the form of the proposed temple. Through this process, fundamentalists believe that they will regain access to the spiritual essence of the site. Recognition of the religious importance of Ram's birthplace has thus become the core of the Ayodhya controversy from the Hindu perspective and a unifying concern of the entire Hindu fundamentalist movement.

Up to this point, the discussion of fundamentalist concerns with sacred space has focused primarily on cases where different religious groups have contested the meaning of particular sites. Fundamentalist controversies involving sacred places may also occur among followers of the same religion. Such controversies develop because fundamentalists consider less traditional adherents of their own religion to be a threat to the doctrines and practices that they are trying to defend. Fundamentalists therefore fear that these other adherents, through their unorthodox beliefs and behavior, will not properly respect their religion's sacred sites. Haredi fundamentalists' opposition to women or mixed groups of men and women praying at the Western Wall, discussed previously, exemplifies this type of dispute, although the severity of the conflict has been tempered by the fact that neither the fundamentalists nor their opponents have direct authority over the site. Fundamentalists may also undertake actions involving sacred sites as a means of expressing their opposition to the beliefs of other adherents of the same religion. Such instances tend to produce more extreme outcomes, particularly in situations where one side in the dispute has absolute control over the sacred site. The potential for violent conflict in such cases has been clearly demonstrated, for example, in fundamentalist actions involving Islam's most sacred site, the Great Mosque of Mecca.

The religious significance of the Great Mosque in Mecca derives from several factors. It represents Islam's most important place of worship and the climactic stop on the hajj, the pilgrimage to Mecca and Medina that all Muslims are obliged to make at some point in their lives if they are physically and financially able. The courtyard of the mosque also contains Islam's holiest object, the Kaaba ("cube," in Arabic), a large stone structure believed first to have been built by the biblical prophet Abraham and his son, Ismail. The Black Stone, a meteorite believed to be the foundation stone of the original structure, is embedded in one corner. According to Moslem belief, the Kaaba was built on the site of an earlier sanctuary erected at the beginning of human existence by the first prophet, Adam.

Conflicts involving the Great Mosque have developed because it and other sacred sites in Mecca and Medina, the holiest places in Islam, are controlled by the ruling monarchs of Saudi Arabia. The official title of the Saudi king in fact includes the designation "custodian of the two holy mosques," referring to the main places of worship in Mecca and Medina. At first glance, it might seem unlikely that Islamic fundamentalists would oppose the Saudis and their control of these sites. Millions of Muslims from around the world make the obligatory pilgrimage to these sites every year, so access is not an issue. Moreover, the Saudis themselves practice an orthodox form of Sunni Islam, known as Wahhabism, that emphasizes adherence to the sharia and rejects religious innovation. Some scholars in fact characterize Saudi Arabia as a fundamentalist state. Others disagree, arguing that mainstream Islam in Saudi Arabia is not driven by a sense of threat to its traditions and that the political relationship between the country's rulers and the United States reveals a willingness to compromise that is inconsistent with a true fundamentalist perspective. But even if it is not a fundamentalist state, Saudi Arabia does support a highly orthodox approach to Islam and Islamic law. Nonetheless, non-Sunni fundamentalists have attacked Saudi Arabia's stewardship of Islam's holy sites, focusing in particular on the Great Mosque of Mecca.

One such attack occurred in 1979, when a group of Saudi fundamentalists captured the Great Mosque by force, taking hostage hundreds of Muslims praying in the mosque on the first day of the Muslim new year.[18] These militants belonged to a sect of Mahdists, who like Shiites believe that the Mahdi or "last prophet" will appear as an Islamic messiah. Apparently they further believed that their own leader was the Mahdi. A group of more than four hundred militants entered the mosque as pilgrims, but once inside they took over the complex using automatic weapons that they had smuggled in. After they had established themselves in the mosque, they declared their opposition to Saudi Arabia's ruling family and to the erosion of traditional Islam. They characterized the country's rulers as enemies of authentic Islam and demanded an end to the contamination of Saudi society by Western influences. The militants' specific objectives in taking control of the Great Mosque remain uncertain, but the event clearly challenged the Saudis' authority over Islam's most sacred sites. The militants maintained control of portions of the Great Mosque for about two weeks, in part because the Saudi military was reluctant to harm the religious shrine or endanger the hostages and in part because the mosque complex itself contains an elaborate network of rooms and passages in which the militants were able to hide. The military eventually recaptured the mosque, but in the process more than a hundred soldiers, militants, and hostages were killed. The militants' leader and several dozen followers were later publicly beheaded by sword, the traditional Islamic punishment for sacrilege.

Another challenge to Saudi authority over the holy sites in Mecca and Medina emerged in 1987, after violence broke out between Saudi security forces and Shiite pilgrims from Iran. Since the Islamic Revolution in 1979, Iranian pilgrims had used the hajj as an occasion to stage large political rallies and protests in Mecca. In 1987, a group from Iran demonstrating against the United States, Israel, and the Soviet Union attempted the enter the Great Mosque, although they had been ordered not to do so. As a result, a violent confrontation broke out between the demonstrators and Saudi forces, and hundreds of people, mainly Iranians, were killed. This event led to a sharp rebuke from Iran's fundamentalist government. Ayatollah Khomeini blamed the Saudis for allowing the conflict to escalate into violence, which violated the sanctity of the Great Mosque, and he declared that Saudi rulers were not competent to serve as the protectors of Islam's most sacred sites in Mecca and Medina. He further claimed that the U.S. presence in Saudi Arabia contaminated Islam's sacred sites and that ending Saudi control of the shrines should have higher priority than destroying Israel or defeating Iraq in its drawn-out war with Iran. Other Iranian officials asserted that the United States had in fact planned the violence in Mecca and that the martyred Iranian pilgrims must be avenged by freeing Mecca from Saudi control.[19] In response to this conflict, Saudi Arabia banned political protests during the hajj and later sought to limit the number of pilgrims from Iran. Iran in turn boycotted the hajj for several years and broke off diplomatic ties with Saudi Arabia. Relations between the two countries began to improve during the early 1990s, as they grew more concerned about aggression on the part of their common enemy, Iraq. When Iranian pilgrims subsequently began to return to Mecca, however, they continued to incorporate anti-Western protests into their observance of the hajj.

In challenging Saudi control of Islam's sacred sites, fundamentalists in both of the above-mentioned cases did not act out of fear that those sites were directly threatened with specific acts of desecration. They did not object to the ways in which other Muslims worshipped at the sites, for example, and they did not believe that the sites were at risk of being physically defiled. Rather, they challenged the moral legitimacy of Saudi authority over the sites, based on the belief that Saudi rulers did not adhere to genuine Islam and had developed too close a relationship with the United States and other Western countries. The Mahdists who took over the Great Mosque in 1979 did so, therefore, primarily to express their opposition to the Saudi monarchy and its approach to Islam. They chose the Great Mosque as their target because it provided the most meaningful site from which to declare their beliefs. Similarly, in the aftermath of the violence involving Iranian pilgrims at the Great Mosque, Iranian fundamentalists condemned Saudi Arabia's rulers as being spiritually unfit to oversee the sacred sites, but they did not assert that the sites needed to be physically defended. The concerns of Islamic fundamentalists with the Great Mosque thus reflect their recognition of its absolute importance as a sacred site, as well as their opposition to those controlling the site who do not adhere to the fundamentalists' interpretation of Islam.

In addition to explicitly religious disputes, secular forces may play an important role in provoking fundamentalist concerns over sacred places. The intrusion of secular interests into sacred space challenges the sanctity of the latter and may be seen as a threat to its very existence. The protection of sacred places from secular influences is not only a fundamentalist concern, of course. Many religions attempt to limit the impact of secular improprieties at holy sites, for example, by imposing dress codes or similar behavioral restrictions on visitors. For fundamentalists, however, the intrusions of the secular world into sacred space take on an especially sinister character. In many cases they consider their sacred sites to be sanctuaries, where their religious traditions can be protected from external threats, and they therefore interpret intrusions on those sites as direct attacks on their beliefs. In such cases, defense of the sacred site becomes synonymous with defense of the religious certainties espoused by the group, and the site itself becomes the focus of the conflict between fundamentalists and secular society.

Conflicts surrounding the Sikhs' Golden Temple compound, in the northern Indian city of Amritsar, offer a salient example of this issue. The Golden Temple compound contains Sikhism's two most important shrines: the Golden Temple itself, which houses Sikhism's sacred scriptures, the Granth, and the Akal Takht (Punjabi for the "Eternal Throne"), the center of religious authority where members of the Sikh community regularly gather to reach decisions on spiritual matters. The compound also includes a library and various residential facilities. During most of the colonial period, British authorities maintained secular control of the Golden Temple, a practice that early Sikh fundamentalists opposed. The passage of the Gurdwara Reform Act in 1925 placed the Golden Temple and all other Sikh shrines under Sikh control, but Sikh fundamentalists continued to object to secular influences on the sacred site. After independence, for example, they protested a provision in India's constitution that made any place of worship open to people of all religious faiths. Sikhs wanted the Golden Temple and other shrines to be less accessible to non-Sikhs and asserted that the secular authorities should not have the power to allow anyone to enter the sacred site. During the resurgence of fundamentalism during the 1970s and 1980s, Sikhs also demanded that controls be placed on inappropriate secular activities near the temple compound, including the sale of alcohol, tobacco, and meat.

Conflicts involving the temple compound intensified dramatically during the 1980s, however, after Sikh fundamentalist leader Jarnail Singh Bhindranwale claimed sanctuary there in 1982. During 1983 and 1984, a growing number of militant Sikhs moved into the temple compound and began to fortify it, provoking a series of skirmishes with local security forces. Sikh extremists began to use the compound as a refuge as they carried out various forms of terrorist activity in the region. In preparation for a government siege of the compound, the militants also stockpiled weapons (including antitank missiles), food, a generator, and other supplies. The Indian government grew increasingly concerned about the compound's militarization and in 1984 cut off access to food, water, and electricity. Many moderate Sikhs subsequently left the compound, but Bhindranwale and his followers refused to surrender. When Bhindranwale called on Sikhs to enforce an economic shutdown in Punjab, which would have stopped needed grain shipments to other parts of the country, the Indian government decided that it had to take action. The Indian army sealed off Punjab and began planning how to remove the militants from the temple compound.

In June, the army thus initiated Operation Blue Star, in which a large commando force assaulted the temple compound with the backing of tanks. During the ensuing battle for control of the site, hundreds of Sikh militants were killed, including Bhindranwale, along with smaller numbers of unarmed pilgrims and Indian soldiers. In taking the compound, the army had orders to avoid harming the Golden Temple itself, but the rest of the compound suffered extensive damage, particularly the Akal Takht, where Bhindranwale had made his headquarters.

The Sikh community strongly protested the assault on the Golden Temple compound and the destruction of the Akal Takht. Moderate Sikhs sided with the fundamentalists in condemning the government's desecration of the holy site, and extensive Sikh rioting broke out. Radical militants responded to the assault by expanding their campaign of terrorism. The assassination of Prime Minister Indira Gandhi by two Sikh bodyguards later in 1984 produced a violent Hindu backlash, provoking anti-Sikh riots that left thousands dead and heightened the Sikhs' sense of alienation. The government subsequently tried to appease the Sikh community by funding the reconstruction of the Akal Takht and spent about $2 million on the project. This effort further antagonized the fundamentalist militants, however, who saw the reconstruction as an additional desecration of the holy site, since it was being carried out by moderate Sikhs characterized by the fundamentalists as collaborators of the Indian government.

Fundamentalist discontent with the reconstruction project eventually led to further conflict over the temple compound, which the government had returned to the control of Sikh moderates. In 1986, a group of twenty armed Sikh militants took over the compound and expelled the moderate clergy in charge. These militants publicly praised the Sikh bodyguards who had killed Indira Gandhi two years earlier and demanded the release of imprisoned Sikh extremists. They also declared that the rebuilt portions of Akal Takht were spiritually polluted and had to be destroyed before the true restoration of the sacred site could be undertaken by Sikh volunteers. Over the next two weeks, thousands of Sikh fundamentalists participated in the demolition of the rebuilt structure. The fundamentalists then began to construct a new purified Akal Takht, a project that lasted well into the 1990s. As they restored the temple compound, moreover, the militants also began to remilitarize it. It became the de facto headquarters of the movement to create the independent Sikh state of Khalistan and once again served as a sanctuary for dozens of extremists implicated in terrorist violence against the government, Hindu society, and more moderate Sikhs. The Indian government maintained security checkpoints around the compound and in 1988 staged another siege, but it would not risk another direct assault on the site. A stalemate of sorts thus developed during the late 1980s. By the early 1990s, however, the government's continuing crackdown on the extremists and the Sikh community's growing weariness with the prolonged violence led to the disintegration of the radical terrorist movement. Still, the fundamentalist movement within Sikhism has persisted and continues to stress the need to protect the Golden Temple compound from external sources of corruption.

Sikh fundamentalist concerns with the security of the Golden Temple compound thus reached a peak during the radical period of the 1980s, but such concerns were rooted in the group's past and continue to be an important issue. Unlike the other groups previously discussed, the Sikhs' sacred site faced a distinct threat from secular authorities, who protested its use as a radical sanctuary. As a result, the physical safety of the site became a major consideration for Sikh fundamentalists. Nonetheless, the fundamentalists' primary objective was to preserve the sacred significance of the site, which they considered to be far more important than its visible structures. Their decision to demolish the first attempt at rebuilding the Akal Takht demonstrates their commitment to safeguarding not just the shrine itself but also its religious meaning. Like other fundamentalist groups concerned with sacred space, the Sikhs consider the meaning that they have attached to the site to be one of the foundations of their entire belief system. Protection of the site's sacred function from dilution or corruption by outside influences thus represents a key priority for Sikh fundamentalists.

In defending or reclaiming the places that they believe to be sacred, then, fundamentalists have been involved in a variety of conflicts in recent years. Those conflicts are inherently contextual, growing out of the fundamentalists' specific beliefs and the nature of the threats or influences that they oppose. The examples discussed in this chapter display one crucial similarity, however: the absolute importance that fundamentalists assign to the proper use and care of sacred space. Again, from the fundamentalist perspective such issues are not merely symbolic. While sacred places provide material expressions of abstract beliefs, they also serve specific, practical functions for true believers. For fundamentalists, human interactions with sacred places have real consequences for the fulfillment of religious obligations and the human relationship with the divine. Misuse of a sacred site thus directly threatens the integrity of their belief system. As a result, disputes concerning sacred space take on a genuine sense of urgency and in many cases have provoked violent confrontations between fundamentalists and their antagonists. Such disputes in turn intensify the fundamentalists' general distrust of those outside their group and reinforce their commitment to a stance of aggressive activism in all of their concerns.

THE CONTROL OF SECULAR SPACE

A central theme in fundamentalist thought is that traditional religious principles must be fully integrated into the secular realms of human activity. This conviction derives from the belief that religious tradition represents the only legitimate source of authority and should therefore find expression throughout all of society. Fundamentalists further believe that any decline in the dominance of religious authority over secular activities inevitably undermines the moral integrity of society and threatens the survival of religious tradition as a vital social force. One of their primary goals, then, has been to restore religious tradition as the guiding principle of secular life. As a result, fundamentalists have placed considerable emphasis on asserting territorial control over portions of secular space, to ensure that their religious traditions are properly observed and to fight the corrupting influences of contemporary secular trends. Such efforts usually do not possess the same sense of urgency that characterizes fundamentalist concerns with sacred space, but they play a significant role in shaping the relationship between fundamentalist groups and their surroundings. Some fundamentalist groups have focused on creating their own secular spaces, such as residential neighborhoods or social institutions, as a means of increasing their isolation from the larger society. Most fundamentalists have been more aggressive, however, attempting to exercise some form of control over areas also inhabited and used by nonfundamentalists. In doing so, they have adopted various methods, ranging from social pressure to legitimate political action to violence. Disputes over the control of secular space have thus become a major source of conflict between fundamentalists and other elements of society and represent an important form of fundamentalist activism.

The most common objective of fundamentalists in this context is to enforce conformity to their own religious principles within the spatial domains of secular activity. To this end, they may try to restructure social institutions to operate in accordance with fundamentalist values, or they may try to shape individual patterns of behavior to fit their own customs and ethical standards. In pursuing these goals, fundamentalists do not necessarily insist that others adopt their particular religious beliefs. Most fundamentalists believe that religious commitment has meaning only if it grows out of a voluntary choice on the part of the believer. Nonetheless, fundamentalists are convinced that their traditions embody absolute truths and thus believe that they have a moral responsibility to ensure that secular activity conforms to their religious certainties. In their view, the consistent expression of religious values in all realms of life is essential to the preservation of a virtuous society. Again, some isolationist groups attempt to enforce conformity to the demands of their religious traditions only within their own communities, but most fundamentalists seek to impose their values within a broader spatial setting, both to prevent the spread of corrupting influences and to help restore society to its proper moral state.

Such efforts often focus on preventing secular violations of specific religious laws, particularly among fundamentalists whose belief systems stress adherence to strict behavioral practices. Islamic fundamentalists throughout the Muslim world, for example, have attempted to limit or ban the consumption of alcohol, based on Koranic proscriptions against the use of intoxicants. Those who have achieved political control, such as the Taliban in Afghanistan and the Shiite fundamentalists in Iran, have outlawed the use of alcohol and have adopted the traditional Islamic practice of flogging violators in public. In Malaysia's state of Kelantan, the fundamentalists in power have banned the consumption of alcohol by Muslims, and pressure from fundamentalists in Pakistan has led to a similar prohibition there. In Muslim countries where fundamentalists are not in power, they have attempted to restrict alcohol consumption through the use of public demonstrations and violence. In the early 1990s, for example, fundamentalists in Algeria tried to pressure restaurants and hotels to curtail the sale of alcohol and in one instance forced a restaurant to close after it served alcohol to foreigners during Islam's holy month of Ramadan. Since the 1980s, liquor stores, bars, and nightclubs have also become frequent targets of fundamentalist violence in Egypt, Lebanon, and other Muslim countries where alcohol is still sold. In all of these cases, Islamic fundamentalists have sought to enforce religious law within secular space, not necessarily to gain converts but to ensure that secular behavior does not violate sacred principles.

Haredi fundamentalists in Israel have pursued a similar goal in trying to enforce traditional observance of the Jewish Sabbath, which runs from sundown on Friday to sundown on Saturday. The haredi believe that they have a personal religious obligation to chastise those who desecrate the Sabbath, but they are also motivated by a more general desire to fight the spread of secularism within Israeli society.[20] They have thus staged repeated demonstrations against the opening of certain businesses, such as restaurants, movie theaters, and convenience stores, on the Sabbath. They have also demanded that certain roads be closed to automobile traffic during the Sabbath, an issue that generated controversy throughout the 1990s. The haredim had previously succeeded in closing many local streets within their own neighborhoods on the Sabbath, but in the early 1990s they began to push for more widespread closings, asking that traffic be banned on the Sabbath on several major roads running near their residential areas. The city government refused, arguing that these roads provide important means of access to different parts of the city and that closing them would infringe on the rights of secular Israelis. In response, the haredim have staged repeated demonstrations, particularly along Bar-Ilan Street, a major thoroughfare that borders Meah Shearim, a Jerusalem neighborhood dominated by ultra-Orthodox Jews. Demonstrators have shouted insults and thrown stones at passing cars and have placed rubble in the street to block traffic.[21] These demonstrations have led to violent conflicts with the police and have generated a significant backlash within the larger Israeli society. The city has made several attempts to compromise with the haredim, for example, by closing the street for limited times to all traffic except emergency vehicles and secular residents of the immediate area.[22] The fundamentalists have found such compromises to be unsatisfactory, however, and continue to protest the use of the street on the Sabbath.

Fundamentalist efforts to regulate activity and behavior in secular space is not motivated solely by concerns with specific religious laws. Fundamentalists have also tried to enforce conformity to the general standards of morality derived from their religious beliefs. Christian fundamentalists have tried to restore traditional values in U.S. society, for example, by mounting campaigns against perceived sources of moral decay, such as pornography, abortion, and homosexuality. In doing so, they have often focused their attention on manifestations of those phenomena in secular space. Fundamentalists have thus repeatedly targeted clinics that perform abortion procedures, establishing pickets and trying to dissuade women from entering. The intensity of such protests, organized by Operation Rescue and other antiabortion groups, eventually led the U. S. Congress to pass the "Freedom of Access to Clinic Entrances Act" in 1994. Christian groups have also picketed stores that sell adult books and videos, trying to force them to close or to relocate to areas less accessible to children. Similarly, fundamentalists have used public protests to pressure mainstream bookstores to stop selling materials that they find offensive.[23] Fundamentalist protests have been directed as well against gay bars, gay and lesbian festivals, and other expressions of gay activism. The Walt Disney Company's accommodation of annual "Gay Day" events at its Disney World theme park in Florida became a particularly conspicuous target of fundamentalist outrage during the 1990s. The company itself does not organize these events, which are part of a larger series of gay celebrations held in June throughout the state, but Christian groups like the American Family Association and Focus on the Family fault Disney for not barring the events from its property and have regularly organized protests against Disney World. Fundamentalists also object to the company's provision of health benefits to same-sex partners of employees and to the adult content of many of the movies and television programs produced by Disney and its subsidiaries and so during the late 1990s tried to organize a general boycott of the company's theme parks and products. Through such efforts, then, Christian fundamentalists have sought to purge immoral activity from secular space.

Islamic fundamentalists have also tried to banish corruption from secular space, but their primary concern has been to limit the effects of Western values and practices on Muslim society. Their antagonism toward Western culture in part grows out of nationalist and anti-imperialist sentiments, but it is based on religious motives as well. The Koran states that Muslims make up the "noblest" human culture. Islamic fundamentalists thus believe that the infiltration of Muslim society by Western influences represents a serious threat to their superior status and will lead to moral decay and the pollution of religious tradition. The pervasive influence of Western popular culture has become a particular concern of Islamic fundamentalists, because they believe that it is so effective in undermining authentic Islamic values. When Ayatollah Khomeini came to power in Iran, he thus banned the use of videocassettes and satellite dishes, although that ban proved very difficult to enforce. Similarly, the Taliban have carried out house-to-house searches to remove satellite dishes and antennas and have staged public events centering on the destruction of television sets, videocassette players, and stereo systems. Fundamentalist extremists in Egypt have destroyed video stores in Cairo as symbols of Western corruption and have targeted the tourist trade as a major source of Western influence. The U.S. military presence in Saudi Arabia after the Gulf War generated a surge of fundamentalist activity there as well, based in part on fears that it would initiate a cultural invasion from the West. In all of these cases, secular space represents a major concern for Islamic fundamentalists because it provides the medium through which Western influences have entered Muslim society.

In addition to seeking to eliminate corrupting influences, some fundamentalists have also attempted to increase the presence of religious activity in secular space. Again, they generally have not adopted this approach to force conversions to their beliefs. They are interested instead in establishing the importance of religious belief as the foundation of secular life and in asserting the inseparability of sacred and secular concerns. Christian fundamentalists in the United States have placed particular emphasis on this issue, based on their conviction that the United States is indisputably a Christian nation. Their primary focus in this context has been public schools, which in their view have become increasingly corrupt since the Supreme Court decision in 1962 that prohibited school prayer. The reestablishment of voluntary prayer in public schools has thus become a major fundamentalist objective. Various fundamentalist groups have lobbied for a constitutional amendment that would allow prayer in school and other public places and that would permit public school employees to express their religious beliefs in the classroom. During the 1990s, groups like the Citizens for Excellence in Education also encouraged fundamentalists to seek election to local school boards so that they could reshape school curricula to be more consistent with conservative Christian beliefs. Their specific goal is to introduce their view of religious truth into the public school classroom. Fundamentalists have been particularly concerned about eradicating the philosophy of secular humanism, which they claim denies the role of divine influence in human affairs. As discussed in earlier chapters, they also promote the teaching of creationism as a biblically viable alternative to evolutionary theory. Regarding sex education, they want schools to focus on the merits of abstinence and to ban teachings about homosexuality that characterize it as a natural element of social diversity. Outside of the context of public schools, fundamentalists have sought to increase the visibility of religious tradition by supporting religious displays such as Nativity scenes in public places during the Christmas season and by trying to remove controversial books or displays from public libraries. Again, their ultimate goal is to incorporate their beliefs into the public functions of secular space.

A related set of issues concerning secular space revolves around the status of women. Most religious traditions assign men and women different social responsibilities and obligations, and those differences are considered to be a crucial element of the social order. As a result, fundamentalists see the weakening of traditional gender roles as a threat to the survival of religious principles in society. They respond to that threat by reasserting traditional attitudes toward women, which often have distinct spatial consequences. Concepts of gendered space, based on strict beliefs regarding access to and use of different spatial realms by men and women, thus play an important role in fundamentalist thought.[24] These spatial manifestations of traditional gender roles are in most cases associated with several related themes, including the segregation of men from women in particular contexts, the enforcement of restrictions on female mobility, and the requirement that women adopt certain patterns of behavior, such as styles of dress (fig. 4.5). For fundamentalists, such approaches to the control of secular space ensure the preservation of religious interpretations of the meaning of gender, which in their view must be maintained to

Figure 4.5 An Afghan woman dressed in a burka walks down a street in war-torn Kabul in 1995. After the Taliban took control of Kabul the following year, the burka became mandatory dress for all women when in public. The Taliban further required that women in public be accompanied by an adult male relative. Kabul, Afghanistan, 1995. *Source:* CORBIS/Baci.

safeguard the proper structure of society. Because they directly clash with the attempts of feminist movements to expand opportunities for women, however, fundamentalist efforts to enforce traditional concepts of gendered space have often been a major source of social conflict.

The concern with gendered space appears most frequently among fundamentalists whose religious traditions emphasize adherence to strict rules of behavior. Restrictions on women are rigidly codified in the Islamic concept of purdah, for example. This concept, which derives from the Koran, requires that women lead a life of seclusion, submission, and modesty. They should be veiled when in the presence of men outside their family, should not be touched by men other than their husband, and should not be alone in private with a man other than their husband, and in public space, men and women should be strictly segregated. According to traditional Islamic belief, such rules help to maintain the social order in two ways: by ensuring that women devote themselves to raising children and caring for the family and by protecting men from the temptations that exposure to women outside their family would bring. Violations of these rules in turn are seen as a threat to family honor and to the stability of society as a whole. In trying to enforce such rules, Islamic fundamentalists have adopted a variety of approaches, some more restrictive than others, but invariably their underlying strategy has been to impose different constraints on the activity spaces of women and men, as dictated by religious law.

A common approach has been to restrict the spatial mobility of women. In Afghanistan, for example, the Taliban have explicitly prohibited women from leaving the home unless accompanied by a close male relative (and clothed in a burka). Elsewhere, similar restrictions have been enforced by custom rather than law. Many Pakistani women who do not need to work to support the family spend most of their lives at home, in that portion of the house reserved for women. If they do travel outside the home, they go in the company of male relatives, usually at night or in curtained vehicles. Rural Muslim women in Bangladesh move more freely about their own neighborhoods, which are generally inhabited by relatives, but rarely travel to other areas, and if they do so they must be veiled. In predominantly Muslim countries where traditional restrictions on female mobility are less widely observed, like Egypt, women who are unveiled and unaccompanied in public often face harassment from fundamentalists. Members of the Islamic Salvation Front in Algeria have in fact enforced their own curfew on dormitories at women's colleges, surrounding the buildings and not allowing women students to leave. During the mid-1990s, Algerian extremists also claimed that unveiled women would be the targets of violence, and a number of killings of unveiled women did in fact occur. Even in fundamentalist settings where women have considerable freedom of movement, such as Iran, the requirement that they be veiled in public enforces subtle constraints on their mobility.

The spatial restrictions placed on women by Islamic fundamentalists take many other forms as well. The employment of women outside the home is severely restricted by law or custom in many countries where fundamentalists have influence. In Pakistan many peasant women must work to help provide for their families, but their husbands generally decide where they are allowed to find employment. Similarly, women in rural Bangladesh who work outside the home suffer a severe loss in status. Many Islamic fundamentalists also support gender segregation in education. Although the fundamentalist regime in Iran has not barred women from the workplace, it has insisted on segregated schools. In the most extreme case of educational segregation, the Taliban prohibit girls from attending school at all. Similar policies of gender segregation have been applied to various other types of activities. Again, in some cases these policies do not prevent women from taking part in secular activities but simply keep them apart from men. Iran, for example, has built separate sports facilities for women athletes, encouraging them to compete but preventing them from doing so before a male audience. In the Malaysian state of Kelantan, Muslim women are not discouraged from shopping, but in grocery stores in the capital city they must use their own checkout lines, separate from those reserved for men. Segregation of medical facilities has more serious implications, however, and in Afghanistan has led to a severe deterioration of health services for women under Taliban rule.

Jewish fundamentalists too have expressed concerns with gender and space, based on the belief that women should remain isolated from men who are not their husbands. Again, the segregation of women is seen as essential in preserving female modesty and the integrity of the family. In some cases, the concern for keeping women and men apart has an explicit religious dimension, as in the controversy over groups of mixed gender praying together at the Western Wall, discussed earlier in this chapter. But Jewish fundamentalists have also attempted to impose restrictions on women in secular space, and these efforts have become an important symbol of the clash between traditionalist and modernist perspectives in Israeli society. Fundamentalists have thus demanded separate facilities for men and women at certain beaches and in hospitals. As heavy users of public transportation system in Israel's larger cities, they have successfully lobbied to impose gender segregation on public buses running through their neighborhoods. Haredi fundamentalists have also been aggressive about enforcing their own standards of modesty in female dress in and around their neighborhoods in Jerusalem. Signs posted at the entrances to their residential districts warn women to stay out if they are not wearing modest clothing, such as long sleeves and skirts cut below the knees. Many stores in these areas will not serve women who are improperly dressed. In the mid-1990s, haredim living in the Meah Shearim district of Jerusalem carried out a campaign to discourage female government workers deemed to be immodestly dressed from parking near the neighborhood. Several women employed by the nearby Ministry of Education were publicly confronted and harassed, and others found their cars vandalized. Such forms of activism have produced a strong public outcry, but the haredim claim that they and their children should not be forced to witness these perceived displays of immodesty.

Issues concerning the connections between gender and space are particularly important for Islamic and Jewish fundamentalists, since their beliefs emphasize the observance of strict and detailed rules of behavior, which often have a spatial dimension. Concerns with such issues do appear among other groups, however. For groups with strong patriarchal traditions, the organizations established by fundamentalists often have a strong gender bias. Thus the RSS, the central organization in Hindu fundamentalism, essentially provides a social structure for male bonding among current and future activists. On a somewhat different scale, Christian groups like the Promise Keepers and Focus on the Family advocate a traditional sexual division of labor that places women in charge of domestic space while men deal with the outside world. Such groups argue, for example, that the husband's work should be the primary factor in making family moves and claim that homosexuality does not develop among adults who had authoritarian fathers and "home-loving" mothers. Most Christian fundamentalist groups in the United States do not prohibit women from working outside the home, but their views clearly assert that gender roles have spatial implications. It should also be noted that fundamentalism does not always impose greater spatial restrictions on women. Their involvement in group rituals and institutions in some cases opens up opportunities for women that did not previously exist.[25] Even in these cases, however, the spatial manifestations of gender roles represent a key fundamentalist concern and an important issue in fundamentalist attitudes toward the proper use of secular space.

Finally, many fundamentalists use the control of secular space as a means of maintaining the boundaries that separate them from others. They typically do so by establishing their own secular institutions, such as schools or businesses, or by moving to separate residential areas. In the process, they create "bounded" segments of secular space that operate according to their religious principles. These bounded spaces exist beyond the scope of nonfundamentalist society and thus are not intended to reform external social structures. Rather, their primary function is to serve essential needs of the fundamentalist group itself, and in this sense they represent perhaps the most basic form of interaction between fundamentalism and secular space. In delimiting their own segments of secular space, fundamentalists generally have two objectives: to create settings that accommodate activities designed to protect and promote their beliefs and to make a conspicuous display of their distinctiveness from the rest of society. The creation of such spaces in other words provides a means of actively responding to threats against the group's traditions. The more menacing those threats are perceived to be, the more the group will seek to define its own secular spaces. Fundamentalists are particularly likely to undertake such actions in settings where they are a small minority having little influence on larger institutions, where their views differ strongly from those of the larger society, or where society's institutions are perceived to be directly antagonistic to fundamentalist views, rather than merely neutral.

Fundamentalist efforts to mark off portions of secular space for their own use take a number of different forms. Very often these efforts involve the creation of separate educational institutions for fundamentalist children. Separate schools provide an effective means for fundamentalists to preserve their beliefs within the next generation, by socializing children as members of the group and by isolating them from perceived sources of corruption. Indeed, many fundamentalist groups see the protection of children from offensive ideas and beliefs as their most important responsibility. Fundamentalists also create secular institutions to provide for specific needs defined by their particular beliefs, such as food stores for groups that observe strict dietary laws or hospitals that provide for strict gender segregation. Other institutions serve to build group solidarity or to demonstrate that the group can care for its members more effectively than the secular authorities can. In extreme cases, fundamentalists establish their own residential districts or settlements, such as the haredi neighborhoods in Israeli cities or the Asoke communities founded by Buddhists in Thailand. Fundamentalists are most likely to take this approach when they believe that they must live their daily lives in isolation from outsiders to remain true to their religious traditions or when a strong sense of antagonism alienates the fundamentalists from the rest of society. All of the above approaches ultimately serve the same purpose, however: to declare and protect the fundamentalist group's distinctive beliefs.

The creation of bounded secular spaces has been particularly significant among Jewish fundamentalists in Israel. The haredim believe that the mainstream of Israeli society has turned its back on Jewish law, and many reject Israel's legitimacy as a political state. As a result, the haredim have adopted a strategy of isolation from the rest of society, which has in turn motivated them to establish their own secular institutions and residential areas. The haredim operate a comprehensive educational system, including kindergartens and primary schools for younger children as well as the traditional yeshivas for young men.[26] By emphasizing the teaching of fundamentalist values, these schools reinforce the integration of children into haredi society. In this sense the schools serve primarily as religious institutions, but they also fulfill the broader secular function of providing an education. Most haredi schools are in fact under the supervision of the Ministry of Education, as required by law, and receive substantial government funding. Only the more extreme haredim operate illegal schools, which function without government involvement. The haredi schools have also had a significant impact on education generally within

Israel as they have grown in number. In Jerusalem, for example, nearly half of all Jewish children attended haredi schools in 1998.[27]

The haredim have also created their own commercial realm within secular space, made up of businesses run according to fundamentalist principles. These businesses serve a crucial function for the haredi community by providing goods and services needed for the proper observance of religious law. The food sold in haredi groceries, for example, are labeled with kosher certificates guaranteeing that it conforms to the strict standards of traditional Jewish dietary law. Meats are marked with the name of the rabbi who certified them as kosher, so customers can consistently follow the practices advocated by their particular religious authority. Groceries also often sell vegetables such as cauliflower and cabbage that have been grown using methods to ensure that they are free of insects and worms, the consumption of which would violate Jewish dietary law. In addition to providing needed goods and services, haredi stores also offer a commercial setting that conforms to the group's religious expectations. These stores contain no advertising or packaging that customers might find offensive, for example, because it displays immodestly dressed women. Some packaging has been redesigned specifically for haredi customers, but often the store simply tapes over the offending image. Haredi stores require as well that customers observe a traditional dress code and provide jackets or robes to shoppers whose clothing does not conform to haredi standards. Some shops with limited space advertise separate shopping hours for men and women, so customers can avoid physical contact with the opposite sex.[28]

Another important aspect of the haredim's use of secular space has been the development of segregated residential districts, where nearly all haredi fundamentalists live. Residence in these neighborhoods allows the haredim to remain close to their secular and religious institutions and at the same time isolates them from what they consider to be corrupting influences within Israeli society.[29] The largest haredi neighborhoods are located in Jerusalem and Bnei Brak, a city within the Tel Aviv metropolitan region. The Meah Shearim district, northwest of Jerusalem's Old City, represents the traditional core of the haredim's residential space, which has gradually expanded into a large belt across the northern part of the city (fig. 4.6). The rapid growth of the haredi population in recent decades has produced a chronic housing shortage in these increasingly crowded neighborhoods.[30] In response, the haredim have continually expanded into new residential areas, bringing with them their strict attitudes regarding public behavior and the proper observance of Jewish law. As they occupy new areas, moreover, the haredim assert territorial control over them in various ways. Proper observance of the Sabbath, for example, prohibits Jews from carrying any object beyond their own private domain into public space or to other private areas. The haredim define their neighborhoods as their private domain, and so, as their residential patterns have expanded, they have incorporated new areas into the ritual space that they consider to be

Figure 4.6   The haredi neighborhood of Meah Shearim. The haredim have used geographical segregation as part of their larger strategy of isolation from the rest of Israeli society. Jerusalem, Israel, 1993. *Source:* CORBIS/David Rubinger.

theirs.[31] The haredim also try to encourage conformity to their own standards of behavior within their neighborhoods. One distinctive expression of such efforts are the many signs posted by the haredim, promoting religious charity or instructing women on how to dress modestly.[32] Such attempts to exert control have in turn led to repeated conflicts with secular Israelis, who resist the spread of the haredim's influence and often feel pressured to move out of areas where the haredim have settled. Indeed, a survey conducted during the late 1990s found that a majority of the secular Jews living in Jerusalem had considered leaving the city to escape the growing haredi presence.[33]

Like the haredim, Buddhist fundamentalists of the Asoke movement in Thailand have established their own residential spaces both to protect themselves from corrupting influences and to create a setting where they can live according to their religious principles. In their case, however, they have chosen to live in self-sufficient rural communities rather than in segregated urban neighborhoods. This choice reflects the Asoke movement's goal of practicing a simple, communal way of life cut off from the distractions of the modern world. The number of Asoke communities has grown as the movement has increased in popularity, but they still house only the dedicated core of the movement. Many people sympathetic to the movement continue to live within the mainstream of Thai society. As secular spaces, the Asoke communities thus in part serve a symbolic function, representing an ideal way of life to which only the most committed members adhere.

In a similar fashion, some Islamic fundamentalists have appropriated portions of secular space to demonstrate the superiority of Islam as a way of life. In countries dominated by fundamentalists, like Iran and Afghanistan, all of secular space in theory becomes part of their domain. Elsewhere, Islamic fundamentalist groups have created networks of institutions in secular space that operate parallel to those of the government. The founding of these institutions again reflects the fundamentalists' desire to advance their religious principles, but in the context of Islam such efforts also often take on distinct political connotations. By using their institutions to provide needed social services, such as education, health care, and financial support, the fundamentalists challenge the effectiveness of the existing political authorities and show how society would function under an authentic Islamic order. In the process, they also seek to strengthen support among the masses for the eventual creation of an Islamic state. Various groups have adopted this strategy, but it has probably been developed most fully by Islamic fundamentalist groups in Egypt, particularly the Muslim Brotherhood. These groups operate hundreds of local clinics and hospitals, many of them associated with local mosques, which serve as a major source of health care in working-class neighborhoods and poor villages. Fundamentalists have also established hundreds of schools at all levels, including adult education programs, and their social welfare programs offer food, shelter, job training, and financial assistance to the poor. According to one estimate, the fundamentalists' social infrastructure provides services on a regular basis to about 10 percent of Egypt's population.[34]

Secular governments in the Islamic world have in some cases seen the rapid growth of fundamentalist institutions as a threat to their authority. In Turkey, for example, rapid growth in the number of religious schools operated by fundamentalists led the secular government to change the nation's education laws. By the late 1990s, religious schools in Turkey contained half a million students and produced over fifty thousand graduates per year. The Turkish government viewed this trend with alarm, seeing the religious schools as a major source of fundamentalist propagandizing. In response, the government passed a law in 1997 that increased the period of compulsory public education from five years to eight, thus raising the age at which students could first be sent to religious schools from twelve to fifteen. The government extended imposed additional limitations on fundamentalist educational programs in 1998 by banning religious courses during the summer months and on weekends.[35] Fundamentalists have protested these actions but have not succeeded in having them reversed.

Schools have also been a major concern of Christian fundamentalists in the United States seeking to partition their own secular spaces (fig. 4.7). The Christian focus on education in this context derives from the perception that local

Figure 4.7 Christ the King Christian Academy, located in a small strip mall. Despite their efforts to participate in the mainstream of American society, fundamentalist Christians have often formed their own schools and other secular spaces to protect themselves from outside influences. This school covers grades K–6 and is a member of the Association of Christian Schools International. Kerrville, Texas, 1999. *Source:* the author.

control over public schools has declined in recent decades as a result of Supreme Court rulings banning school prayer and enforcing racial integration, as well as through the development of standardized curricula. Christian fundamentalists have voiced particular concern with the prevalence of secular humanistic values in the public schools, especially as expressed in the teaching of biological evolution, sex education, and moral relativism. To counter this trend, they have developed their own educational structures focusing on religious values and the moral absolutes drawn from the Bible (fig. 4.8). By promoting Bible-centered education, they also hope to protect their children from external sources of corruption and the negative influences of peer pressure. Christian fundamentalist efforts in this context have taken two major forms: the creation of separate Christian schools, from kindergartens to universities, and the practice of home schooling.[36] The number of Christian schools has grown rapidly since the 1960s; at present around ten thousand are operating in the United States, serving up to 1.5 million children. Such schools account for about 25 percent of all private school students and 3 percent of total school enrollment across the country. These schools obviously vary in terms of their

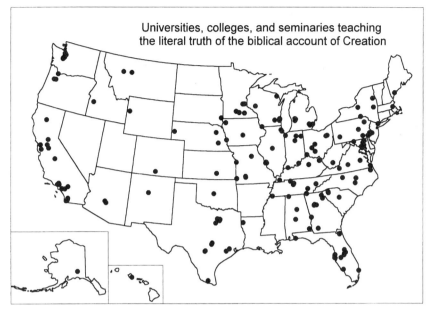

Figure 4.8   Institutions of higher education where the literal truth of the biblical account of creation is taught, as of June 1999. *Data source:* ChristianAnswers.Net.

specific religious orientations, but a majority of them promote fundamentalist beliefs, particularly the concept of biblical inerrancy. They also generally incorporate fundamentalist beliefs throughout the curriculum. Widely used texts, for example, explain the certainty of mathematics by comparing it to religious certainty and present Roman Catholicism as an inauthentic form of Christianity. Organizations like the American Association of Christian Schools and the Association of Christian Schools International have provided a broader institutional context for the Christian school movement. Home schooling, or the education of children at home by a parent, has been adopted more recently by fundamentalists but has also grown in popularity very rapidly. This practice at first faced strong opposition from local school boards, state education departments, and other elements of the educational establishment, but has now been legalized in every state of the United States. It has often been used by Christians when no fundamentalist school operates in the local area or when the cost of private schooling is too high. Current estimates suggest that about one million children in the United States are now educated at home and that roughly 80 percent of parents have chosen this approach for religious reasons.

The appropriation of portions of secular space by Christian fundamentalists has not been limited to schools. In many parts of the United States, fundamentalists have attempted to develop networks of Christian businesses and services, based on the belief that Christians should support each other financially as well as spiritually. These businesses often indicate in their advertisements that they are Christian through the use of a stylized fish symbol, or ichthus, based on the many references to fish in the New Testament, and many fundamentalist groups have promoted the idea of "shopping Christian" (fig. 4.9). Fundamentalists in the United States have also created their own recreational spaces, in the form of youth camps, adult retreats, and resorts. Again, these spaces provide recreation in a biblically principled context, both to reinforce their customers' religious commitment and to isolate them from the corrupting influences perceived to exist in other recreational settings.

The partitioning of secular space thus represents an important strategy for fundamentalist groups as they attempt to defend their religious beliefs. This approach mirrors fundamentalists' efforts to lay claim to their own sacred space and plays an equally important role in maintaining commitment to the fundamentalist cause. The creation of institutional or communal boundaries in secular space allows fundamentalists to express the ideological boundaries that they use to define themselves, and it also creates a safe haven to protect them from

Figure 4.9   An ichthus displayed in a store window, along with credit card signs and store hours. Many Christian business owners have adopted the stylized ichthus as a means of declaring their religious orientation. Fredericksburg, Texas, 1999. *Source:* the author.

external forces that they consider to be hostile. In some instances, fundamentalists believe that their secular spaces will contribute to the spread of their ideas. Islamic groups in Egypt, for example, use their many social services and charitable institutions to attract support from the larger population. Likewise, when in 1998 the fundamentalist Citizens for Excellence in Education gave up its goal of reforming U.S. public schools and instead encouraged its followers to support private Christian schools and home schooling, it assumed that private Christian education would ultimately serve as a role model for failing public school systems. In other cases, however, fundamentalists have established secular institutions or residential areas primarily for defensive purposes, as seen in the case of haredi Jews in Israel.

In general terms, then, fundamentalist efforts to control secular space reflect two related beliefs: that certain religious principles must be observed in all realms of social life and that adherence to those principles should be conspicuously rigorous. By demanding that secular activities conform to their religious beliefs, by defining gendered spaces consistent with traditional gender roles, and by creating their own bounded secular spaces, fundamentalists assert that their values and principles provide the only legitimate foundation for a virtuous social order. Unless their values and principles are respected, in their view, the secular realms of social life will become morally corrupting and will ultimately hinder the ability of true believers to fulfill their religious obligations. Haredi Jews thus argue that automobile traffic after sundown on Friday interferes with the proper observance of the Sabbath, Islamic fundamentalists insist that women must be veiled outside the home to protect men from sexual temptations that could lead them to abandon their family and community responsibilities, and Christian fundamentalists turn away from public school systems to limit their children's exposure to ideas and behaviors that they find threatening.

A crucial feature of fundamentalist actions relating to the use and control of secular space, moreover, is their explicitly public nature. Even when such actions involve a withdrawal from the larger society, they are intended to have conspicuous consequences. Fundamentalists tend to stress the visibility of their interactions with secular space in part to declare their distinctiveness from the rest of society. As Martin Marty has observed, religious fundamentalism typically insists on "scandalous" behavior, which, by violating the customs of secular society, makes significant demands on the movement's followers and clearly identifies them as part of a select group of true believers.[37] The insistence on conspicuous observance of the group's beliefs reinforces the ideological boundaries that separate the fundamentalists from others and helps to define their identity. At the same time, this conspicuous behavior also presents a direct challenge to nonfundamentalists. Particularly when they infringe on established social practices, fundamentalist efforts to impose traditional beliefs in the secular realm pose a direct threat to the values and principles of outsiders.

As a result, fundamentalist actions in secular space often become the central source of conflicts with those outside the group.

TERRITORY AND IDENTITY

A strong sense of group identity is an intrinsic element of the fundamentalist perspective. Fundamentalists use their identity as a distinct group within society to express their commitment to specific religious traditions that others have abandoned and to declare their opposition to social trends of which they disapprove. Moreover, the sense of threat that motivates their actions typically involves the fear that their identity as a group is at risk. Groups like the haredim, for example, see the growth of secularism as a threat to the survival of religious community as a basis for social identity. Christians in the United States and Hindus in India, on the other hand, assert that the acceptance of cultural pluralism undermines their group's traditional identity as the core of their society. Islamic fundamentalist responses to Western imperialism focus on the loss of indigenous Muslim identity brought about by the hegemony of Western popular culture and political philosophies. The preservation of their religious identity in the face of such threats thus represents a key goal of fundamentalists. They believe that the defense of their distinct sense of identity is an indispensable part of their larger effort to protect and promote their traditional beliefs. From the fundamentalist perspective, such beliefs cannot exist without the support of a clearly defined moral community, and such a community cannot function effectively unless it expresses a shared identity based on common beliefs.

In defining or strengthening their sense of identity, fundamentalists have often placed considerable emphasis on associations between their group and a particular territory. Such associations may have specific religious connotations, involving notions of sacred space or sacred history. Frequently, though, they are based on more general conceptions of the role of territory in the group's political or communal identity. Many fundamentalist groups have tried to assert control over a particular political state, for example, and for these groups, an abstract identification with that state becomes a logical extension of their desire to exercise cultural hegemony over the area. Fundamentalist groups have also focused on the importance of a particular territory as their communal homeland, tying it to their belief in an idealized past in which they enjoyed cultural hegemony and their traditional beliefs dominated the social order. In either case, fundamentalists use territorial associations to give physical expression to their group's distinct identity, as well as to establish a geographical focus for their actions. These territorial associations thus become a key element of the group's defense against the threatening "other" that it opposes. In the process, moreover, they have often imparted a nationalistic quality to fundamentalist ideologies, a result that again has generated considerable conflict with nonfundamentalists.

The interaction between territorial identity and religious nationalism has been especially conspicuous among Hindu fundamentalists, who seek to achieve the revitalization of an authentic Hindu nation. This group has stressed the concept of territorial identity in part because Hinduism does not focus on a strictly defined set of uniform doctrines. Tolerance for diverse beliefs and practices in fact represents one of Hinduism's most important traits and is recognized as such by Hindu fundamentalists. In the absence of a codified set of orthodox beliefs, then, Hindu fundamentalism requires some other source of unity on which to base its sense of common identity. Fundamentalists have addressed that need through the concept of *Hindutva*, or Hinduness. Originally developed by the Hindu militant V. D. Savarkar in the early 1900s, the idea of *Hindutva* reflects an inclusive approach to defining the boundaries of the Hindu community. It does not refer to a specific set of religious rituals or beliefs. Rather, it defines Hinduness in terms of the social and cultural features that have traditionally distinguished the Indian people from other groups. These features include their genealogical descent from ancestral groups that have lived in this region for thousands of years, their practice of the distinctive way of life, or dharma, associated with the region, and their overriding belief in an elemental natural order. The concept of *Hindutva* also stresses the universality of the Hindu ethos and its ability to accommodate a broad range of practices and beliefs.[38]

Geography clearly plays a central role in this definition of Hindu identity. In his original discussion of *Hindutva*, Savarkar strongly emphasized the connections between Hinduness and a particular territory: that is, the region that lies between the Indus River, the Himalayan Mountains, and the Indian Ocean. Known as Bharat (or Bharatvarsha), this territory encompasses the original homeland of the Aryan ancestors of modern-day Hindus, according to fundamentalist belief. Many fundamentalists in fact reject the widely accepted theory that the Aryan people invaded the Indian subcontinent from the northwest in prehistoric times, insisting instead that the Aryans were indigenous to Bharat.[39] Bharat thus represents the hearth in which Hindu civilization and the history of the Hindu people evolved. It also has important religious meaning as the sacred land where the various Hindu gods have taken earthly forms and where the only true holy men have been born. As a result, Hindu fundamentalists consider the association with Bharat to be an essential part of *Hindutva* and the unifying factor in Hindu identity. Savarkar expressed this view quite clearly, basing his definition of *Hindutva* on the integration of geographical, cultural, and genealogical factors. He asserted specifically that the quality of *Hindutva* described those people who recognize Bharat as both their ancestral homeland and their holy land, a characterization that has become the basis for Hindu fundamentalist identity. Savarkar did make it clear that *Hindutva* could apply to adherents of religions other than Hinduism, but only if they view Bharat as sacred space, a requirement that excludes Christians and Muslims, as well as secularists.[40]

Reaffirming the association between *Hindutva* and the land of Bharat has become a primary objective of the Hindu fundamentalist movement. In their view, this association has been threatened both by secular trends, which have diminished the social influence of religion, and by the government's pluralistic policies, which in assigning equal status to all religions have displaced the Hindu ethos as the dominant force in Indian society. Fundamentalists believe that these developments have undermined *Hindutva* as a source of national unity and have thus weakened India's moral, cultural, and political integrity. In response, they seek to reestablish the supremacy of Hindu culture and civilization in their homeland of Bharat. This goal is most directly expressed in the fundamentalist concept of *Hindu Rashtra* ("Hindu nation"), a view of Indian nationhood based on the shared identity of *Hindutva*. The desire to revitalize *Hindu Rashtra* motivated the formation of the Rashtriya Swayamsevak Sangh (RSS) in 1925 and has become a principal concern of the other organizations of the Sangh Parivar, such as the Vishwa Hindu Parishad and the Bharatiya Janata Party. These groups assert that *Hindutva* provides the only basis for creating a meaningful national identity in India, without which the country will stagnate or decline.

That assertion has had important political ramifications, since fundamentalists see the Indian state as the modern expression of their cultural homeland. Bharat is in fact the other official name of India, although in the context of *Hindutva* Bharat refers not to the modern political state but to the original hearth of Hindu civilization. As the Hindu fundamentalist movement has grown, however, its members have sought to identify India as a political state with Bharat as a traditional culture realm. Fundamentalists assert that India should become the nation-state for those people encompassed by the concept of *Hindutva*, whom they consider to be the country's rightful rulers. In this context, *Hindu Rashtra* has evolved from a cultural concept denoting the people united by *Hindutva* to a political concept describing India as a true Hindu state. Support for the revitalization of *Hindu Rashtra* has thus emerged as the focus of a contemporary form of Hindu nationalism that often does not differentiate between political and religious goals. The destruction of the Babri Mosque in Ayodhya, for example, has been depicted by Hindu nationalists as essentially a patriotic act, honoring the Hindu deity Ram as an Indian national hero. The politicization of the concept of *Hindu Rashtra* also appears in the fundamentalist goal of establishing Ram Rajya, an ideal state organized around the principles of the true dharma of Hinduism. According to fundamentalist belief, such a state would lead to the creation of a perfect Hindu society, whose members would function as a single, integrated social entity, and in doing so would become a living manifestation of the divine.[41]

In seeking to preserve Hindu tradition by linking India's political identity to the concept of *Hindutva*, Hindu fundamentalists have provoked considerable opposition from other segments of Indian society. The primary source of conflict has been disagreement over the religious content of *Hindutva*. The BJP, the fundamentalist party at the center of this effort to politicize the concept of *Hindu Rashtra*, argues that *Hindutva* is not the same as Hinduism. Its leaders characterize *Hindutva* as an expression of nationalism, not of religious communalism. In support of this contention, for example, they cite the traditional practices of referring to India as Hindustan and to its inhabitants as Hindus, regardless of their religion. They believe that Hindu culture represents the core of the region's shared history and should be considered the heritage of all true Indians. They further assert that the religious heroes of Hinduism, such as Lord Ram, should be viewed as national heroes, symbolizing the common values for which the country stands. The fundamentalists' opponents, on the other hand, see the politicized concept of *Hindu Rashtra* as a threat to the freedoms of other religious groups and secularists. They argue that the cultural and religious components of *Hindutva* cannot be separated from one another and that any attempt to impose *Hindutva* as a national ideology will disadvantage Indians who are not practicing Hindus. Some opponents have also argued that the fundamentalists' promotion of *Hindutva* as the source of national identity is motivated largely by status concerns. In particular, they assert that upper-caste Hindi-speakers from northern India, a core constituency of Hindu fundamentalism, have used the *Hindutva* movement as a means of protecting their traditional status in contemporary Indian society. The fundamentalists reject such arguments, however. They insist that their goal is to preserve a distinct cultural identity for India by countering the corrosive effects of modernism, secularism, and the compromises with tradition imposed by the current secular state. To achieve that end, they believe that they must incorporate *Hindutva* into India's identity as a political state.

The associations among religion, territory, and national identity have also emerged as a major concern of Sinhalese Buddhist fundamentalists in Sri Lanka. Like their Hindu counterparts, Sinhalese fundamentalists believe that Western colonialism had the effect of undermining their traditional identity, which they now must try to recreate. In doing so, they have emphasized the central role that their cultural and religious heritage has played in the formation of a distinctive Sri Lankan society. To be meaningful, Sri Lanka's postcolonial identity must be defined in their view as being explicitly Buddhist and Sinhalese, and they are committed to seeing that such a definition prevails. Their interest in promoting religious tradition thus arises from a desire to establish an authoritative source of group cohesion rather than from concerns over particular doctrinal issues. Moreover, like Hindu fundamentalists, Sinhalese Buddhists have developed a strong emphasis on territory in promoting their religious conception of national identity. Specifically, their focus on Buddhism as a core element of national identity reflects their belief in Sri Lanka as a sacred homeland for their group, with a special purpose in Buddhist history. Sinhalese fundamentalists conceive of territory, then, as the physical expression of both their sense of nationhood and their religious traditions.

This view of Sri Lanka as a consecrated land derives primarily from the *Mahavamsa* ("Great Chronicle"), an important Buddhist history dating from the fifth century. The *Mahavamsa* provides an account of the origins of the Sinhalese people, of the coming of Buddhism to Sri Lanka, and of nearly nine hundred years of rule by the first Sinhalese kings, starting in the sixth century B.C.[42] The narrative describes three supernatural visits by the Buddha to Sri Lanka, during which he rid the island of demons, resolved conflicts between rival rulers, and visited various locations since recognized by Buddhists as sacred sites. It also tells of how the Buddha foretold that Buddhism would decline in India but would flourish in Sri Lanka under the leadership of the Sinhalese. The Buddha thus provided for the protection of the first Sinhalese king, Vijaya, an Indian prince who is believed to have arrived in Sri Lanka as the Buddha achieved his final state of nirvana. The story goes on to describe the official establishment of Buddhism as the state religion under Sinhalese rule several centuries later, fulfilling the Buddha's prophecy. Sri Lanka's consecration was further reinforced through the importation of several important Buddhist relics, including a tree propagated from a cutting from the bo tree under which the Buddha achieved enlightenment, which survives in the city of Anuradhapura, the Buddha's right collarbone, also enshrined in Anuradhapura, and one of the Buddha's teeth, kept in the city of Kandy at the Temple of the Tooth, Sri Lanka's holiest Buddhist shrine (fig. 4.10). Based on these various events, the Sinhalese have defined Sri Lanka as a sacred land blessed by the Buddha and have identified themselves as Buddhism's chosen people, responsible for the preservation of their religion in its purest form.

In recounting the national origins of the Sinhalese people, then, the *Mahavamsa* describes their essential bonds to both Sri Lanka and Buddhism. Sinhalese fundamentalists have in turn used this narrative to create a meaningful group identity within their present postcolonial context. They argue that to be Sinhalese is to be Buddhist and that the Sinhalese-Buddhist nation represents the core society of Sri Lanka. They have thus defined the boundaries of their movement through an "imagined" conception of their distinctive communal history rather than on the basis of adherence to distinctive religious doctrines. The resulting sense of identity is most clearly expressed, according to anthropologist Gananath Obeyesekere, through the concept of *sasana*, a term that can refer to either the community of all Buddhists or the Buddhist society of a particular country, such as Sri Lanka.[43] In the latter meaning, this concept has become the foundation for the fundamentalists' territory-based definition of Sinhalese identity. It has also become integrated into the country's political structure through the creation of the government's Ministry of Buddha Sasana.

Figure 4.10 The shrine of the sacred bo tree in Anuradhapura, propagated from the original bo tree in India, under which the Buddha achieved enlightenment. This and other Sri Lankan sites connected with the Buddha represent important expressions of the relationship between Buddhism and Sinhalese nationalism. Anuradhapura, Sri Lanka, 1982. *Source:* CORBIS/Sheldan Collins.

Established in 1989 by Ranasinghe Premadasa, Sri Lanka's president and leader of the United National Party, the ministry was charged with protecting and promoting Buddhist interests in the country.[44]

Sinhalese fundamentalists have thus asserted that their Buddhist community is embodied in the territory of their sacred homeland. As a result, they have a strong commitment to the idea of Sri Lanka as a unitary Buddhist state. This idea has important political consequences, since it inevitably raises the issue of the right of the Sinhalese to exercise control over the territory with which they identify. That issue has generated enduring conflicts between the Sinhalese and other ethnic and religious groups, particularly the Hindu Tamils. The *Mahavamsa* in fact recognizes the Tamils as legitimate inhabitants of Sri Lanka, but during the postcolonial era many Sinhalese have come to see them as antagonists. The Tamils have responded by seeking political autonomy, a goal strongly opposed by the Sinhalese who want to preserve Sri Lanka's territorial integrity. The result has been a prolonged civil war between the Sinhalese-led government and Tamil rebels, particularly those belonging to the Liberation Tigers of Tamil Eelam (LTTE). Numerous efforts have been made to end the fighting, including the mobilization of an Indian peacekeeping force during the late 1980s. These efforts have repeatedly failed, however, and throughout the 1990s the LTTE have maintained a campaign of terrorist violence. Early in 1998, shortly before Sri Lanka was to celebrate its fiftieth year of independence, LTTE terrorists carried out a suicide bombing against the Temple of the Tooth. The tooth remained unharmed, but the temple was extensively damaged, and the Sri Lankan government responded by ending direct negotiations with the Tamil rebels. The bombing also strengthened fundamentalist support for continuing military operations against the rebels.

Sinhalese fundamentalists have stressed the integration of religion, identity, and territory as a way of dealing with a threat deriving from the ethnoreligious divisions within Sri Lankan society. In particular, they have sought to maintain the traditional dominance of Sinhalese Buddhist culture in the country, which in their view had been undermined during the period of British colonialism. Their efforts thus reflect their belief that they represent Sri Lanka's rightful national majority. Sikh fundamentalists in Punjab have attempted to establish similar connections between identity and territory, but their efforts represent a response to a different kind of threat. They believe that because of their minority status they are threatened with marginalization or, even worse, assimilation by Indian society at large. The historical roots of Sikhism within the context of Hindu society reinforce the threat of assimilation, as does the belief of Hindu fundamentalists that Sikhism represents a variant expression of *Hindutva*. The efforts of Sikh fundamentalists to carve out a territorial identity have thus been largely defensive in nature, aimed at establishing a geographical context that will protect their distinctiveness.[45]

The Sikh fundamentalists' conception of a modern territorial identity has evolved over time, in response to the Sikhs' changing political context. That conception had its roots in the Sikh Empire established early in the nineteenth century by military leader Ranjit Singh, who took control of much of Punjab away from the declining Mogul regime. By mid-century, the British had absorbed the Sikh Empire into their colonial holdings, and the Sikhs remained loyal to Britain for the rest of the 1800s. As the prospect of British decolonization emerged in the early decades of the twentieth century, however, Sikhs again became concerned with territorial issues. They were particularly concerned with the fate of Punjab in the proposed division of the British colonies into a predominantly Hindu India and a predominantly Muslim Pakistan. Although Punjab was the homeland of the Sikh community, Muslims in fact accounted for a slight majority of the province's population. On this basis, Muslim leaders argued that the whole of Punjab should be incorporated into Pakistan. The Sikhs strongly opposed this plan, since Pakistan was to be constituted as an explicitly Muslim state. During the 1940s, some Sikh political leaders in the Akali Dal argued for the creation of a separate Sikh state, but this proposal had little chance of success. After the future leaders of India assured the Sikhs that they would have autonomy if they remained part of India, the Sikhs thus demanded that Punjab be divided during the process of partition, with the predominantly Muslim areas in the western part of the province becoming part of Pakistan and the areas in eastern Punjab, where Sikhs and Hindus together made up a majority, becoming part of India. This solution was adopted, but it led to considerable hardship in the region after partition, as millions of Sikhs and Hindus fled from West Punjab to India and millions of Muslims moved from East Punjab to Pakistan. The violence that accompanied this vast relocation led to the deaths of over half a million Punjabis.[46]

After independence, the Sikh fundamentalist movement began to expand as increasing numbers of Sikhs saw themselves as being marginalized within Indian society. They asserted that they had been denied the degree of autonomy promised to them before partition and that their homeland had been reduced to a colony of India's central government. They believed that these circumstances placed them at a disadvantage economically and politically, but they also saw them as a threat to their cultural and religious integrity. Fundamentalists associated with the Akali Dal thus returned to the idea of establishing a specific territorial domain for the Sikhs, both to promote their secular interests and to defend their ethnoreligious identity against the cultural hegemony of Hindu society. During the 1950s and early 1960s, they argued for the creation of a more clearly defined territorial presence within India itself. The initial boundaries of the province of Punjab contained a diverse population, including many areas dominated by languages other than Punjabi. The province's cities also had large concentrations of Hindus, and within the province as a whole Sikhs represented only about a third of the population.[47] Sikh fundamentalists thus sought to have the existing provincial boundaries redrawn, to create an area within which Sikhs would dominate. Hindu politicians opposed the creation of a Sikh province, however, believing that this action would weaken national unity and would violate India's constitutional secularism. In the early 1960s, leaders of the Akali Dal thus began to demand the creation of a separate Punjabi-speaking state within India, since linguistic patterns had served as the basis for provincial boundaries in other parts of India. Because Hindus in the region also speak Punjabi, the fundamentalists further demanded that the new province's official language be defined as Punjabi written in the Gurmukhi script used by Sikhs rather than in the Devangari script used by Hindus.[48] Finally in 1996 the Indian government redrew the boundaries of Punjab along linguistic lines, in effect redefining the Punjab so that it now contained a Sikh majority (fig. 4.11).[49]

The redefinition of Punjab did not eliminate the concerns of Sikh fundamentalists, however. They still believed that Sikhs had been marginalized within the economic and political spheres of Indian life, and they continued to see Hindu hegemony within the larger society as a threat to their identity. Punjab's newly defined boundaries offered some protection, but they did not establish a definitive territorial expression of Sikh identity. Fundamentalists

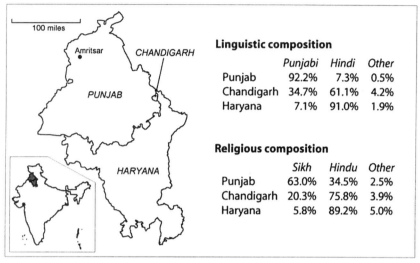

Linguistic composition

	Punjabi	Hindi	Other
Punjab	92.2%	7.3%	0.5%
Chandigarh	34.7%	61.1%	4.2%
Haryana	7.1%	91.0%	1.9%

Religious composition

	Sikh	Hindu	Other
Punjab	63.0%	34.5%	2.5%
Chandigarh	20.3%	75.8%	3.9%
Haryana	5.8%	89.2%	5.0%

Figure 4.11   In 1966, the Indian government divided the existing state of Punjab into three parts: a state dominated by Punjabi-speakers, which retained the name of Punjab; Haryana, a state dominated by Hindi speakers; and a small territory encompassing the city of Chandigarh, which served as the capital city of the other two states. The newly defined Punjab contained a Sikh majority. *Data source:* Census of India, 1991.

thus continued to press for greater autonomy and cultural security. In 1973 at Anandpur, an important historical center of Sikhism in northern Punjab, the Akali Dal issued a manifesto known as the Anandpur Sahib Resolution, which included various demands regarding economic development, political autonomy, and protection of their religious distinctiveness. Sikh fundamentalists repeated such demands throughout the 1970s and early 1980s and by 1981 began to agitate for the creation of an independent Sikh state. To be known as Khalistan ("Land of the Pure"), the proposed state would provide an undisputed homeland for the Sikhs and thus would give their distinct identity a concrete geographical expression. Some members of the Akali Dal originally opposed this idea, but as Jarnail Singh Bhindranwale's influence grew, so did support for Khalistan. In 1987, three years after the Indian army's assault on the Golden Temple and the death of Bhindranwale, fundamentalists assembled at the Golden Temple complex officially declared Khalistan to be an independent political state, which was being unlawfully occupied by the Indian government. The fundamentalists declared that within Khalistan all aspects of life would conform to the dictates of Sikhism and that there would be no distinction between religious and political concerns.[50] In the same year, however, India's central government reasserted direct control over Punjab and began a campaign of attrition against Sikh militants. For the rest of the 1980s, Sikh extremists functioned as a de facto regime in Punjab, but their influence declined sharply in the 1990s as government efforts to suppress them began to succeed and as the larger Sikh community became increasingly disaffected with the ongoing violence. Khalistan had more or less disappeared as an immediate political reality by the early 1990s.

In subsequent years, most Sikh fundamentalists have repudiated the idea of creating an independent Khalistan through armed insurrection. Although a few extremist groups like the Khalistan Liberation Force continue to carry out terrorist actions, they have very little support within Punjab's Sikh community. Nonetheless, threats against the integrity of the Sikhs' religious identity remain a genuine concern of fundamentalists. Fundamentalist leaders have thus sought to advance Sikh interests and protect Sikh culture through legitimate political action, and territorial strategies remain an important part of their approach. In 1994, a number of fundamentalist factions within the Akali Dal proposed the creation of a semiautonomous Sikh region as part of a new confederation of Indian states. Their manifesto, known as the Amritsar Declaration, did not advocate violent secession from India, but its authors reserved the right to work toward a fully autonomous Sikh state through democratic means if an agreement with India could not be achieved. More moderate fundamentalists within the Akali Dal have focused less on the issue of independence and more on specific economic, political, and cultural issues, but still with the goal of enhancing the Sikhs' territorial status. From the fundamentalists' point of view, the recognition of a distinct Sikh territory remains crucial to the preservation of their traditional identity. They see such a territory as a necessary expression of their legitimacy as a distinct group within India's larger plural society.

Associations between territory and identity have also figured prominently in Islamic fundamentalism, but in a form somewhat different from the cases already examined. Through centuries of political expansion and missionary activity, Islam has spread into a variety of different regions, from Southeast Asia to northern Africa, which diverge significantly in terms of their culture, environment, history, and political evolution. The geographical unity ascribed to India by Hindu fundamentalists, or to Sri Lanka by Sinhalese fundamentalists, thus cannot be applied to the ecumene of Islam. Moreover, most Muslims live in regions that have no direct connection to the origins of Islam. Hindu and Sikh fundamentalists assert that their ancestral homelands are also their religion's holy lands. Sinhalese fundamentalists make similar claims based on their tradition that the Buddha consecrated Sri Lanka as a land where his teachings would flourish. Most regions of the Islamic world, however, do not possess an analogous religious meaning. As a result, the territorial concerns of Islamic fundamentalist movements differ from those of the groups examined earlier and focus on a different kind of threat. The primary goal of Islamic fundamentalists is to reshape their particular society into an authentic form free from corruption, not to reclaim a homeland sacred to all believers. And to achieve this goal, they seek to establish a geographical setting for the implementation of Islamic law. Within Islamic fundamentalism, the goal of linking territory with identity thus contains a distinct political dimension, which is manifested most clearly in the concept of the Islamic state.

Fundamentalists base the concept of the Islamic state on the historical model of the society established by Muhammad in Medina early in Islam's history. They view the original Muslim community, along with the empire ruled by Muhammad's immediate successors, as a natural expression of Islam as a complete way of life, governing both temporal and spiritual matters. Most Islamic fundamentalist movements have sought to reestablish such a state in the modern world. In pursuing that goal, however, they have focused on creating a political structure for their own nation, rather than on forming a universal polity bringing together all Muslims. Even during the first few centuries of its history, the widespread diffusion of Islam made political unity among its adherents difficult to maintain, and by the thirteenth century, the original Caliphate collapsed through a combination of internal and external conflicts. Muslims retained a concept of the Islamic world, *dar al-Islam*, made up of those areas following the sharia, but that world has been extensively subdivided through political processes of imperialism and decolonization.[51] Some fundamentalists, like the Taliban in Afghanistan, have asserted that they will ultimately reunify the entire Muslim world. In terms of their immediate territorial goals, though, Islamic fundamentalist groups have focused on creating a more exclusive political structure. In this way, the concept of the Islamic state has become a response to modern political realities as well as a defense of traditional beliefs, tying together ideas of territory, nationalism, and religious identity. Despite its roots in the historical model of the early community of Medina, the Islamic state as envisioned by fundamentalists thus represents an essentially modern undertaking.

The definitive characteristic of the Islamic state is its implementation of the sharia in all aspects of life. According to fundamentalists, this function requires the structural support of a political state, including an Islamic constitution and legal code, Islamic institutions, and a social system organized according to Islamic principles. Fulfillment of this function gives the state its political legitimacy. Various fundamentalist groups have also tied the concept of the Islamic state to national interests, however. Some early fundamentalists in fact opposed this approach, arguing that as a universal religion Islam should not be entangled with nationalism. Nonetheless, religion has become an increasingly important element of national identity throughout the Islamic world over the past century, as Muslims have tried to free themselves from Western hegemony. In countries as different as Egypt, Iran, Pakistan, and Malaysia, fundamentalists have promoted Islam as a source of social unity that does not rely on Western ideologies or influences. In this context, the creation of an Islamic state offers a means of asserting a sense of territorial identity based on indigenous traditions rather than on externally imposed structures.

The efforts of Islamic fundamentalists to integrate religious and territorial identity has had a profound influence on countries throughout the Islamic world. This influence appears most clearly in the places where fundamentalists have actually established an Islamic state, as in Iran under the Islamic Revolution or Afghanistan under the Taliban. In these cases, fundamentalists have redefined their countries as theocracies based on the rule of Islam, formally merging their religious identities with political structures. Elsewhere, fundamentalist efforts to create an Islamic state have not transformed society as fully, but have instead become a major source of internal political conflict. In some cases, such conflicts revolve around the contested nature of national identity. In Malaysia, for example, fundamentalists seek to define national identity in religious terms, based on the strong association between Islam and Malay ethnicity. In their view, the establishment of an Islamic state in Malaysia provides the only viable means of maintaining a virtuous society. Secularists and members of other ethnic groups reject this assertion, seeing it as a direct threat to the country's pluralistic character. In other instances, conflicts have arisen over the extent to which traditional Islamic law should be implemented within a modernizing society. Fundamentalists in Egypt, for example, want all of the country's legislation to conform to the sharia. The secular mainstream opposes this goal, arguing that while Islam has been recognized as an important source of authority in Egyptian law, the government must make some accommodation to the modern, secular world. The fundamentalists believe, however, that the sharia must be precisely enforced to eliminate corruption from Egyptian society; and in their view that goal can be achieved only by reconstituting Egypt as an Islamic state.

Fundamentalists have thus used the concept of the Islamic state to unite concerns relating to religious identity, nationalism, and territory. The politicizing of religious identity in this manner has generated widespread conflict in Muslim societies. Even in Pakistan, which came into existence as a Muslim state, sharp disagreements exist over the extent to which Islamic traditions should be integrated into the country's institutions and legal code. Fundamentalists believe, however, that their conception of Islam as a comprehensive way of life requires the complete integration of religious and political structures. And within the context of the contemporary nation-state, the latter goal has repeatedly led fundamentalists to draw connections between religious and territorial identities.

The above-mentioned cases illustrate that fundamentalist movements have tried to assert connections between their ideological boundaries and specific geographical boundaries, using territory to concretize their identity. In some cases, they have done so because they believe that their group identity has an inherent geographical dimension. Hindu fundamentalists, for example, define their essential characteristic, *Hindutva*, through their connections to Bharat, the homeland of Hinduism. Sinhalese fundamentalists similarly link their identity to Sri Lanka as a sacred land. The connections between territory and identity have also taken on a strong political character for many groups, providing a means of reconciling fundamentalist identity to the realities of the modern nation-state. This process has been especially important for fundamentalists in postcolonial settings, where the traditional nature of their group identity has been challenged by the introduction of Western influences and ideologies, as in Sri Lanka and many predominantly Muslim countries. In such cases, the integration of fundamentalism and nationalism serves to reclaim traditional sources of identity and thereby to redefine society in terms of indigenous values and structures.

Fundamentalist groups other than those just considered have also focused on issues of territory and identity, in somewhat different ways. Protestant fundamentalists, for example, have promoted the idea of the United States as a Christian nation, although they have generally stopped short of calling for the kind of absolute theocracy envisioned by Islamic fundamentalists. More complex connections between territory and identity appear within Jewish fundamentalism. Religious Zionists define themselves in part through their ties to a specific sacred space—the promised Land of Israel—but haredi fundamentalists explicitly reject this approach, denying the legitimacy of Israel or any secular political state as a source of Jewish identity. Finally, fundamentalists' efforts to associate themselves with a particular territory have frequently led to conflict with those outside the group, since these efforts imply the assertion of some form of control over the territory in question. Others see these efforts as a threat to their own interests and have strongly resisted them. Secularists and religious minorities in India thus reject the concept of *Hindutva* as the foundation of Indian national identity, and nonfundamentalists in Muslim countries have continually resisted the idea of the Islamic state.

CONCLUSIONS

The preceding discussion confirms the crucial role of spatial concerns in fundamentalism. Fundamentalist groups have placed great emphasis on defining and controlling bounded spaces, both sacred and secular. Different groups have assigned structure and meaning to space in quite different ways, of course, suggesting that fundamentalist movements do not all share a common spatiality. The religious Zionists' concern with the sacred Land of Israel has no parallel among Christian fundamentalists, for example, and the strict territorial control required by the Taliban in imposing the sharia in Afghanistan does not have a direct counterpart in the efforts of Hindu fundamentalists to promote *Hindutva* in India. These diverse expressions of spatial concerns reflect the contextual nature of fundamentalism and the importance of specific beliefs and circumstances in shaping the strategies used by particular groups to advance their goals. Despite the differences in their approaches to dealing with space, however, all fundamentalist groups clearly do have a strong interest in spatial concerns, related both to their sense of being threatened and to their activist response to the "other" that they oppose.

Fundamentalists devote considerable attention to spatial themes in part because of the totalistic nature of their ideologies. From the fundamentalist perspective, the certainties of religious tradition are relevant to all facets of life and imbue all human activity with meaning. Space serves as the medium within which such meanings become specific and concrete. To fundamentalists, for example, concepts relating to the divine or the sacred are not mere abstractions; they reflect vital forces that are made tangible through their embodiment in sacred space. Hindu fundamentalists thus see the creation of a temple to Ram at Ayodhya as a necessary and practical action in trying to protect their beliefs. Similarly, fundamentalists promote strict adherence to moral standards not just to maintain social decorum but to give physical expression to the religious certainties on which such standards are based. Control of secular space provides the means to achieve this goal of linking mundane activities to sacred obligations, as in the segregation of men and women on certain Israeli bus routes. Fundamentalists' concern with meaning in a spatial context also involves the perception of threats to their traditional values and beliefs. In identifying such threats, fundamentalists again tend to focus on their manifestations in the real world, which they consider to be particularly alarming. Protests by Christian fundamentalists against the Disney Company for allowing gay and lesbian organizations to sponsor Gay Day events at Disney World provide a case in point. Outrage at this practice goes beyond the issue of gay rights to a more specific concern that space ostensibly reserved for "families," as fundamentalists define them, has been appropriated by groups that by the same definition are antifamily. The location of this celebration by gays and lesbians in "public" space provokes a heightened sense of danger among fundamentalists. Along somewhat different lines, Sinhalese fundamentalists consider Tamil efforts to carve an independent state out of Sri Lanka as a direct threat to the unified Buddhist identity of their country.

A second factor responsible for fundamentalists' concern with space is their commitment to activism. Fundamentalists believe that they must exert some form of control or influence in the world to ensure the survival of their religious traditions. The certainty of their faith prohibits them from compromising or giving in to threatening forces, of course, but it also requires that they take concrete actions to advance their own beliefs. In their view, verbal arguments are not sufficient to protect their beliefs. They believe that to prevail they must become actively engaged in fighting the threats that they have identified. Geographical space thus provides the setting for fundamentalist activism. As-

serting territorial control over a bounded space represents an especially common goal among fundamentalists. Religious Zionists thus seek to remove the
Muslim shrines on the Temple Mount as a way of reclaiming control of that
sacred space, a concrete action that they believe must take place before the
Jewish people can be redeemed. Haredi fundamentalists, on the other hand,
have attempted to establish control over the secular space surrounding their
own neighborhoods, to prevent public transgressions against their religious beliefs. Likewise, Islamic fundamentalists in various countries have tried to establish the sharia as the basis for the legal code, rather than relying on theological
arguments to persuade Muslims to follow traditional religious laws. Attempts
to unite territorial and religious identity represent another way in which fundamentalists have tried to exert influence on their surroundings. The supporters
of the Islamic Revolution in Iran, for example, saw their creation of an Islamic
regime as a crucial step in reclaiming a distinct national identity independent
of Western influence and in reforming the character of society. Spatial expressions of fundamentalist activism have inevitably led to conflict with others who
contest the meanings and functions assigned by fundamentalists to particular
spaces. Such conflict in turn reinforces the fundamentalists' motivations, by
providing concrete evidence that they are right to feel threatened by outside
forces.

Spatial concerns thus represent an inherent component of fundamentalism.
Such concerns reflect the religious meanings assigned by fundamentalists to
the entire scope of human activity and the importance they place on taking
action in defense of their religious certainties. Just as fundamentalists use ideological boundaries to distinguish themselves from others, so do they use geographical boundaries to assign meaning to and shape behavior within particular
spaces. The creation of boundaries around sacred spaces defines the sanctity
of those areas and provides a basis for protecting them from desecration. The
bounded secular spaces created by fundamentalists are more diverse in their
functions and uses. In some instances they may serve to isolate the group from
external threats; in others, they represent a mechanism for imposing the
group's standards and values on its own members and frequently on others as
well. Territorial boundaries also provide a concrete expression of the group's
own distinctiveness, sense of community, or political unity. In sum, the characteristics of the bounded spaces created by fundamentalists within both the
sacred and secular domains provide important insights into their conceptions
of religious certainty, social order, and group identity.

NOTES

1. Edward W. Soja, "The Spatiality of Social Life: Towards a Transforma-
tive Retheorization," in *Social Relations and Spatial Structures*, Derek Gregory
and John Urry, eds. (London: Macmillan, 1985), 90–127.

2. Yi-Fu Tuan, *Space and Place: The Perspectives of Experience* (Minneapolis: University of Minnesota Press, 1977).

3. David E. Sopher, *Geography of Religions* (Englewood Cliffs, N.J.: Prentice-Hall, 1967), 47–55; Yi-Fu Tuan, "Sacred Space: Exploration of an Idea," in *Dimensions of Human Geography*, Karl W. Butzer, ed. (Chicago: University of Chicago, Department of Geography, 1978), 84–99.

4. Ian S. Lustick, *For the Land and the Lord: Jewish Fundamentalism in Israel* (New York: Council on Foreign Relations, 1988), 68–9.

5. Gilles Kepel, *The Revenge of God: The Resurgence of Islam, Christianity and Judaism in the Modern World* (University Park: Pennsylvania State University Press, 1994), 163–8.

6. Michael Leeden and Barbara Leeden, "The Temple Mount Plot: What Do Christian and Jewish Fundamentalists Have in Common," *New Republic* 190 (June 18, 1984): 20–3.

7. For example, see Haim Shapiro, "Conservative Prayers at Wall Cause Near-Riot," *Jerusalem Post*, June 1, 1998, 1; and Deborah Sontag, "Orthodox Confront U.S. Reform Rabbis at Western Wall," *New York Times*, February 2, 1999, 3(A).

8. Aryeh Dean Cohen, "Women of the Wall Reject Compromise Prayer Site," *Jerusalem Post*, September 25, 1998, 1.

9. David Rudge, "Islamic Movement Gaining Support," *Jerusalem Post*, November 14, 1997, 5.

10. Martin Regg Cohn, "No Prayers Allowed," *Toronto Star*, February 8, 1998, 6(F).

11. Lustick, *For the Land and the Lord*, 105; Yosseph Shilhav, "Interpretation and Misinterpretation of Jewish Territorialism," in *The Impact of Gush Emunim: Politics and Settlement in the West Bank*, David Newman, ed. (London: Croon Helm, 1985), 111–24; Gwyn Rowley, "The Land of Israel: A Reconstructionist Approach," in *The Impact of Gush Emunim*, David Newman, ed., 125–36.

12. Gershon Shafir, "Institutional and Spontaneous Settlement Drives: Did Gush Emunim Make a Difference," in *The Impact of Gush Emunim*, David Newman, ed., 153–71.

13. Robert I. Friedman, "25,000 Saboteurs of Peace," *New York Times*, April 12, 1994, 17(A).

14. Ved Mehta, "The Mosque and the Temple: The Rise of Fundamentalism," *Foreign Affairs*, 72, no. 2 (Spring 1993): 16–21.

15. Yogendra K. Malik and V. B. Singh, *Hindu Nationalists in India: The Rise of the Bharatiya Janata Party* (Boulder, Colo.: Westview Press, 1994), 127–31.

16. Edward A. Gargan, "Hindu Militants Destroy Mosque," *New York Times*, December 7, 1992, 1(A).

17. Subhash Mishra and Uday Mahurkar, "Ayodhya: Carving Controversy," *India Today*, June 22, 1998, 20.

18. Dilip Hiro, *Holy Wars: The Rise of Islamic Fundamentalism* (New York: Routledge, 1989), 128–33.

19. Charles P. Wallace, "Iran Asks Overthrow of Saudi Rulers over Riots," *Los Angeles Times*, August 3, 1987, 1(1).

20. Herb Keinon, "Haredi Leader Threatens More Demonstrations in Tel Aviv," *Jerusalem Post*, December 5, 1996, 3.

21. Joel Greenberg, "Jerusalem Road Is Secular-Religious Battleground," *New York Times*, July 15, 1996, 3(A).

22. Batsheva Tsur and Elli Wohlgelernter, "Rehov Bar-Ilan Closes Tonight," *Jerusalem Post*, May 23, 1997, 1.

23. For example, see Dan Mihalopoulos, "Activists Protest Barnes & Noble," *St. Louis Post-Dispatch*, November 29, 1997, 7.

24. For a thorough discussion of the concept of gendered space, see Daphne Spain, *Gendered Spaces* (Chapel Hill: University of North Carolina Press, 1992).

25. The varied impacts of fundamentalism on women's lives is examined through a variety of case studies in Judy Brink and Joan Mencher, eds., *Mixed Blessings: Gender and Religious Fundamentalism Cross Culturally* (New York: Routledge, 1997).

26. For a detailed description of these schools, see Samuel Heilman, *Defenders of the Faith: Inside Ultra-Orthodox Jewry* (New York: Schocken Books, 1992), 168–235.

27. Amy Klein, "Haredi School Systems Have Almost Half of Jerusalem's Jewish Pupils," *Jerusalem Post*, September 11, 1998, 5.

28. Heilman, *Defenders of the Faith*, 309.

29. Yosseph Shilhav, "Spatial Strategies of the 'Haredi' Population in Jerusalem," *Socio-economic Planning Sciences* 18, no. 6 (1984): 411–18; Sara Hershkowitz, "Residential Segregation by Religion: A Conceptual Framework," *Tijdschrift voor Economische en Sociale Geografie* 78, no. 1 (1987): 44–52.

30. Galit Lipkis Beck, "The Haredi Housing Crisis," *Jerusalem Post*, August 23, 1995, 8.

31. Yosseph Shilhav, "Communal Conflict in Jerusalem: The Spread of Ultra-Orthodox Neighbourhoods," in *Pluralism and Political Geography: People, Territory and State*, Nurit Kliot and Stanley Waterman, eds. (London: Croom Helm, 1983), 100–13.

32. Heilman, *Defenders of the Faith*, 300–12.

33. Ruth Mason, "Can Children Learn Tolerance While Being Called 'Nazis'?" *Jerusalem Post*, December 6, 1996, 9.

34. Michael Ross, "Rising Influence: Islam Seeks to Build Its Own Egypt," *Los Angeles Times*, December 23, 1987, 1(1); Robin Wright, "Quiet Revolution: Islamic Movement's New Phase," *Christian Science Monitor*, November

6, 1987, 18; Martin Cohn, "Health Clinics' Premise Fixed in Spiritual World," *Toronto Star*, April 22, 1995, 5(C); Alan Sipress, "Mosques in Egypt Fill Bill for Social Services," *Phoenix Gazette*, November 24, 1994, 29(A).

35. Kelly Couturier, "Turkish Government Cracks Down on Religious Schools," *Washington Post*, September 21, 1997, 24(A); "Court Further Limits Turkey's Islamic Schools," *New York Times*, February 4, 1998, 7(A).

36. Melinda Bollar Wagner, *God's Schools: Choice and Compromise in American Society* (New Brunswick, N.J.: Rutgers University Press, 1990); Colleen McDannell, "Creating the Christian Home: Home Schooling in Contemporary America," in *American Sacred Space*, David Chidester and Edward T. Linenthal, eds. (Bloomington: Indiana University Press, 1995), 187–219.

37. Martin Marty, "Fundamentals of Fundamentalism," in *Fundamentalism in Comparative Perspective*, Lawrence Kaplan, ed. (Amherst: University of Massachusetts Press, 1992), 15–23.

38. C. Ram-Prasad, "*Hindutva* Ideology: Extracting the Fundamentals," *Contemporary South Asia* 2, no. 3 (1993): 285–309; Yogendra Malik and V. B. Singh, *Hindu Nationalists in India*, 1–27.

39. Hindu fundamentalists have argued that the theory of an Aryan invasion of India is in fact a Western invention; see Eva Hellman, "Dynamic Hinduism: Towards a New Hindu Nation," in *Questioning the Secular State: The Worldwide Resurgence of Religion in Politics*, David Westerlund, ed. (New York: St. Martin's Press, 1996), 243–4.

40. Satish Deshpande, "Communalising the Nation-Space: Notes on Spatial Strategies in Hindutva," *Economic and Political Weekly* 30, no. 50 (December 16, 1995): 3220–7.

41. Hellman, "Dynamic Hinduism," 245–7.

42. Gananath Obeyesekere, "Buddhism, Nationhood, and Cultural Identity: A Question of Fundamentals," in *Fundamentalisms Comprehended*, Martin E. Marty and R. Scott Appleby, eds. (Chicago: University of Chicago Press, 1995): 231–56.

43. Gananath Obeyesekere, "Buddhism, Nationhood, and Cultural Identity," 239.

44. George D. Bond, "Conflicts of Identity and Interpretation in Buddhism: The Clash between the Sarvodaya Shramadana Movement and the Government of President Premadasa," in *Buddhist Fundamentalism and Minority Identities in Sri Lanka*, Tessa J. Bartholomeusz and Chandra R. de Silva, eds. (Albany: State University of New York Press, 1998): 36–52.

45. Gurharpal Singh, "The Punjab Crisis Since 1984: A Reassessment," *Ethnic and Racial Studies*, 18, no. 3 (1995): 476–93.

46. Ishtiaq Ahmed, "Religious Nationalism and Sikhism," in *Questioning the Secular State*, David Westerlund, ed., 268–9.

47. Paul Wallace, "The Dilemma of Sikh Revivalism," in *Fundamentalism,*

Revivalists and Violence in South Asia, James Warner Björkman, ed. (Riverdale, Md.: The Riverdale Co., 1988), 64.

48. T. N. Madan, "The Double-Edged Sword: Fundamentalism and the Sikh Religious Tradition," in *Fundamentalisms Observed*, Martin E. Marty and R. Scott Appleby, eds. (Chicago: University of Chicago Press, 1991), 610.

49. Ahmed, "Religious Nationalism and Sikhism," 271.

50. Ibid., 277–9.

51. Manoucher Parvin and Maurie Sommer, "Dar al-Islam: The Evolution of Muslim Territoriality and its Implications for Conflict Resolution in the Middle East," *International Journal of Middle East Studies*, 11, no. 1 (1980): 1–21.

❺

THE IMPACTS OF FUNDAMENTALISM

The preceding chapters describe fundamentalism essentially as a type of reaction to processes of social change, driven by adherence to specific religious certainties. Because they develop contextually, such reactions have appeared in many different forms. The usefulness of the concept of fundamentalism lies in its ability to characterize the common features of these diverse religious movements. All expressions of fundamentalism exhibit a strong commitment to religious tradition, both in belief and practice, and based on that commitment, they develop an exclusive sense of group identity that sets their adherents apart from the rest of society. A fundamentalist group's adoption of such an identity serves as the foundation for a larger strategy to combat forces that it believes threaten its traditions. The most important feature of that strategy is the group's involvement in various forms of activism aimed at protecting its beliefs or advancing its objectives. Taken together, these traits explain the oppositional character of fundamentalist movements. They also clarify a crucial feature shared by such movements with respect to their impacts on society at large: that is, their intrinsic potential for provoking social conflict. By definition, fundamentalists are discontent with the current state of the surrounding society and adamantly oppose trends or groups that threaten their religious traditions. This position inevitably places them in conflict with others. Even those fundamentalists who attempt to withdraw from society declare an oppositional stance simply by rejecting the basic principles on which the larger society is founded. In most cases, though, fundamentalists' conflicts with society are expressed in more explicit forms.

Conflicts between fundamentalists and those who do not share their views focus on diverse issues and develop at various geographical scales. Most such conflicts emerge between fundamentalists and other groups within the same society. Some revolve around questions of personal morality: for example, the haredim's insistence on modest dress codes for women in and near their neighborhoods in Jerusalem, Islamic fundamentalist opposition to the consumption of alcohol and other products of Western popular culture, or the protests of Christian fundamentalists against public gatherings organized by homosexuals. A second, somewhat broader category of conflicts between fundamentalists and their antagonists involve disagreements over the nature and function of particular social institutions. In the United States, for example, local educational institutions have served as an ideological battlefield as fundamentalists have tried to promote biblical values in the public schools, particularly with reference to the teaching of biological evolution, sex education, and homosexuality. Similarly, Islamic fundamentalists have challenged the nature of existing political structures, such as legal or financial systems, that do not conform to Islamic principles. Such conflicts also emerge between fundamentalists and the existing religious establishment, as in the case of the Santi Asoke movement in Thailand or the haredi Jewish community in Israel. Disputes over the fulfillment of religious obligations, including the proper use of sacred space, account for a third category of conflicts, exemplified in the Hindu fundamentalist insistence on the construction of a temple to Ram on the site of the Babri Mosque in Ayodhya or in the haredim's continuing efforts to close certain roads on the Sabbath. A final type of conflict that may develop within a particular society involves questions of national identity. The assertion by Hindu fundamentalists that *Hindutva* represents the essence of Indian identity, for example, has provoked considerable opposition from secularists and religious minorities. Similar disputes have arisen in Sri Lanka over the role of Buddhism in the nation's identity and in Malaysia and other predominantly Muslim countries over the idea of creating an Islamic state.

As their global presence has become more conspicuous in recent decades, fundamentalists have also become increasingly involved in conflicts having significant international dimensions. Disputes over the control of territory, sacred or secular, may extend beyond the boundaries of a single country. This problem appears most clearly in the case of Israel, where religious Zionist fundamentalists strongly oppose the ceding of territories occupied by Israel after the Six-Day War and in fact plan eventually to expand the area under Israeli control. In their view, the areas occupied by Israel represent part of the sacred Land of Israel and should not be given up to achieve peace. That point of view, in turn, has had important implications for the development of a workable solution to the ongoing conflict between Israel and the Palestinians. Islamic fundamentalists see the question of Israel's existence as a major problem as well and remain committed to the country's destruction. International conflict has also been provoked by the potential impact of fundamentalist states on neighboring areas. Russian leaders believe that the Taliban regime in Afghanistan represents a significant threat, for example, because it may attempt to encourage militant Islam in adjacent states in Central Asia that were once part of the Soviet Union. Similarly, countries in north central Africa see Sudan's Islamic government as a threat to development of a stable political situation in the region. The potential for international conflict is greatest, however, in those situations where fundamentalists have influence on both sides. Again, the persistence of the conflict between Israelis and Palestinians derives at least in part from the fundamentalist elements within each group. Political conflicts between different fundamentalisms have also shaped relations between India and Sri Lanka, where the Tamil minority is predominantly Hindu, and between Iran and Afghanistan, which adhere to different versions of Islam. Perhaps the most serious expression of this type of conflict in recent years has been the nuclear arms race between Pakistan and India during the late 1990s. Although religious issues are not solely responsible for the tension between these two countries, that tension has been heightened by the rhetoric of both Islamic and Hindu fundamentalists (fig. 5.1).

Because of its significant potential to generate conflict, religious fundamentalism has become a major concern for nonfundamentalists in many parts of the world. In various settings the opponents of fundamentalism have characterized it as a destabilizing force that polarizes society, increases ethnic strife, undermines the political legitimacy of the state, infringes on the rights of indi-

Figure 5.1   Members of Pakistan's Jamaat-e-Islami burn an Indian flag in protest over the border conflict in Kashmir. The long-standing dispute between Pakistan and India over control of Kashmir has become a major concern of fundamentalists on both sides and has exacerbated tensions between the two countries. Lahore, Pakistan, 1999. *Source:* CORBIS/AFP.

viduals, or even inhibits economic development by scaring off foreign investment. Thus, as fundamentalism has become more widespread, so has the
hostility of others toward it. That hostility merely confirms the sense of threat
that drives fundamentalist movements, however. As a result, the conflicts between fundamentalists and their opponents tend to be self-perpetuating and
show few signs of diminishing in the contexts where they have emerged.

Two factors in particular contribute to the persistence of conflicts involving
fundamentalist movements: the fundamentalists' absolute certainty that they
alone understand truth and the territorial imperatives manifested in their activist responses to the threatening "other." The absolute certainty of fundamentalism has important consequences because it precludes the possibility of
compromise with others with whom they disagree. Fundamentalists see the
conflicts in which they are involved in strictly dualistic terms—as a struggle
between good and evil. In their view, the only satisfactory solution to such a
struggle is complete victory. To achieve victory, moreover, they presume that
they must assert some form of territorial control. Indeed, they believe that they
are both entitled and obliged to wield such control because they alone have
access to the truth. That belief invariably leads to conflicts with others who do
not accept the fundamentalists' claim to absolute authority. Because both of
these factors help to perpetuate such conflicts, they are crucial in understanding the broader impacts of fundamentalism and therefore will be the focus of
this concluding chapter.

FUNDAMENTALIST CERTAINTY

Fundamentalists are often viewed by their opponents as a serious threat,
both to society as a whole and to individuals. The danger of fundamentalism
derives in part from the specific beliefs and values espoused by its followers,
which often conflict with those of other groups in society. In different contexts,
fundamentalists and their opponents have disagreed on a wide variety of issues,
including the role of religion in public life, the enforcement of moral standards,
and the nature of national identity. From the nonfundamentalist point of view,
however, the threat posed by these disagreements is intensified by the fundamentalists' absolute conviction that they alone know the truth. This certainty
ultimately makes it impossible for fundamentalists to compromise with others,
since to do so would be to deny the exclusive validity of their beliefs. Some
fundamentalists may negotiate short-term solutions to their conflicts with others for practical reasons, particularly within the realm of politics. The leaders
of the Bharatiya Janata Party have had to relax their positions on certain issues
in establishing a ruling coalition within India's parliamentary system of government, for example, just as Christian fundamentalists have had to make some
compromises with moderates in the Republican Party to strengthen their voice

in U.S. politics. In the long run, however, fundamentalists refuse to make concessions on matters of faith. Fundamentalists thus posses an inherent inflexibility regarding their objectives, which in their view will have meaning only when they are fully achieved.

The basic obstacle preventing fundamentalists from compromising with their opponents is their understanding of the nature of truth. In essence, the fundamentalist perspective requires the acceptance of a clearly defined epistemology, or way of understanding the sources and nature of human knowledge, in which divine revelation serves as the ultimate authority. For most fundamentalist groups, divine revelation finds expression in sacred texts, such as the Gospels, the Torah, the Koran, or the Granth, but it may also be conveyed more generally through the lives of divine figures or by the group's historical traditions, as in the case of Hinduism and Buddhism. In whatever form it is manifested, divine revelation yields knowledge that to fundamentalists is unambiguous, incontrovertible, and eternal. Divine revelation, in other words, represents the only source of certainty. Other sources of knowledge, such as empirical evidence or human theorizing, are of secondary importance and are insufficient to disprove divinely revealed truths. Fundamentalists also reject the idea of reinterpreting traditionally accepted truths to fit contemporary sensibilities, as expressed in Reform Judaism or modernist Christian theology. In the view of fundamentalists, the truths derived from divine revelation are not negotiable; they are fixed in meaning and must be interpreted literally. And it is this epistemological position that sustains the absolute certainty characteristic of fundamentalist ideologies (fig. 5.2).

This sense of certainty serves as the basis for fundamentalists' commitment to protecting their traditional conceptions of sacred law, sacred history, and sacred space. Their opposition to current trends that contradict or undermine their traditions thus involves more than disagreements over particular theological issues or interpretations of ritual practice. It derives from their conviction that any belief or practice inconsistent with their traditions is simply wrong, both morally and factually. Indeed, from the fundamentalist perspective moral and factual truth cannot be separated from one another, since each stems from the same divine source. Fundamentalists consider threats to their traditions to be a danger to their understanding of reality, and this point of view necessarily commits them to goals and forms of action that are not subject to compromise or debate. Christian fundamentalists thus oppose teaching the theory of evolution because they know it to be wrong, and conversely, they support the teaching of creationism not as an expression of religious belief, but as science. In their view, the origins of life will be taught incorrectly and unscientifically in public schools until creationism replaces evolutionary theory in the curriculum. Similarly, the religious Zionists' claim to the Land of Israel derives from what they consider to be historical fact, not from an interpretation of religious belief. They see the eventual spread of Jewish control to a much larger area, extending

Figure 5.2   Church sign expressing fundamentalist certainty. Glenmont, New York, 1999. *Source:* the author.

into Syria, Iraq, and Egypt, as a historical inevitability. And for Islamic fundamentalists, implementation of the sharia is not just a means of reforming society; it is a necessary step in creating a society consistent with divine mandates that are eternal and inviolable. From the fundamentalist perspective, then, a perfect social order will be achieved only when all human activity conforms to revealed truth.

Fundamentalists' adherence to an epistemology based on divine revelation cannot be explained by any single factor. Certainly the process of socialization plays a major role. Individuals raised in a cultural setting whose inhabitants rely on religious certainty to understand the world will tend to adopt the same perspective, and fundamentalists in fact devote considerable attention to such processes of socialization, through their educational, social, and religious institutions. But this pattern occurs within all traditional religious cultures, not just those characterized as fundamentalist. Fundamentalism is distinguished from other forms of traditionalism by its conscious assertion of the importance of religious certainty and by the use of various forms of activism in support of that assertion. The psychological need to make such an assertion derives, in a general sense, from a fear of the "other" and the social changes that the "other" represents. Typically this fear arises from a sense of loss, or the potential for loss, as transformations within society threaten to erode traditional social patterns and relationships. Fundamentalists may fear the loss of their identity as society becomes more anonymous and fragmented, or they may fear a loss of status as a result of changes in the structure of society. The rise of new cultural influences in society may also lead fundamentalists to fear the marginalization of their beliefs and values. Whatever the nature of their perceived loss, however, fundamentalists believe that the associated threat has developed because the rest of society no longer adheres to their traditional religious beliefs. In their view, the stability of society depends on its foundation in an authentic conception of the ultimate sources of authority. Fundamentalists thus resist the changes that threaten them by reasserting their religious certainty. They refuse to let the "other" define the nature of truth, which they insist can be found only in their own traditions.

Christian fundamentalists in the United States, for example, fear the effects of moral relativism on society. They believe that modernists, by defining morality from a fallible and changeable human perspective, have undermined any genuine sense of social authority. They argue that U.S. society will inevitably decay unless it accepts the truth of biblical teachings, which in their view represents the only source of epistemological certainty. Hindu fundamentalists express somewhat similar anxieties regarding the official establishment of pluralistic policies in Indian society, which grant minority religions a status equal to that of Hinduism. They believe that these policies deny the unchanging truths associated with Hindu tradition, reject Hinduism as the core of Indian culture, and thus weaken Indian national identity. Sikh and Buddhist fundamentalists also fear the effects of pluralism and modernism on their ability to maintain their true religious identities. A primary concern of both major branches of Jewish fundamentalism, on the other hand, has been a secular view of history manifested most clearly in the secular concept of Zionism. This secular view has focused on the creation of Israel as a modern nation-state, where Jewish identity and Israeli nationalism merge. To religious Zionists, the secular view of history denies the ultimate truth of the Jews' divine redemption and has replaced the sacred Land of Israel with a mere political state. At the same time, the haredim object to the secularization of Jewish society and the abandonment of the idea that the Jews must remain a people in exile until they are redeemed through divine action. For both groups, secular Jewish society is based on an inauthentic view of truth. Finally, Islamic fundamentalists in various settings have expressed concern that the eternal truths of Islam have been threatened with replacement by alien ideologies, such as capitalism, socialism, or Western democracy. They believe that these ideologies, and the cultural values associated with them, challenge the certainty of Islamic belief and therefore debase Muslim society by making it subservient to outside influences. In all of these cases, the fear of social catastrophe ultimately derives from the belief that society has succumbed to an erroneous view of reality. That fear provides a powerful motivation for fundamentalists to assert their view of truth and knowledge as products of religious certainty.

In defending their traditional epistemology, fundamentalists invariably face opposition from others who base their understanding of truth and knowledge on different sources of authority. Such opposition is not surprising to fundamentalists, however. It is in fact entirely consistent with their dualistic conception of the world, in which good and evil struggle continually against one another. Disagreements over the nature of truth substantiate the fundamentalists' view of the "other" as a source of falsehood and corruption and prove that they are right to fight its influence. The opposition that they face consequently reinforces their commitment to their religious certainties and strengthens their aversion to compromise (fig. 5.3). The epistemological gulf separating fundamentalists from their antagonists thus has the effect of perpetuating conflicts between the two. Fundamentalists have no logical means, given their irrefutable conception of reality, to compromise with those who disagree with them. For the latter, then, the rise of a fundamentalist movement presents an intractable problem, with no easy solution as long as its adherents sustain their distinct epistemology. And while the influences of modernism and secularism may

Figure 5.3   An ultra-Orthodox Jew protests the use of Bar-Ilan Street on the Sabbath. Opposition from the secular world serves to reinforce the sense of threat that fundamentalists perceive and their absolute certainty that they are right to oppose secular perspectives. Jerusalem, Israel, 1996. *Source:* Greg Marinovich/Newsmakers.

in the long run tend to undermine religious certainty, fundamentalists have repeatedly taken action to prevent such a trend, particularly through the creation of their own institutions and communities. From Christian schools in the United States to Israel's segregated haredi neighborhoods to the RSS youth movement in India, fundamentalists have devoted considerable energy to preserving their traditional view of reality and passing it on to subsequent generations. Their success in this effort suggests that fundamentalism will persist as an important social phenomenon in various parts of the world, where it will continue to be a source of conflict.

TERRITORIAL IMPERATIVES

A second factor contributing to fundamentalism's enduring potential for generating social conflict is its inherent territoriality. The drive to impose a set of religious traditions as the underlying principles of society produces an implicit territorial imperative in all fundamentalist movements. Without exerting control over a particular spatial domain, sacred or secular, fundamentalists have no way to ensure that their beliefs will prevail over the influences and trends by which the group feels threatened. Such control enables fundamentalists to assert their values in all realms of human activity and provides a material expression of their distinct identity. The effort to achieve territorial influence thus represents an intrinsic element of fundamentalist activism. Again, that effort has the potential to produce conflict because it invariably places constraints on those who contest the fundamentalists' control of the territory in question. Indeed, it is this aspect of fundamentalism that nonfundamentalists find most threatening. The absolute certainty of fundamentalists in their beliefs may be a source of disagreement with others, but it does not automatically impose restriction on others' actions. Efforts to control territory, on the other hand, have direct implications for those who do not share the fundamentalists' beliefs. In the case of fundamentalists who seek only to withdraw from society, the external effects of their control over a given territory may be limited to excluding others from their separate community. Most fundamentalists adopt a more active role in confronting their antagonists, however, and their territorial aspirations are likely to have much broader consequences. Through their control of territory, these fundamentalists seek to enforce their own standards of behavior, reshape the nature of social institutions, and redefine the meaning and use of places. These goals obviously have far-reaching implications for other members of society and thus can lead to lasting conflicts.

The specific nature of a fundamentalist movement's territorial initiatives depends on the particular threats that they are meant to address. In responding to threats involving sacred places, fundamentalists define territorial control as an end in itself. Hindu fundamentalist efforts to reclaim the birthplace of Ram in Ayodhya, for example, reflect the belief that establishing control over that specific site represents a crucial step in protecting the integrity of Hindu belief. Similarly, religious Zionist fundamentalists see the restoration of Jewish society to the Land of Israel as an essential step in the redemption of the Jewish people, and they consider this task to be one of their primary religious obligations. They view the reclamation of the Temple Mount in much the same way, as a goal with intrinsic religious significance. In these cases, the territorial imperative of fundamentalism derives from the belief that the sanctity of sacred places has been challenged and must be restored through the stewardship of true believers. The place itself thus represents the primary focus of fundamentalist concern. As discussed in previous chapters, concerns with sacred places can lead to especially bitter and persistent conflicts when another group has also laid claim to the same site. The contested nature of a sacred site reinforces the fundamentalists' perception that it is threatened with desecration and strengthens their determination to remove it from the control of others.

As responses to threats expressed in secular space, the territorial imperatives associated with fundamentalism take on a somewhat different character. In such cases, fundamentalists see territorial control not as an end in itself, but as a means to achieving some greater objective, such as the transformation of society or the promotion of group traditions. For Islamic fundamentalists, for example, the ultimate purpose of creating an Islamic state is to establish an ideal social order based on the sharia. Christian fundamentalists seek political influence in the United States to instill the certainty of biblical values into the nation's institutions and public life. On a more local scale, the haredim in Jerusalem have segregated themselves in their own neighborhoods so that they can enforce strict conformity to traditional Jewish law in their immediate surroundings. In the context of secular space, then, fundamentalists pursue territorial control not for its own sake, but because it enables them to establish their beliefs as guiding principles in all aspects of secular life. This strategy again has considerable potential to provoke conflict, particularly when fundamentalists try to use it to impose their values and beliefs on others or on society in general. Fundamentalists insist that the authenticity of their religious beliefs gives them the right to define the proper character of society, but their opponents strongly disagree. Secular Jews thus denounce the haredim's efforts to influence Israeli society, characterizing the ongoing conflict over street closings, female dress, and gender segregation as a religious war. Women's rights activists protest the severe restrictions placed on Afghan women by the Taliban, arguing that these practices violate the basic standards of the international community. Secularists in India assert that the religious nationalism of the Hindu fundamentalist movement will provoke increasing social conflict among the country's diverse religious communities. To their opponents, fundamentalists' efforts to exert territorial control intrude on areas of public and private life over which the fundamentalists have no rightful authority and as a result create real threats to personal freedom and social stability.

A final type of territorial imperative manifested in fundamentalist ideologies involves efforts explicitly directed at expanding the spatial domain of the group's beliefs. Nearly all fundamentalist movements undertake such activities on a local scale in trying to recruit new followers from the surrounding society. For some groups, however, the interest in territorial expansion derives from specific religious concerns and takes on a more aggressive character. Fundamentalist adherents of universalizing religions often consider missionary work to be an essential religious obligation and may devote considerable effort to spreading knowledge of their beliefs to societies other than their own. Christians and Muslims are particularly active in such work, reflecting their extensive histories of territorial expansion. Some fundamentalists also believe that the expansion of their religion's spatial domain represents a crucial step in the fulfillment of its sacred history. As discussed earlier, religious Zionists believe that they must seek to regain possession of the Land of Israel in preparation for the redemption of the Jewish people. Christians and Muslims espouse even broader objectives. The commitment to expansionism among Islamic fundamentalists reflects two religious concerns: their desire to unify the Islamic world as a single community of believers living under the sharia, based on the model of Islam's early history, and their obligation to spread Islam to all of humanity, as commanded in the Koran. Expansionism among Christian fundamentalists also conforms to a scriptural directive to spread their faith, but they also see it as a necessary step in the fulfillment of Christian sacred history, based on a passage in the Book of Matthew that states that the end of history will arrive after the Christian gospel has been preached in all parts of the world.

The expansionist goals of Christian and Islamic fundamentalists are particularly notable because their global scale significantly increases their probability of producing conflict. The efforts of Christian fundamentalists in this context are part of a broader evangelical movement intent on spreading the message of Christianity. Various evangelical groups have joined together to form the AD2000 movement, which seeks to make the gospel available to the world's entire population by the year 2000. Its "Joshua Project" has the more precise goal of establishing at least one self-sustaining Christian church in every ethnolinguistic culture containing more than ten thousand individuals. A coalition of fundamentalist broadcasters has formed the similar "World by 2000" project, which aims to broadcast the gospel by radio in hundreds of different languages so that every person on earth can hear and understand the Christian message.[1] These movements generally concentrate their efforts on taking Christianity to areas of the world where it currently has little presence. In particular, they have targeted a region known as the "10/40 Window," an area stretching across northern Africa, the Middle East, and Asia between 10 degrees and 40 degrees north latitude (fig. 5.4). The dominance of this region by

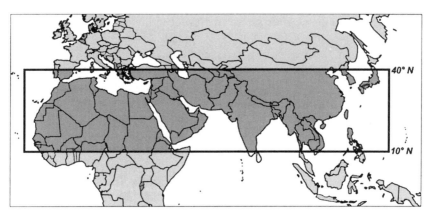

Figure 5.4   The 10/40 Window. Evangelical Christians have targeted this region, lying between 10 degrees and 40 degrees North latitude, as the focus of missionary activity in achieving the complete evangelization of the world.

Islam, Hinduism, and Buddhism has left it spiritually impoverished, according to Christian fundamentalists. Since the early 1990s, AD2000 has sponsored several extensive prayer campaigns (called "Praying through the Window") to promote evangelization of this region.[2] The group responsible for managing these campaigns, the Christian Information Network, has also organized "prayer journeys" during which believers travel to 10/40 Window countries and pray for the local acceptance of Christianity. It is important to note that some fundamentalists have rejected the legitimacy of AD2000 because of its ecumenical nature, which has led to contacts with many nonfundamentalist organizations, including liberal Protestant groups and the Roman Catholic Church. Nonetheless, Christian fundamentalists generally attach great importance to the goal of global evangelization, based on their belief that the realization of this goal will help to bring about the end of history and the Second Coming of Christ. As a result, they play a leading role in the efforts of U.S. groups to spread the Christian gospel.

From the Christian fundamentalist perspective, then, the territorial imperative of global evangelization has transcendent religious meaning. Inhabitants of targeted countries, however, consider fundamentalist evangelism to be an affront to their own beliefs and a threat to their traditions. Because most of these missionary organizations are based in the United States, their actions are also seen as an unwelcome intrusion of U.S. culture. Thus while Christian missionary work has converted millions of adherents around the world, it has also provoked considerable opposition in some places. In Israel, for example, lawmakers introduced a bill in 1997 that would prohibit the possession or distribution of materials designed to promote religious conversion. This anti-missionary bill was introduced after a California-based fundamentalist organization, Morris Cerullo World Evangelism, mailed 1.5 million copies of an eighty-two-page evangelistic tract to Jewish households across Israel (with a total population of only 5.4 million).[3] Orthodox and ultra-Orthodox Jews expressed outrage at the mailing, but even many moderates agreed that Jews living in Israel should not be subject to foreign missionary activity. A broader version of the anti-missionary bill was reintroduced in 1998, which proposed banning all missionary activity, written or verbal.[4] Similar reactions to the work of foreign Christian organizations has emerged in Russia, where in 1997 a bill was proposed to limit the activities for foreign missionaries. The Hindu fundamentalist organizations of the Sangh Parivar have also protested Christian missionary activity in India, decrying as a national crisis the evangelists' plan to spread knowledge of Christianity to all Hindus by the year 2000. The RSS and VHP further claim that foreign missionary activity has fostered civil unrest among tribal groups in northeastern India. In 1998, one VHP leader called for an outright ban on conversions, and some militants carried out violent attacks on India's Christian community, including the burning of churches. These responses to Christian evangelism apply to Christians, not just fundamentalists, but because fundamentalists are generally the most aggressive and persistent evangelists, they often figure most prominently in the controversies produced by this territorial imperative.

Conflicts of a different sort have developed out of the expansionist goals of Islamic fundamentalism. Like Christianity, Islam emphasizes the importance of missionary activity. That emphasis is expressed in the concept of *Dawah*, the obligation of Muslims to invite others to accept the truth of Islam, which derives from passages in the Koran enjoining Allah's followers to spread their faith to all the nations of the world. In addition, the unification of the Muslim world under the rule of the sharia represents one of the core ideals of Islamic tradition. Based on their commitments to missionary work and to the universal application of the sharia, Islamic fundamentalists consider the expansion of the spatial domain of authentic Islam to be an essential step in counteracting perceived threats to their beliefs. Individual groups pursue this goal in different ways, provoking varying degrees of controversy. Some groups focus on persuading existing Muslims to adhere more closely to authentic Islam. The Tablighi Jamaat in South Asia offers perhaps the clearest example of this approach, but other groups have also tried to expand the observance of traditional Islamic practices within existing Muslim communities. In some instances, radical groups like the Islamic militants in Algeria and the Taliban in Afghanistan have tried to achieve this goal through the use of violence and other forms of coercion.

A second approach to Islamic expansion, which has more significant international implications, involves traditional missionary work among non-Muslims. As in the case of Christianity, Islamic missionary activity is not solely the domain of fundamentalists, but it does provide an important outlet for fundamentalist activism. This activity focuses primarily on Africa, the target of roughly 90 percent of the funding spent by Muslims on missionary work. Muslims concentrate on converting those Africans who practice local animistic religions, a group that also receives considerable attention from Christian evangelists. As a result, the two missionary efforts are in constant competition with each other. This competition has important political overtones for Muslims, who see the spread of Christianity as one element of the broader diffusion of Western hegemony.

Political concerns figure even more prominently in the third form of expansionism associated with Islamic fundamentalism: the spread of "Islamic revolution." This strategy pertains specifically to fundamentalists and aims not just to convert individuals but to transform entire societies according to the rules of a strict Islamic order. This goal derives from the basic conviction of Islamic fundamentalism that, as a comprehensive way of life, Islam must be structurally incorporated into every facet of society. Iran has been the primary force behind efforts to spread militant political Islam, providing money, arms, and other forms of support to radical groups in many parts of the Muslim world, including Lebanon, Egypt, Algeria, and Saudi Arabia. Iran has also promoted the spread of its revolution through its close ties to the fundamentalist regime in Sudan, which has become an important force behind the expansion of Islamic political movements in Africa.[5] More recently, Afghanistan's Taliban government has emerged as a potential source of support for the creation of fundamentalist regimes in nearby Asian countries, such as Pakistan, Bangladesh, Tajikstan, and the other Central Asian republics.

Other countries see this form of fundamentalist expansionism as a significant danger because it obviously threatens to destabilize existing social and political structures. Africa has become the primary focus of both local and international concerns over this threat, given both the political volatility of many African countries and Sudan's apparent interest in spreading Islamic revolution. Various Western intelligence sources indicate that Sudan has received military and financial support from Iran throughout the 1990s to support this goal, enabling it to become a major training center for Islamic radicals. A former member of its Islamic regime has in fact claimed that Sudan has begun preparing Islamic insurgents for military action in every neighboring country except Libya, and both Eritrea and Uganda have cut diplomatic ties with Sudan to protest the latter's support of Islamic rebels in those countries.[6] Militant Islamic groups have also begun to appear in central and southern Africa, often with Iran's support. Such groups are attracted to Iran's version of Islamic revolution because it connects them to key sources of financial assistance while offering a political alternative to the Western ideologies associated with colonialism. The 1998 bombings of U.S. embassies in Nairobi and Dar es Salaam by Islamic radicals provide clear evidence of the potential for conflict associated with this expression of fundamentalist expansionism.

The various territorial imperatives outlined above represent crucial manifestations of fundamentalist activism. They clearly illustrate fundamentalism's basic concern with concrete action as well as abstract matters of belief. They also yield important insights into the nature of conflicts between fundamentalists and others. In using control over the meaning and use of space as a means of actualizing their beliefs, fundamentalists necessarily intrude on the interests and activities of other groups. The extent of that intrusion varies from one setting to the next, but in all cases it makes visible the antagonism between fundamentalists and their opponents. By giving such conflicts a concrete expression, fundamentalists publicize the ideological boundaries that separate them from others and substantiate their commitment to their traditional beliefs. In addition, the use of this strategy makes it impossible for their opponents to ignore the fundamentalists' concerns. In essence, the territorial imperatives of fundamentalism unambiguously challenge the authority of the "other," however that entity might be defined. As a result, they largely define the contexts within which disputes between fundamentalists and their opponents develop.

CONCLUSIONS

Fundamentalists' absolute certainty in their beliefs and their commitment to actualizing their beliefs in geographical space both contribute to widespread and persistent conflicts with other groups. The impacts of fundamentalism have thus become a major issue in societies around the world. Its opponents see fundamentalism as a divisive or even destructive force incompatible with contemporary social and political realities, and, as the preceding chapters have suggested, they have adopted various strategies in attempting to limit its influence. Opponents of the Sangh Parivar have tried to use electoral politics to forestall a fundamentalist reworking of Indian society. In the United States, various public interest and political action groups have been formed to lobby against the vision of U.S. society put forth by Christian fundamentalists. The Egyptian government has taken a more extreme approach, outlawing certain Islamic fundamentalist groups and imprisoning their members. Similarly, Algeria's military government has fought against Islamic radicals there in a protracted civil war. None of these responses has been particularly successful in stemming the tide of fundamentalism, however. At a global scale, fundamentalism remains a vigorous cultural and political force, and in many parts of the world it continues to affect the character of society and its institutions.

The relative ineffectiveness of efforts to lessen the impacts of fundamentalism reflects the influence of various factors. In democratic societies, fundamentalist movements are typically protected by constitutional guarantees of religious freedom and by the state's official position of religious neutrality. The fundamentalists themselves may oppose the latter position, but it nonetheless protects them from government action when they are in the minority. Their opponents thus respond to fundamentalism primarily by trying to persuade political leaders and the population at large to reject the fundamentalists' agenda. Fundamentalists are free to use the same methods to promote their views, however, and in many settings they have been very successful at doing so. In the United States, for example, Christian fundamentalist groups have become highly adept at using television, mailing lists, the Internet, and other communication technologies to organize their activities, develop sources of funding, and maintain the commitment of their followers. Similarly, the various organizations of India's Sangh Parivar have successfully built a strong sense of solidarity among their members and have demonstrated considerable skill at staging mass political events with great popular appeal. Of course, such efforts would have little impact if the fundamentalists' message of religious certainty and discontent with the status quo did not resonate with a large segment of the population. Nonetheless, the freedom to operate openly allows fundamentalists in democratic societies to express their views without fear of official reprisal and thus to persist in their efforts to move that society toward greater conformity with their fundamentalist vision. Even the hard-line haredim in Jerusalem, who reject the legitimacy of the state of Israel, benefit from the state's protection as well as its tolerance of dissenting views.

Fundamentalist minorities in countries ruled by more authoritarian regimes obviously face greater difficulties, but they are equally persistent in trying to transform society. Government attempts to restrict or suppress the fundamentalists' activity merely confirm their belief in the corruption of the existing state and strengthen their motivation to establish a new order. Their exclusion from the social and political mainstream also reinforces the fundamentalists' oppositionalism, further destabilizing the state. In extreme cases, the result may be violent conflict between fundamentalists and the state itself. The military's nullification of fundamentalist victories in Algerian elections in the early 1990s, for example, produced a violent response from Islamic radicals, who initiated a fierce campaign of terror against their opponents. Exclusion from the mainstream may also lead to the development of a parallel fundamentalist society, through which religious activists demonstrate their ability to function independently of the state and their greater success in meeting the needs of the people. The clearest example of such a development has occurred in Egypt, where fundamentalists have created a whole network of institutions designed to replace inadequate government services. Finally, government opposition may in fact help to position fundamentalists as the primary alternative to the regime in power and thus bring more widespread support to their movement. Again, some Islamic fundamentalists in Egypt have tried to exploit this possibility, but they have not reached a position where they can actually challenge the existing government for control. In Iran during the 1970s, however, the enduring antagonism between the shah's regime and the fundamentalist movement added to Ayatollah Khomeini's credibility as a new national leader.

At a global scale, the international community has had equal difficulties in dealing with fundamentalist states such as Iran, Afghanistan, and Sudan. Many other countries see these fundamentalist regimes as a direct threat. The United States and its Western allies have condemned all three states for harboring Islamic terrorists and have enforced various sanctions against Iran in particular. Russia views both Iran and Afghanistan as potentially destructive influences on the former Soviet Central Asian republics. Various governments in northeastern Africa have accused Sudan of sponsoring rebel movements in neighboring countries. India sees the Taliban government in Afghanistan as an immediate threat to stability in the region. In addition, private groups have attacked the fundamentalist regimes for their violations of human rights, such as the harsh treatment of women by the Taliban. Nonetheless, the international community in general has been reluctant to challenge the internal authority of these governments or to confront them militarily. The external threats that they pose are not defined clearly enough and are difficult to prove conclusively. Moreover, other countries have a strong interest in cultivating more positive relationships with these fundamentalist states, to prevent the development of future conflicts. The international community has thus relied largely on diplomacy and sanctions of various sorts to limit the impact of fundamentalist regimes on other countries, but these efforts have not eliminated the potential for geopolitical conflict based on the actions of fundamentalist states.

The religious certainty and territorial imperatives of fundamentalism have thus combined to create far-reaching problems for those who do not share the fundamentalists' beliefs. The prevalence in many contemporary societies of modernist attitudes based on rationalism, secularism, and humanism, and of postmodernist attitudes based on relativism and pluralism, has led to a widening gulf between fundamentalists and their opponents. The boundaries of faith that separate these groups are ideological in origin, but they also take on explicit geographical dimensions as a result of fundamentalism's intrinsic goal of giving concrete expression to traditional beliefs through the restructuring of both sacred and secular space. Such attempts to control social and political space are perceived as a significant threat by other groups and thus continue to be a major source of social and political conflict in contemporary societies around the world.

NOTES

1. For a general analysis of the global efforts of religious broadcasters, see Roger W. Stump, "Spatial Patterns of Religious Broadcasting: Stability and

Change in Patterns of Belief," in *Collapsing Space and Time: Geographic Aspects of Communication and Information*, Stanley D. Brunn and Thomas R. Leinbach, eds. (London: HarperCollins Academic, 1991), 354–75.

2. Edward Gilbreath, "Millions to Pray in Worldwide Rally," *Christianity Today*, 39, no. 11 (October 2, 1995), 106–7.

3. S. Aaron Osborne, "Christians Protest Proposed 'Anti-missionary' Legislation," *Christianity Today*, 41, no. 6 (May 19, 1997), 55.

4. Liat Collins, "Anti-Missionary Bill Passes First Knesset Hurdle," *Jerusalem Post*, May 21, 1998, 1.

5. Barbara Crossette, "U.S. Official Calls Muslim Militants a Threat to Africa," *New York Times*, January 1, 1992, 3(1); Jennifer Parmelee, "Sudan Denies 'Khartoum-Tehran Axis' to Promote Islamic Regimes in Africa," *Washington Post*, March 12, 1992, 21(A); Kim Murphy, "Islamic Militants Build Power Base in Sudan," *Los Angeles Times*, April 6, 1992, 1(A); Edgar O'Ballance, *Islamic Fundamentalist Terrorism, 1979–1995: The Iranian Connection* (New York: New York University Press, 1997).

6. Mark Huband, "African States Face Islamic Revolution Plot," *Observer*, June 25, 1995, 22.

GLOSSARY OF TERMS
AND GROUPS

AD2000 movement. A Christian evangelical movement seeking to make Christianity known to the world's entire population by the year 2000.

Agudat Israel ("Union of Israel"). An Orthodox Jewish political organization founded in Eastern Europe and now a non-Zionist religious political party in Israel.

Akal Takht ("Eternal Throne"). A structure adjacent to the Golden Temple that serves as the Sikhs' center of religious authority.

Akali Dal ("Band of Immortals"). The leading Sikh political party.

Angkatan Belia Islam Malaysia, or ABIM ("Malaysian Islamic Youth Movement"). An Islamic student organization that produced many of the leaders of Malaysia's Islamic fundamentalist movement.

Aqsa Mosque, al-. A mosque located atop the Temple Mount, designed to accommodate large numbers of worshippers; frequently the site of Islamic fundamentalist protests in Jerusalem.

Armed Islamic Group, or GIA. The most powerful of the Islamic guerrilla organizations active in Algeria during the 1990s.

Arya Samaj ("Society of Nobles"). A Hindu reform movement founded in the late 1800s that attempted to reconcile Hindu tradition with Western modernism.

Ayodhya. A city in the northern Indian state of Uttar Pradesh where Hindus and Muslims have contested control of an important sacred site. An Islamic mosque stood on the site for several centuries, but Hindu fundamentalists claim that the mosque had replaced an older Hindu temple and occupied the birthplace of the Hindu deity Ram.

Babri Mosque. A sixteenth-century Muslim mosque in Ayodhya, which, according to Hindu fundamentalists, was constructed on the birthplace of the Hindu deity Ram.

Bharat (or Bharatvarsha). The traditional hearth of Hindu culture, located between the Indus River, the Himalayan Mountains, and the Indian Ocean.

Bharatiya Janata Party, or BJP. The leading Hindu fundamentalist political party in India, closely allied with the other organizations of the Sangh Parivar.

Chief Khalsa Diwan. A Sikh reformist organization that sought to remove Hindu influences from Sikhism early in the twentieth century.

Christian Coalition. A political action group formed by Christian fundamentalists in the United States during the 1980s. Its founder, Pat Robertson, staged an unsuccessful bid for the Republican presidential nomination in 1988.

dar al-Islam. The Islamic world, including all areas where the sharia is followed.

Dawah. The obligation of Muslims to invite others to convert to Islam.

dharma. The observance of Hindu customs and religious duties and the way of life based on such observance.

dispensational premillennialism. The Christian belief that human history is divided into a series of distinct eras, the last of which will bring about the Second Coming and the millennial age of Christ's rule on earth.

Dome of the Rock. A Jerusalem mosque located on the Temple Mount. According to Muslim belief, this mosque contains the rock from which Muhammad ascended on a miraculous journey to heaven.

Edah Haredit ("Haredi Community"). One of the leading organizations of ultra-Orthodox Jews in Israel, characterized by a general strategy of separation from the rest of Israeli society.

Emancipation. The process, starting at the end of the eighteenth century, during which European states repealed the laws of exclusion that had limited Jewish participation in politics, the economy, and society.

Eretz Israel. In traditional Jewish belief, the sacred Land of Israel to which the Jews will be restored through their divine redemption.

faqih. An Islamic jurist and religious scholar; after the Islamic Revolution, the title used by Iran's supreme religious leader.

Golden Temple. The principal sacred shrine of Sikhism, located in Amritsar, India.

Granth. Sikhism's sacred scripture.

gurdwara ("gateway to the guru"). A Sikh temple.

Gush Emunim ("Bloc of the Faithful"). The leading organization in the religious Zionist branch of Jewish fundamentalism. The group has played an active role in establishing settlements in the occupied West Bank.

hajj. The pilgrimage to Mecca and often Medina, defined in the Koran as a religious obligation for Muslims.

halakhah. Jewish religious law derived from the Torah and other written and oral traditions.

Haram al-Sharif ("Noble Sanctuary"). The portion of the Temple Mount sacred to Muslims, containing the Dome of the Rock and al-Aqsa Mosque.

haredim. Ultra-orthodox Jews who adhere strictly to traditional laws and customs. Literally, "those who tremble" (at the word of God).

Hasidism. A traditionalist movement within Judaism established in Eastern Europe in the eighteenth century, stressing religious zeal and mysticism.

Haskalah. The Jewish Enlightenment, a movement to integrate modern European thought and scientific knowledge into Jewish culture, primarily during the eighteenth and nineteenth centuries.

Hindu Mahasabha ("Hindu Great Council"). A political party formed early in the twentieth century to promote Hindu interests in British India.

Hindu Rashtra ("Hindu Nation"). The nation of people who share the characteristic of *Hindutva*, encompassing all those whose cultural and religious traditions originated in the Indian subcontinent.

Hindutva ("Hinduness"). The sense of Hindu identity attributed to all those who consider the traditional geographical domain of Hindu culture to be their homeland as well as their holy land. Hindu fundamentalists consider *Hindutva* to be the only valid basis for Indian nationalism.

Hovevei Zion ("Lovers of Zion"). A Zionist organization founded in the late 1800s to promote Jewish settlement in Palestine.

Ibrahimi Mosque, al-. A Muslim mosque in Hebron, Israel, located atop the Tomb of the Patriarchs, a sacred site for Jews as well as Muslims.

Islamic Group (Jamaa al-Islamiyya). Since the early 1980s, the leading Islamic fundamentalist group in Egypt. The Islamic Group has carried out terrorist activities against the government but has also sought popular support.

Jamaat al-Muslimin ("Society of Muslims"). An isolationist Islamic fundamentalist group active in Egypt since the 1970s, committed to separating itself from the mainstream of Egyptian society and overthrowing the secular government.

Jamaat-e-Islami ("Islamic Society"). An Islamic fundamentalist organization founded in 1941 to promote Muslim interests in British India. Separate branches of the group exist in various South Asian nations; of these, the most active operates in Pakistan, where it seeks the establishment of an authentic Islamic state.

Jana Sangh. A Hindu fundamentalist political party founded in 1951; the precursor of the Bharatiya Janata Party.

jihad. A holy war or struggle in defense of Islam.

Jihad, al- ("Holy War"). A cluster of militant Islamic fundamentalist groups active in Egypt since the 1970s.

Khalistan ("Land of the Pure"). A proposed Sikh homeland that would function as either an independent state or an autonomous province within India.

Khalsa. The "community of the pure," those baptized Sikhs who adhere to a strict set of rules of conduct.

Koran. Islam's sacred scripture, believed to be divinely revealed to the prophet Muhammad.

madrassa. A traditional Islamic religious school. Madrasses established in Afghan refugee camps in Pakistan became the hearth of the Taliban movement.

Mahavamsa. A Buddhist chronicle dating from the fifth century that describes the origins of the Sinhalese people and the coming of Buddhism to Sri Lanka.

Mahdi. In Shiite Islam, the last Imam who will appear as a messiah reuniting religious and secular authority in a just Islamic state.

Meah Shearim. The core residential district of the haredim living in Jerusalem.

Mizrachi. A Jewish organization founded in 1902 with the goals of perpetuating Jewish traditions and promoting religious Zionism within the Orthodox community.

Mogul dynasty. The Muslim rulers who governed much of South Asia from the early 1500s up until the late 1700s.

Moral Majority. An organization founded in 1979 by Christian fundamentalists who advocated the use of political means to restore traditional moral values in American society.

mujahideen. Muslim "holy warriors" engaged in a jihad.

mujtahid. A Muslim cleric or jurist. Mujtahids represent an important local source of authority in Iranian society.

Muslim Brotherhood (al-Ikhwan al-Muslimun). An Islamic fundamentalist political organization founded in Egypt in 1928, with the goal of establishing an authentic Islamic order based on the sharia. Separate branches have subsequently developed in many other Arab countries.

Muslim League. A political group founded early in the twentieth century to promote Muslim rights and interests in British India and, after 1940, an advocate of the creation of Pakistan as an independent Muslim state.

Neo-Orthodox Judaism. A moderate form of nineteenth-century Jewish orthodoxy that insisted on strict observance of Jewish law but also encouraged secular education and accepted changes in certain traditional practices.

Neturei Karta ("Guardians of the City"). A radical anti-Zionist movement within haredi Judaism that rejects the legitimacy of Israel as a Jewish state and opposes any form of participation in mainstream Israeli society.

Parti Islam SeMalaysia, or PAS ("Islamic Party of Malaysia"). The principal Islamic fundamentalist political party in Malaysia.

Promise Keepers. A Christian fundamentalist organization that stresses male leadership of the family and the importance of biblical values in U.S. society.

purdah. The seclusion of women from public view practiced in Islam and some varieties of Hinduism.

Ram Rajya ("Kingdom of Ram"). A utopian state organized around the principles of the true dharma of Hinduism.

Ramayana. The Hindu epic that describes the life of Ram, an important deity and the seventh incarnation of the Hindu god Vishnu.

Rashtriya Swayamsevak Sangh, or RSS ("National Union of Volunteers"). A Hindu fundamentalist organization formed in 1925 to promote the spiritual and physical training of young men. Now one of the leading organizations of the Hindu fundamentalist movement.

sakha. A local RSS community designed to support discipline and solidarity among its members.

Sangh Parivar ("Union Family"). The various organizations that together make up the core of the Hindu fundamentalist movement, including the RSS, VHP, and BJP.

Sangha. A Buddhist monastic order; in Thailand, the organization responsible for overseeing proper adherence to Buddhist practices.

Santi Asoke. A fundamentalist movement in Thailand that seeks to create a self-sufficient rural society based on Buddhist principles.

Scopes trial. The trial of biology teacher John Scopes in Dayton, Tennessee, in 1925 for disobeying the state's law against teaching evolution.

sharia. Islamic law based on the Koran and traditions associated with the prophet Muhammad.

Shiite Islam. A form of Islam that emphasizes belief in the messianic return of the last Imam, who will rule over a just Islamic state; the dominant form of Islam in Iran.

Shiromani Gurdwara Prabandhak Committee, or SGPC. An elected Sikh body established in 1920 to oversee Sikh gurdwaras, which had previously been managed by hereditary temple guardians who often were not Khalsa Sikhs.

Singh Sabha ("Singh Assembly"). A Sikh reform movement, founded in the late 1800s, which sought to promote Sikh identity and interests. Various Sabhas united as the Chief Khalsa Diwan early in the twentieth century.

Sri Lanka Freedom Party, or SLFP. A Sri Lankan political party that has been a strong advocate of Sinhalese Buddhist nationalism.

Sufism. A movement within Islam that emphasizes mysticism and personal religious experience.

Tablighi Jamaat ("Missionary Society"). A Muslim organization committed to strengthening Islam by promoting individual adherence to the sharia and to the religious duties specified in the Koran.

Talaeh al-Fath ("Vanguards of Conquest"). A violent offshoot of al-Jihad that has claimed responsibility for terrorist attacks on tourists in Egypt in the 1990s.

Taliban movement. A fundamentalist Islamic movement that arose in the 1990s among Afghan refugees in Pakistan and that now controls most of Afghanistan. The movement adheres to a strict interpretation of Islamic tradition and has imposed many restrictions on daily life in Afghanistan.

Temple Mount. The site in Jerusalem believed to have been the location of Judaism's second Temple and also the location of the Dome of the Rock and other important Muslim shrines.

Temple Mount Faithful. A religious Zionist organization committed to reclaiming possession of the Temple Mount and, more broadly, *Eretz Israel*.

Tomb of the Patriarchs. A sacred site located in Hebron, Israel, believed to contain the tombs of the biblical patriarch Abraham, his wife, Sarah, his son Isaac and grandson Jacob, and their wives, Rebecca and Leah.

Torah. Judaism's sacred scripture.

ultra-Orthodox Jews. The haredim and other traditionalist Jews who adhere to a strict interpretation of Jewish law both in their religious practices and in daily life.

United Malays National Organization, or UMNO. The leading political party in Malaysia and a frequent target of Islamic fundamentalist criticism.

United Monks' Front. An organization of Buddhist monks in Sri Lanka that has supported the fundamentalist ideology of Sinhalese Buddhist nationalism.

Vishwa Hindu Parishad, or VHP ("World Hindu Society"). A Hindu fundamentalist organization, founded in 1964, that promotes the practice of Hinduism among Indians. The group has been particularly concerned with preventing conversions to Christianity or Islam.

Western Wall. A high stone wall located on one side of the Temple Mount, believed to be the only remaining structural element of Jerusalem's second Temple and thus an important sacred site in Judaism.

World Zionist Organization. An organization founded in 1897 committed to the goal of establishing a legally recognized Jewish homeland.

yeshiva. A Jewish religious academy.

zaddik. A spiritual leader of the Hasidic branch of Judaism.

Zionism. An international movement that sought the creation of a Jewish homeland in Palestine, ultimately in the form of the modern state of Israel.

SELECTED
BIBLIOGRAPHY

Bartholomeusz, Tessa J., and Chandra R. de Silva, eds. *Buddhist Fundamental-ism and Minority Identities in Sri Lanka.* Albany: State University of New York Press, 1998.

Björkman, James Warner, ed. *Fundamentalism, Revivalists and Violence in South Asia.* Riverdale, Md.: The Riverdale Company, 1988.

Brink, Judy, and Joan Mencher, eds. *Mixed Blessings: Gender and Religious Fundamentalism Cross Culturally.* New York: Routledge, 1997.

Bruce, Steve. *Pray TV: Televangelism in America.* London: Routledge, 1990.

Caplan, Lionel, ed. *Studies in Religious Fundamentalism.* London: Macmillan Press, 1987.

Choueiri, Youssef M. *Islamic Fundamentalism.* London: Pinter Publishers, 1990.

Daneshvar, Parviz. *Revolution in Iran.* London: Macmillan, 1996.

Dekmejian, R. Hrair. *Islam in Revolution: Fundamentalism in the Arab World.* Syracuse, N.Y.: Syracuse University Press, 1985.

Gatewood, Willard B. Jr., ed. *Controversy in the Twenties: Fundamentalism, Modernism and Evolution.* Nashville, Tenn.: Vanderbilt University Press, 1969.

Handy, Robert T. *A Christian America: Protestant Hopes and Historical Reali-ties.* London: Oxford University Press, 1971.

Harris, Christina Phelps. *Nationalism and Revolution in Egypt: The Role of the Muslim Brotherhood.* The Hague: Mouton, 1964.

Heilman, Samuel. *Defenders of the Faith: Inside Ultra-Orthodox Jewry.* New York: Schocken Books, 1992.

Hiro, Dilip. *Holy Wars: The Rise of Islamic Fundamentalism.* New York: Routledge, 1989.

Hunter, Shireen T. *Iran after Khomeini.* New York: Praeger, 1992.

Hussain, Asaf. *Islamic Iran: Revolution and Counter-Revolution.* London: Frances Pinter, 1985.

Jaffrelot, Christophe. *The Hindu Nationalist Movement in India*. New York: Columbia University Press, 1996.

Jansen, G. H. *Militant Islam*. New York: Harper and Row, 1979.

Kaplan, Lawrence, ed. *Fundamentalism in Comparative Perspective*. Amherst: University of Massachusetts Press, 1992.

Kepel, Gilles. *The Revenge of God: The Resurgence of Islam, Christianity and Judaism in the Modern World*. University Park: Pennsylvania State University Press, 1994.

Kliot, Nurit, and Stanley Waterman, eds. *Pluralism and Political Geography: People, Territory and State*. London: Croon Helm, 1983.

Lawrence, Bruce B. *Defenders of God: The Fundamentalist Revolt against the Modern Age*. San Francisco: Harper and Row, 1989.

Lustick, Ian S. *For the Land and the Lord: Jewish Fundamentalism in Israel*. New York: Council on Foreign Relations, 1988.

Maley, William, ed. *Fundamentalism Reborn? Afghanistan and the Taliban*. New York: New York University Press, 1998.

Malik, Yogendra K., and V. B. Singh. *Hindu Nationalists in India: The Rise of the Bharatiya Janata Party*. Boulder, Colo.: Westview Press, 1994.

Marsden, George M. *Fundamentalism and American Culture*. New York: Oxford University Press, 1980.

Marty, Martin E., and R. Scott Appleby. *Fundamentalisms Comprehended*. Chicago: University of Chicago Press, 1995.

———. *Accounting for Fundamentalisms*. Chicago: University of Chicago Press, 1994.

———. *Fundamentalisms and Society*. Chicago: University of Chicago Press, 1993.

———. *Fundamentalisms and the State*. Chicago: University of Chicago Press, 1993.

———. *Fundamentalisms Observed*. Chicago: University of Chicago Press, 1991.

Milani, Mohsen M. *The Making of Iran's Islamic Revolution*. Boulder, Colo.: Westview Press, 1988.

Mitchell, Richard P. *The Society of the Muslim Brothers*. London: Oxford University Press, 1969.

Nasr, Seyyed Vali Reza. *The Vanguard of the Islamic Revolution: The Jama'at-i Islami of Pakistan*. Berkeley: University of California Press, 1994.

Newman, David, ed. *The Impact of Gush Emunim: Politics and Settlement in the West Bank*. London: Croom Helm, 1985.

Omid, Homa. *Islam and the Post-Revolutionary State in Iran*. New York: St. Martin's Press, 1994.

Park, Chris C. *Sacred Worlds: An Introduction to Geography and Religion*. London: Routledge, 1994.

Provenzo, Eugene F. Jr. *Religious Fundamentalism and American Education:*

The Battle for the Public Schools. Albany: State University of New York Press, 1990.

Ravitzky, Aviezer. *Messianism, Zionism and Jewish Religious Radicalism.* Chicago: University of Chicago Press, 1996.

Sack, Robert David. *Human Territoriality: Its Theory and History.* Cambridge: Cambridge University Press, 1986.

Sandeen, Ernest R. *The Roots of Fundamentalism: British and American Millenarianism, 1800–1930.* Chicago: University of Chicago Press, 1970.

Schiff, Gary S. *Tradition and Politics: The Religious Parties of Israel.* Detroit, Mich.: Wayne State University Press, 1977.

Silberstein, Laurence J., ed. *Jewish Fundamentalism in Comparative Perspective: Religion, Ideology and the Crisis of Modernity.* New York: New York University Press, 1993.

Sopher, David. *Geography of Religions.* Englewood Cliffs, N.J.: Prentice-Hall, 1967.

Tuan, Yi-Fu. *Space and Place: The Perspectives of Experience.* Minneapolis: University of Minnesota Press, 1977.

van der Veer, Peter. *Religious Nationalism: Hindus and Muslims in India.* Berkeley: University of California Press, 1994.

Westerlund, David, ed. *Questioning the Secular State: The Worldwide Resurgence of Religion in Politics.* New York: St. Martin's Press, 1996.

INDEX

10/40 Window, 223–24, 224f

Abduh, Muhammad, 50
abortion. *See* Christian fundamentalism
Abraham, 162, 167, 172
AD2000 movement, 223–24
Adam, 172
Advani, L. K., 127
Afghani, Jamal al-Din al-, 49–50
Afghanistan, 62, 93–95, 95f, 100–101,
    157, 182f, 189, 215; Islamic fundamen-
    talism, 95–99; as refuge for terrorists,
    99, 229; Shiites, 97–98; war against So-
    viet occupation, 94, 96, 119, 147. *See
    also* Taliban
Agudat Israel, 40–41, 44–48, 111–13, 139
Ahmad, Qazi Hussain, 119
Ahmadiya movement, 61–62
Akali Dal, 70–71, 134–36, 148–49,
    200–203
Akal Takht, 149, 175–77
Algeria: Islamic fundamentalism, 88, 147–
    48, 179, 183, 225–28; Islamic terror-
    ism, 147–48, 183, 228
American Association of Christian
    Schools, 191
American Family Association, 109, 180
Amritsar, 69, 70f, 136, 149, 175
Amritsar Declaration, 203
Anandpur Sahib Resolution, 202
Angkatan Belia Islam Malaysia (ABIM),
    123
Anuradhapura, 198, 199f
Aqsa Mosque, al-, 162–65

Ark of the Covenant, 162–63
Armed Islamic Group (GIA), 147–48
Aryans, 73, 195, 211n39
Arya Samaj, 72–74, 76
Asoke movement. *See* Santi Asoke
Association of Christian Schools Interna-
    tional, 190f, 191
Atatürk, Mustafa Kemal, 51
Austria, 50
Ayodhya controversy, 1, 3, 14, 16, 19, 127,
    129, 157, 160, 168–72, 170f, 196, 207,
    214, 221–22
Ayub Khan, Muhammad, 62

Babar, 168
Babri Mosque. *See* Ayodhya controversy
Bahrain, 93
Bakker, Jim, 105
Bandaranaike, Sirimavo, 132
Bandaranaike, S. W. R. D., 131–32
Bangkok, 142–43
Bangladesh, 62, 118, 226; Islamic funda-
    mentalism, 183–84
Banna, Hasan al-, 52–54, 56
Baptists, 25–27, 30, 106
Bar-Ilan Street, 179, 220f
Bauer, Gary, 108
Bharat, 195–96, 206
Bharatiya Janata Party (BJP), 87, 102–3,
    126–30, 130f, 136, 169–71, 196–97,
    216
Bhindranwale, Jarnail Singh, 135–36,
    148–49, 175–76, 202
Bhutto, Benazir, 120

Bhutto, Zulfikar Ali, 117–20
Bible, 5, 6, 10, 25–33, 34f, 106f, 190, 191f, 217, 223; biblical inerrancy, 5, 25–30, 105, 191
Bible conferences, 27–29, 34
Bnei Brak, 2, 47, 139, 187
Bodhirak, Phra, 142–44
Borneo, 121
bo tree, 198, 199f
British India, 64–65; decolonization, 57–60, 63, 73–74, 200; Hindu fundamentalism, 71–76; Islamic fundamentalism, 56–59, 66; Sikh fundamentalism, 68–71
Bryan, William Jennings, 32–33
Buddha, 143, 198, 199f, 203
Buddhism, 5, 15, 64, 74, 126, 217, 219, 224; sacred history, 131, 133, 198
Buddhist fundamentalism: alcohol, 142–43; strategy of isolation in Thailand, 142–44, 188–89; strategy of participation in Sri Lanka, 131–33; territorial identity in Sri Lanka, 197–200. See also Sri Lanka, Thailand

Cairo, 52–54, 115–16, 145, 181
Caliphate, 51, 204
Central Asian republics, 96, 99, 214, 226, 229
Chamlong Srimuang, 143
Chandigarh, 135, 128f, 202f
Chief Khalsa Diwan, 69–70
Christ, 25–28,30; Second Coming, 25, 27, 163, 166, 224
Christian Broadcasting Network, 105, 107
Christian Coalition, 87, 103, 105, 107–9
Christian fundamentalism, 24, 85, 87, 102, 114, 163, 185, 194, 217, 219, 227; abortion, 103, 106, 108, 110, 114, 180; control of secular space, 20f, 180–81, 189–93, 192f, 207, 214; equal rights for women, 106; home schooling, 109, 190–91, 193; homosexuality and gays rights, 13f, 103, 105–10, 114, 157, 180–81, 185, 207, 214; origins in North America, 25–31; pornography, 106, 108, 180; Protestant denomina-

tional conflicts, 28–31; public schools, 1, 109, 181, 189, 193, 214, 217; religious broadcasting, 31, 34–5, 87, 103, 105–7, 109, 223, 228; religious schools, 28, 34–5, 105, 109, 189–91, 190f, 193, 221; response to modernism, 25–35; sex education, 108–9, 181, 190, 214; strategy of participation, 104–11, 137, 216–17, 222, 227; territorial imperatives, 223–25. See also evolution, creationism
Christian Information Network, 224
Christianity, 5, 10, 15, 25, 29, 32, 35, 72; diffusion of, 126, 223–26; in India, 70, 225; missionary work, 28, 34, 52, 68, 72–73, 105, 126, 224–26, 224f; sacred history, 223. See also Protestantism, Roman Catholicism, specific denominations
Christian Science, 25
Churches of Christ, 30–31
Citizens for Excellence in Education (CEE), 109, 181, 193
colonialism, 8–9, 16–17, 23, 78, 226; and Islamic fundamentalism, 25, 60, 62–63; and Sinhalese Buddhist fundamentalism, 131, 197, 200. See also British India
communism, 56, 97
Congregationalists, 26, 29
Congress Party, 127–28, 135
contextuality as geographical concept, 2–3, 15–18, 23–25. See also fundamentalism
Coptic Christians, 146
creationism, 1, 109, 181, 217. See also evolution

Darby, John Nelson, 27
Dar es Salaam, 226
Delhi, 130
Dharmapala, Anagarika, 131
Disciples of Christ, 26, 27, 30–31
Disney Company, 157, 180, 207
dispensational premillennialism, 27, 28
Dixon, A. C., 25
Dome of the Rock, 161f, 162–63

Edah Haredit, 45–48, 139–41
Egypt, 20, 49–57, 62–63, 100–101,183,
    218, 227; British presence, 50, 52,
    54–55; conflict with Israel, 112–13; Is-
    lamic extremists, 85, 88, 115–16, 144–
    46, 226; Islamic fundamentalism,
    52–56, 114–17, 189, 193, 204–5, 228;
    Islamic terrorism, 20, 54, 116, 145–46,
    179, 181; nationalism, 50–51, 55–56,
    63. *See also* Muslim Brotherhood
Emancipation, 36–38
Eretz Israel (Land of Israel), 20, 37, 42–
    44, 48, 111–13, 167–68, 206, 214, 217,
    219, 222–23
Eritrea, 226
Ethiopia, 101
Euphrates River, 167
evolution, 26, 28, 32, 181; Scopes Monkey
    Trial, 32–33, 33f, 105; teaching of, 1,
    11, 16, 31–33, 33f, 78, 106, 109, 190,
    214, 217. *See also* creationism

Falwell, Jerry, 106–7
Family Research Council, 108
faqih, 90–93
Faraj, Muhammad Abdul Salam, 145
Farouk, King, 54
feminism, 2, 99, 107, 110, 183
Focus on the Family, 108, 180, 185
fundamentalism: conflicts with others,
    103, 110–11, 160, 178, 193–94, 206,
    208, 213–16, 220–29; contextuality,
    85–86, 151–52, 159, 213; control of sa-
    cred space, 158–77; control of secular
    space, 158, 177–94; definition, 4–14; in
    democratic societies, 227–28; episte-
    mological certainty, 216–21, 218f, 220;
    geographical dimensions, 15–21; gov-
    ernment suppression, 228–29; patterns
    of domination, 86, 88–101; patterns of
    isolation, 87, 138–50; patterns of par-
    ticipation, 86, 101–38; territorial im-
    peratives, 216, 221–27; territoriality, 3,
    18–21, 157–58, 208; territory and
    identity, 158, 194–206, 208; terrorist
    activity, 24, 87, 150. *See also* specific
    religions
Fundamentals, The, 25, 29

Gandhi, Indira, 149, 176
Gandhi, Mohandas, 76
gay rights. *See* Christian fundamentalism
Gaza, 43f, 112
gender roles, 4, 109–10, 182, 185, 193
gendered space, 4, 182–83, 185, 193
gender segregation, 182, 186; absence in
    Santi Asoke, 142; in Islamic fundamen-
    talism, 92, 94, 147, 184, 183; in Jewish
    fundamentalism, 1–3, 7f, 19, 140–41,
    141f, 164, 165f, 184, 187, 207, 222. *See
    also* Western Wall
Germany, 46, 50
Golden Temple, 69–70, 70f, 135–36, 149,
    175–77, 202
Granth, 68, 175, 217
Gulf War, 93, 181
Gurdwara Reform Act, 70–71, 175
Gush Emunim, 44, 112–14, 163, 167

hajj, 172–74
Haram al-Sharif, 162, 164–66, 166f
haredim: anti-Zionism, 40–41, 44, 206,
    228; control of sacred space, 159, 163–
    64, 172; control of secular space, 157,
    179–80, 186–88, 193, 208, 214; East-
    ern European origins, 39–40; public
    demonstrations, 140, 141f; restrictions
    on women, 140, 184–85, 213, 212; seg-
    regation from Israeli society, 44, 47,
    87, 138–42, 144, 186–88, 188f, 214,
    221–22; settlement in Palestine, 44–
    48, 111; threat of secularism, 194, 219.
    See also Edah Haredit, Jewish funda-
    mentalism, Neturei Karta
Haryana, 134, 202f
Hasidism, 37–39, 41
Haskalah, 36
Hazaras, 97
Hebron, 167
Hedgewar, K. B., 75
Herat, 97
Herzl, Theodor, 40
Himalayan Mountains, 73, 195
Hindi, 73, 127, 128f, 134, 197
Hindu fundamentalism, 148, 203, 219,
    228; attacks on Christian community,

225; concerns with sacred space, 1, 157, 160, 168–72, 207, 221–22; Hindu nationalism, 57–59, 69, 73–76, 126–29, 195–97, 222; origins, 71–77; response to pluralism, 65, 71–75, 134, 194; strategies of participation, 125–31, 138; territorial identity, 195–97, 205–6; threat of secularism, 74, 77, 125, 138, 197

Hinduism, 24, 72–74, 125–26, 195–97, 206, 217, 224; and Buddhism, 64, 74, 126, 131; in Indian society, 11, 71, 74, 77,127, 219; internal diversity, 63–65, 71, 195; and Islam, 66; and Jainism, 64, 74, 126; missionary work, 126; reformism and revivalism, 57, 72–73; and Sikhism, 64–65, 68–69, 74, 126; threat of Christian missionary work,72–73, 126, 225; threat of Islamic missionary work, 126

Hindu Mahasabha, 73, 75–76

Hindu Rashtra, 74–75, 125, 196–97

Hindutva, 73–77, 125–27, 129–30, 195–97, 200, 206, 214

Holy of Holies, 163–64

homosexuality. *See* Christian fundamentalism

Hovevei Zion, 40

Hungary, 37–39, 41

Ibrahimi Mosque, al-, 167

ichthus, 192, 192f

Ilyas, Muhammad, 66

imperialism, 8–9, 16–17, 131. *See also* Islamic fundamentalism

India, 99, 120, 132–36, 148–49, 175, 197, 200–203, 206, 214–15, 219, 221–22, 229; cow protection laws, 130; emigration after partition, 60, 61f; as fundamentalist hearth, 63–77; Islamic fundamentalism, 59–60, 65–67, 77; Muslim-Hindu conflicts, 127, 168–71; nuclear weapons, 129, 215; peacekeeping force in Sri Lanka, 132, 199–200; religious pluralism, 25, 63–77, 125, 138, 219; as secular state, 6, 11, 17, 60, 72, 74, 77, 102, 127, 169, 201; Sikh-

Hindu conflicts, 149, 176. *See also* Ayodhya controversy, Hindu fundamentalism, Hinduism, Sikh fundamentalism

Indian Ocean, 195

Indus River, 73, 195

Iran: and Afghanistan, 95, 97–99, 215; assistance to Islamic movements, 92–93, 100, 146, 226; Islamic fundamentalism, 18, 56, 86, 88–94, 99, 101, 123, 147, 179, 181, 183–84, 189, 204–5, 208, 229; origins of Islamic Revolution, 88–90, 91f; and Saudi Arabia, 160, 173–74

Iran-Iraq War, 93

Iraq, 93, 167, 174, 218

Isaac, 162, 167

Islam, 10–11, 15, 24, 51, 55, 58, 74, 186, 224; as comprehensive ideology, 49, 53, 58, 63, 88, 114, 117, 125, 137, 204–5, 226; conflicts with outside influences, 49, 51–52, 56–59, 92–93, 99, 219; economic principles, 92, 118, 123; and fundamentalist patterns of domination, 88; and Hindu influences in India, 66; missionary work, 49, 64, 125–26, 203, 225–26; reformism and revivalism, 49–50, 81n42; sacred history, 55, 89, 204, 223; sacred sites, 162, 164–67, 172–74; and Sikhism, 68; threat of Christian missionary work, 52; traditional punishments, 1, 92, 97, 100, 119, 124, 173, 179. *See also* sharia

Islam, Shiite, 92–93, 173; in Afghanistan, 97–98; in Iran, 89–90, 93, 99, 101, 179; Iranian pilgrims in Mecca, 173

Islam, Sunni, 93–94, 98, 101, 173

Islamic fundamentalism: concerns with sacred space, 160, 162, 164–68, 172–74; control of secular space, 178–79, 180–81, 183–85, 189, 208, 218; and nationalism, 59, 204–5; opposition to Western influences, 6, 16–17, 90, 97, 100–101, 173, 180–81, 206, 208, 214, 219, 226; response to Western imperialism, 48–63, 194, 204; restrictions on alcohol, 52, 92, 110, 119, 124, 147, 179, 214; restrictions on entertainment, 1, 92–93, 97, 119, 124, 181; restrictions on women, 1, 92, 95, 98–99, 124, 157–58, 182–84, 193, 222, 229; strategy of domination, 88–101, 151; strategy of isolation, 144–48, 151; strategy of participation, 114–25, 137, 151; territorial imperatives, 222–23, 225–27; territory and identity, 203–6; terrorist activity, 20, 49, 54, 101, 116, 145–48, 179, 181, 183, 228. *See also* specific countries

Islamic Group, 146

Islamic law. *See* sharia

Islamic Revolution. *See* Iran

Islamic Salvation Front (FIS), 147–48, 183

Ismail, 172

Israel, 19–20, 41–48, 111, 173–74, 219, 221, 225, 228; accommodations of ultra-Orthodox, 111–12; American Jews, 146; Chief Rabbinate, 42, 45, 163–64; Islamic fundamentalism in, 164, 167; Jewish nationalism, 40, 42–43, 219; Jewish settlement in Palestine, 41–42; occupied territories, 113–14; War of Independence, 167. *See also Eretz Israel*, Jerusalem, Jewish fundamentalism, Palestine, Six-Day War, Zionism

Jacob, 167

Jainism, 64, 74, 126

Jamaat al-Muslimin, 145–47

Jamaat-e-Islami, 58–63, 65–66, 85, 102–3, 117–20, 123, 215f; outside Pakistan, 59–60, 62

Jana Sangh, 76, 127

Janata Party, 127

Jerusalem, 16, 45, 161f; haredim, 2, 47, 139, 157, 179, 184, 187–88, 213–14, 222, 228; religious Zionists, 42, 44; sacred sites, 18, 113, 159–64

Jesus Christ. *See* Christ

Jewish fundamentalism, 2, 18–19, 24–25, 35–48, 87, 158, 206; control of secular

space, 184–86; sacred sites in Israel, 162–63, 167–68; strategy of isolation, 138–42; strategy of participation, 111–14; terrorism, 113, 163; threat of secularism, 6, 17, 35–48, 179, 194, 219. *See also* haredim, Palestine, religious Zionism, Sabbath and Jewish fundamentalism

jihad, 55, 120, 145–46

Jihad, al-, 145–46

Jordan, 162, 167; Muslim Brotherhood, 56

Jordan River, 78

Joshua project, 223

Judaea, 43f, 167

Judaism: halakhah (Jewish law), 37–9, 41, 44, 47–48, 112–13, 141, 164, 186–87, 222; promised land, 37, 39–40, 112, 159, 167, 206; redemption of Jewish people, 39–40, 42–44, 111–13, 160, 163, 208, 219, 222–23; rise of modernism, 36–37; sacred history, 40, 42, 45f, 48, 78, 111–12, 139, 164, 167; sacred sites in Israel, 160–64, 161f, 167; threat of Christian missionary work, 224–25

Judaism, Conservative, 164

Judaism, Neo-Orthodox, 38, 40

Judaism, Orthodox, 37–41, 103, 106, 225

Judaism, Reform, 7f, 37–40, 48, 164, 217

Judaism, ultra-Orthodox, 2, 3, 19, 85, 179, 220f; in Israel, 7f, 111–12, 141f, 220f, 225; origins in Hungary, 38–39. *See also* haredim

Kaaba, 172

Kabul, 1, 16, 97, 182f

Kajar dynasty, 89

Kandahar, 96–97

Kandy, 198

Kashmir, 62, 120, 215f

Kelantan, 121–24, 122f, 179, 184

Khalistan, 135–36, 148–50, 176, 202–3

Khalistan Liberation Force, 150, 203

Khalsa. *See* Sikhism

Khartoum, 100–101

Khomeini, Ruhollah, 89–93, 173–74, 181, 229

Kook, Abraham, 42–44, 112
Kook, Zvi Yehudah, 44, 112
Koran, 6, 10, 49, 66, 78, 92, 180, 217; ban on intoxicants, 179; obligation to spread Islam, 223, 225; status of women, 92, 183
Kumaratunga, Chandrika, 133
Kuwait, 93

Labor Party (Israel), 111
Lahore, 69, 215f
Latvia, 41
Leah, 167
Lebanon, 93, 179, 226
Liberation Tigers of Tamil Eelam (LTTE), 199–200
Libya, 226
Likud Party, 111
Lithuania, 37, 41

madrassas, 95–96
Maharashtra, 75
Mahavamsa, 131, 198–99
Mahdists, 173–74
Malaya, 121
Malays, 121–23, 205
Malaysia, 122f, 153n32; decolonization, 121; Islamic fundamentalism, 20, 120–24, 179, 184, 204–5, 214
Marxism, 94, 114
Mathura, 171
Mawdudi, Mawlana Abul Ala, 58–62
Mazar-e-Sharif, 97–98
Meah Shearim, 179, 184, 187, 188f
Mecca, 55, 160, 162, 172–74; Great Mosque, 172–74
Medina, 162, 172, 174; and original Islamic state, 55, 88, 204
Methodists, 26, 29
missionary work, 16, 223; anti-missionary activity, 224–25. See also specific religions
Mizrachi, 41–44
modernism as threat to fundamentalists, 6, 23–79 passim. See also Christian fundamentalism, Jewish fundamentalism

Mogul Empire, 64, 66, 69, 75, 168–69, 200
Moody, Dwight L., 28
Moral Majority, 103, 105–8
Mormonism, 25, 106
Morocco, 56
Morris Cerullo World Evangelism, 225
Mubarak, Hosni, 115–17
Muhammad, 14, 49, 51, 55, 61, 89, 145, 161f, 162; and first Islamic state, 11, 53, 54f, 88, 125, 137, 204
Muslim Brotherhood, 52–56, 62–63, 81n42, 123, 144–45; outside Egypt, 56, 100; participation in Egyptian society, 114–17, 189
Muslim League, 59, 73
Mustafa, Shukri, 145

Nairobi, 226
Nanak, Guru, 68
Nasser, Gamal Abdel, 55
nationalism and fundamentalism, 19, 78, 206. See also specific ethnic groups, religions, countries
National Liberation Front (FLN), 147
Neturei Karta, 46–48, 81n34, 139–40
New Delhi, 61f
Nile River, 113, 167

Omar, Muhammad, 96
Operation Blue Star, 176
Operation Rescue, 180
Ottoman Empire, 50–51

Pahlavi, Reza, Shah of Iran, 89–93, 91f, 229
Pahlavi dynasty, 89
Pakistan, 16–17, 59, 61f, 71, 76, 129, 134, 146, 200–201, 204–5, 226; Afghan refugee camps, 95–96; aid to Afghan rebels, 94, 119; and destruction of Babri Mosque, 171; Islamic constitution, 60, 62, 118; Islamic fundamentalism, 59–63, 84, 102–4, 117–20, 157, 183–84, 179, 215f; nuclear weapons, 215; and the Taliban, 96, 99. See also Jamaat-e-Islami

Palang Dharma Party, 143
Palestine: Jewish fundamentalism, 35, 42–47, 45f, 111, 139; as Jewish homeland, 25, 40–42, 43f
Palestinian Liberation Organization, 140
Palestinians: conflicts with Israelis, 17, 113, 162, 165–68, 214–15; support from Iran, 93; support from Muslim Brotherhood, 53
Pan Malayan Islamic Party, 121
Parti Islam SeMalaysia (PAS), 121–24
People's Alliance Party, 133
Pinsker, Leon, 40
pluralism as threat to fundamentalists, 8–9, 194, 219, 229. *See also* India
Plymouth Brethren, 27
Poland, 37, 41, 46
pornography. *See* Christian fundamentalism
Praying through the Window, 224
Premadasa, Ranasinghe, 199
Presbyterians, 26, 30, 32
Pressburg (Bratislava), 38
Promise Keepers, 103, 109–10, 110f, 185
Protestant fundamentalism. *See* Christian fundamentalism
Protestantism, 26, 28, 30–31, 48; conservative, 2, 4–5, 24–29, 34–35, 107, 206; evangelical, 26–29, 35; liberal, 28, 224
PTL Satellite Network, 105
Punjab, 67f, 69–70, 133–36, 149–50, 175, 200–203, 202f
Punjabi language, 134, 201, 202f
purdah, 183
Pushtuns, 95f, 96–97

Qom, 90
Qutb, Sayyid, 55–56, 144–45, 147

Rahman, Omar Abdel, 146
Ram (Hindu deity), 1, 3, 19, 125, 127, 129, 157, 168–72, 196–97, 207, 214, 221–22
Ramayana, 124, 168
Ram Rajya, 125, 169, 196
Rashtriya Swayamsevak Sangh (RSS), 85,

125–27, 129, 170, 185, 221, 225; origins, 75–76, 196
Reagan, Ronald, 106
Rebecca, 167
relativism, 8, 190, 219, 229
religious fundamentalism. *See* fundamentalism
religious Zionism: concerns with sacred space, 160, 163–64, 167–68, 206, 208, 214, 217, 219, 222–23; origins, 41–44, 43f, 48; participation in Israeli society, 112–13. *See also* Gush Emunim, Mizrachi
Republican Party, 104–8, 216
Rida, Muhammad Rashid, 50
Robertson, Pat, 105, 107
Roman Catholicism, 25, 26, 103, 106, 191, 224
Rushdie, Salman, 93–94
Russia, 37, 40, 97, 99, 214, 225, 229

Sabbath and Jewish fundamentalism: efforts to ban business activity, 112, 140, 141f, 179; efforts to ban street traffic, 140–41, 157, 179–80, 193, 214, 220f, 222; spatial restrictions, 187
sacred history, 158–60, 194, 217, 223. *See also* specific religions
sacred place. *See* sacred space
sacred space, 4, 18–20, 83n67, 158, 178, 192, 194, 196, 206–8, 214, 217, 221–22, 229; fundamentalist efforts to control, 159–77. *See also* specific sacred sites
Sadat, Anwar, 114–16, 144–46
Samaria, 43f, 167
Sangha (Thailand), 142–44
Sangh Parivar, 76, 125, 127, 196, 225, 227–28
Santi Asoke, 142–44, 186, 188–89, 214
Sarah, 167
Saudi Arabia: conflicts involving Islamic sites, 172–74; Islamic fundamentalism, 172–73, 181, 226; Muslim Brotherhood, 56; tensions with Iran, 93, 160
Savarkar, V. D., 73–74, 76, 195
school prayer, 106, 108, 181, 190

Scopes Monkey Trial. *See* evolution, teaching of
secular humanism, 9, 181, 190, 229
secularism as threat to fundamentalists, 7–9. *See also* Hindu fundamentalism, Jewish fundamentalism
secular space, 19, 158, 206–8, 222; fundamentalist efforts to control, 177–94, 190f
sex education. *See* Christian fundamentalism
sharia, 49, 53, 66, 131, 204, 208, 218, 222–23, 225; Afghanistan, 206; Algeria, 147; Egypt, 114, 116, 205; Iran, 90, 92, 94; Malaysia, 123–24; Pakistan, 60, 117–20, 157; Saudi Arabia, 173; Sudan, 99, 100; Turkey, 51
Sharif, Nawaz, 120
Shiite Islam. *See* Islam, Shiite
Shiromani Gurdwara Prabandhak Committee (SGPC), 70–71, 134, 136, 149
Sikh fundamentalism, 17, 65, 67–71, 70f, 77, 88, 219; alcohol, 150, 175; concerns with sacred space, 175–77; strategy of isolation, 148–50; strategy of participation, 133–38; territorial identity, 200–203; terrorist activity, 135–37, 148–50, 175–77, 202–3
Sikhism, 24, 64–65, 67–71, 67f, 70f, 74, 126, 133–37, 148–50, 175–77, 200–203, 202f; gurdwaras, 69–71; threat of Christian missionary work, 68
Sinai, 112–13
Singapore, 121, 153n32
Singh, Gobind, 68
Singh, Kahan, 69
Singh, Ranjit, 200
Singh Sabha movement, 68–69
Sinhala Maha Sabha, 131
Sinhalese. *See* Sri Lanka
Six-Day War, 43f, 112, 115, 162, 164, 167, 214
socialism, 114, 117–18, 219
Sofer, Moses, 38
Soviet Union, 93, 96, 173, 214, 219; occupation of Afghanistan, 94, 96, 119, 147

Sri Lanka, 199f, 214–15; civil war, 132–33; Sinhalese Buddhist fundamentalism, 17, 131–33, 138, 197–200, 203, 206–7; Sinhalese nationalism, 131–32, 199f
Sri Lanka Freedom Party (SLFP), 131–32
Stewart, Lyman, 25
Sudan: Islamic fundamentalism, 86, 99–101, 214–15, 226, 229; Muslim Brotherhood, 56, 100; as refuge for terrorists, 99–101, 226, 229
Sunni Islam. *See* Islam, Sunni
Syria, 112, 218; Muslim Brotherhood, 56

Tablighi Jamaat, 66–68, 71, 103, 125, 137, 225
Tabriz, 90
Tajiks, 97
Tajikistan, 226
Talaeh al-Fath, 146
Taliban, 1, 14, 18–19, 56, 86, 95–99, 95f, 182f, 205–6, 214, 225; control of secular space, 97–98, 157, 179, 181, 183–84, 222, 229; criticism regarding status of women, 99, 222, 229; goal of spreading Islamic regime, 98, 204, 226; international relations, 98–99, 214, 226, 229; takeover of Afghanistan, 95–97
Tamils, 131–33, 199–200, 207, 215
Tehran, 90, 91f, 93
Tel Aviv, 187
Temple of the Tooth, 198, 200
Temple Mount, 113, 159–66, 161f, 166f, 208, 222; and Christian fanatics, 166
Temple Mount Faithful, 163–65
Thailand, 10f; Buddhist fundamentalism, 87, 142–44, 186, 188–89, 214
Tohra, Gurcharan Singh, 136
Tomb of the Patriarchs, 167
Torah, 10, 38–39, 139, 164, 217
Trengganu, 122
Turkey, 51, 189
Turkmenistan, 96

Uganda, 226
United Malays National Organization (UMNO), 121–24

United Monks' Front, 132
United National Party (UNP), 132–33, 199
United States: Christian fundamentalism, 87, 103–11, 114, 137, 157, 163, 166, 180, 185, 189–94, 214, 219, 221–22, 224, 227–29; as Christian nation, 19, 104, 104f, 181, 206; as fundamentalist hearth, 4, 24–35; Islamic radicals in, 146; relations with Islamic countries, 93, 99, 101, 173–74; religious character, 16, 26–27. See also Christian fundamentalism
Uttar Pradesh, 1, 127, 171
Uzbekistan, 97–98
Uzbeks, 97

Vajpayee, Atal Bihari, 129
Varanasi, 171
Vedas, 65, 72–73
veil. See women, veiling of

Vijaya, 198
Vishwa Hindu Parishad (VHP), 76, 126–27, 169–71, 170f, 196, 225

Wahhabism, 173
Wailing Wall. See Western Wall
West Bank, 43f, 78, 112, 167–68
Western Wall, 45f, 161f, 162, 164–65; gender segregation, 7f, 159, 164, 165f, 172, 184
Women of the Wall, 164
women, veiling of, 1, 92, 98–100, 115, 124, 147, 182f, 183, 193
World by 2000 project, 223
World Trade Center, 146
World Zionist Organization, 40–41

Zia ul-Haq, Mohammad, 119–20
Zionism, 40–48, 139, 219; Jewish fundamentalist opposition, 40–41, 44, 46, 48, 111, 138. See also religious Zionism

ABOUT THE AUTHOR

Roger W. Stump is associate professor of geography at the University at Albany, State University of New York, where he has taught since 1982. He also holds a joint appointment in the university's interdisciplinary religious studies program. He completed his undergraduate education at the University of Kansas with a double major in French and English. He received a master's degree in library science from Indiana University and after working as a librarian for several years returned to the University of Kansas to complete a Ph.D. in geography. At the University at Albany he has taught a variety of courses in cultural geography, other aspects of human geography, and quantitative methods. In the 1990s he served terms as chair of the department of geography and planning and as associate dean of undergraduate studies. In the latter capacity, he oversaw the University at Albany's General Education program. In 1998–99, he served as the chair of the university senate. He has published numerous articles and book chapters dealing with various aspects of cultural geography, and in 1986 he edited a special issue on the geography of religion for the *Journal of Cultural Geography*. His research on the geography of religion has covered a variety of topics, including regional variations in the determinants of religious behavior, the persistence of ethnic parishes in the Roman Catholic Church, the historical geography of the Disciples of Christ, and the global spread of religious broadcasting.